The Science Fiction Roll of Honor

RANDOM HOUSE 🏠 NEW YORK

The Science Fiction Roll of Honor

An Anthology of
Fiction and Nonfiction
by Guests of Honor
at World Science Fiction
Conventions

EDITED BY

Frederik Pohl

Library of Congress Cataloging in Publication Data
Main entry under title:

The Science fiction roll of honor.

   1. Science fiction, American.   2. Science fiction
—History and criticism—Addresses, essays, lectures.
I. Pohl, Frederik.
PZ1.S4147 [PS648.S3]   813'.0876   75–10340
ISBN 0–394–48677–3

Manufactured in the United States of America

9 8 7 6 5 4 3 2

First Edition

ACKNOWLEDGMENTS

"Kings Who Die," by Poul Anderson. Copyright © 1962 by
Digest Productions, Inc. Reprinted by permission of the
author and Scott Meredith Literary Agency, Inc., 580 Fifth
Avenue, New York NY 10036.

"The Last Question," by Isaac Asimov. Copyright © 1956 by
Columbia Publications, Inc. Reprinted by permission of the
author.

"How Beautiful with Banners," by James Blish. Copyright ©
1966 by Berkley Publishing Corporation. Reprinted by
permission of the author and his agent, Robert P. Mills, Ltd.

"Daybroke," by Robert Bloch. Copyright © 1958 by Ballantine Magazines, Inc. Reprinted by permission of the author and Scott Meredith Literary Agency, Inc.

"Who Goes There?," by John W. Campbell. Copyright 1938 by Street & Smith Publications, Inc. (renewed 1970 by The Conde-Nast Publications, Inc.) Reprinted by permission of the author's estate and Scott Meredith Literary Agency, Inc.

"Dog Star," by Arthur C. Clarke. Copyright © 1962 by Galaxy Publishing Corp. (as "Moondog"). Reprinted by permission of the author and Scott Meredith Literary Agency, Inc.

"The Monster," by Lester del Rey. Copyright 1951 by Popular Publications, Inc. Reprinted by permission of the author and Scott Meredith Literary Agency, Inc.

"Dust," by Lloyd Eshbach. Copyright 1939 by Western Fiction Publishing Co., Inc. Reprinted by permission of Forrest J. Ackerman, 2495 Glendower Avenue, Hollywood, California 90027.

"The Prophets of Doom," by Hugo Gernsback. Printed by permission of Forrest J. Ackerman.

"The Long Watch," by Robert A. Heinlein. Copyright 1949 by American Legion Magazine. Reprinted by permission of the author's agent, Lurton Blassingame.

"Sanity," by Fritz Leiber. Copyright 1944 by Street & Smith Publications, Inc. Reprinted by permission of the author.

"The Meaning of the Word 'Impossible,'" by Willy Ley. Copyright © 1967 by Willy Ley. Reprinted by permission of Pyramid Publications, A Division of Pyramid Communications, Inc.

"Science Fiction, The Spirit of Youth," by Frank R. Paul. Printed by permission of Forrest J. Ackerman.

CONTENTS

INTRODUCTION

Every one of the contributors to this volume has been GoH at a Worldcon.

If you are fluent enough in Fanspeak to be able to translate that sentence, then for you this introduction is over. Nothing more needs to be said. Just flip the pages to the contents and enjoy.

If, on the other hand, you don't know what a GoH is, or what a Worldcon is, or even what Fanspeak is, then the rest of these opening remarks are for you. I will try to explain the special sense in which these very special persons have been honored for their contributions to science fiction. They, and the other Guests of Honor who could not be included in this volume, are the ones whose statues would line the rotunda of the Capitol if they were politicians, or would occupy baseball's hall of fame if they were players.

They are the ones that the organized readers of science fiction, the fans, have chosen to receive a unique honor: the homage of the entire world of science fiction—not for a single story or an individual act, but because they themselves have in some way changed the whole shape of science fiction.

Science fiction is a very special kind of writing. It involves the emotions, as any story does. It makes an appeal to the esthetic sense, like any good writing. And it also involves the intellect. Science fiction is a literature of ideas, and what is one to do with a new idea, a fresh insight into the universe, if not to talk about it with some other person?

So science-fiction readers for generations have formed a particular in-group. The more devoted to science fiction, the more in the group; and the inmost of groups is that collection of ten or fifteen thousand human beings around the world called Fandom.

Fandom has existed for a long time. I came to it when I was thirteen years old, in 1933. (Yes, Virginia, there *was* a year called 1933.) I had been reading science fiction for as long as I had been able to read, or at least as long as I was able to get out and select my own reading, in a library or in a second-hand magazine store. And I wanted to talk about it. So I joined a fan club.

I spent the most important parts of the next half-dozen years of my life in the same sort of club, or in the company of other fans in various enterprises. We talked about science fiction. We tried to write science fiction. We published "fan mags" (now they are called "fanzines," but they are the same things: amateur, usually mimeographed publications devoted to discussing, or trying to duplicate, all the myriad aspects of science fiction). About the first real fan I met was Donald A. Wollheim. (Now he is the august publisher of DAW Books— so we old-line fans fabricated our fantasies into life styles.) Isaac Asimov was a young fan in one of the clubs, so was C. M. Kornbluth, so was Damon Knight, so were a dozen others now famous as writers or editors in the field. We were not all writers-to-be; some of us turned out to be day laborers, and one or two (and among them, some of the brightest and most promising of us) turned out to be sodden derelicts. But what brought us together in the first place was an interest in the polemical aspects of science fiction: the ideas it planted in our young heads for ways in which the world could be something different, and more rewarding, than it was.

Talking among ourselves, it was natural to want to go out and talk to other fans elsewhere; and so, around 1936, we almost accidentally planned and carried out the very first ever Science Fiction Convention.

It was not very elaborate. It happened on a Sunday afternoon. Half a dozen of us fans from New York City got on a train and were met by half a dozen local fans in Philadelphia. The first thing we did was to elect officers. The unanimous choice for chairman was a Philadelphia fan named John V. Baltadonis. (It was an inevitable win for him; we were meeting in a corner of his father's saloon.) I became secretary. (I don't remember why. Perhaps I was the only one with a pencil.) Then we talked for a while about science fiction, and then (remember, we were almost all in our early teens) we went out to drink ice-cream sodas together, and then home.

And that was where it all began.

I don't know how many sf conventions have followed that tiny, impromptu affair. Some scholar-fan might enjoy trying to tabulate them one day. The total must be at least a thousand. The U.S.A. alone is host to literally dozens every year now: one in Philadelphia, one in New York, two in Ohio, one each in Boston, Baltimore, Washington, the West Coast and the Deep South as regular annual events. And any number of additional cons whenever some person or group wants to call one. And the U.S. is not alone. England, Australia, Japan, Germany and Italy have long-established events. At least twenty other countries have sporadic attacks of the fever.

But the one big one, the one that counts, the one that fans save up for and look forward to . . . that is the Worldcon.

The First World Science Fiction Convention took place in 1939, and the term "world" was more a hope than a reality. (That was the year World War II began, and the world itself was only a pretty forlorn hope that year.) Still, several hundred fans did get together, in a rented religious-institution hall in New York City, and several of them came from as far away as California. The next was in Chicago a year later, the next in Denver—and then reality struck, and gas rationing and travel dislocations came out of World War II and kept conventions from being easy to run for several years. (Not that there would have been much attendance. Most fans, then as now, were male and young, and therefore mostly drafted.) The next was not until 1946; and from then to the present, there has been one in every year. And looks like going on as a regular annual event until the end of time.

They aren't any little dozen-person meetings any more. Registration runs to two or three thousand persons—not counting those who slide in without paying a registration fee. They take the full resources of a large hotel to accommodate them. In fact, most hotels aren't big enough for a Worldcon. And what was once a pious hope is now pretty much a reality; they are "world." Fans from nearly every country in the world except for the U.S.S.R. and Mainland China have turned up at one Worldcon or another. And the convention itself has begun to float free of the United States from time to time: twice in Canada, twice in England, once in Germany so far; and Australia, Japan and Sweden are all actively planning to take their turn as hosts for the future.

What brings all these people together?

The same thing that brought the six of us to Philadelphia more than a third of a century ago: the shared conviction that science fiction is worth both reading and talking about, and that the people who share this belief are worth meeting.

.   .   .

To a neofan walking in dazzlement into his first convention, everything seems huge, noisy and confusing. There is a reason for this. It *is* huge, noisy and confusing. I've been to at least a hundred conventions, all over the world, and I still get culture shock every time I walk through that door.

Still, there is a sort of plan. A program exists. (Usually.) Events follow each other in some sort of assimilable order. All it takes to learn to live happily in this environment is patience and a willingness to be taught.

At the larger conventions the program in fact never stops. All night long there will be impromptu discussions and probably the showing of films, old sf pictures rescued from the Late, Late Show or ancient serials or foreign films halfway dubbed into English or resuscitated TV shows. They run all night partly for the people who can't sleep, partly for the people who would rather enjoy every minute of the con than sleep and partly for people who would rather sleep than anything else but, having spent all their money with the hucksters, can't afford the price of a bed.

If there are no films, there are parties. Some are more or less official (the convention itself may keep an all-night "hospitality room" going, or one of the clubs will). Some are ad hoc, in someone's room. I must confess that it is no longer ice-cream sodas that are the refreshment at most of these parties. But they aren't American Legion beer-busts, either; you see more people boiled or stoned at an insurance agents' annual sales conference than at most sf conventions. Fans come to conventions primarily to be with other fans, not to escape from them into oblivion.

A typical Worldcon runs over a three-day weekend. (When it is in the United States, the weekend is almost always Labor Day.) There will often be ancillary events a day or two before and a day or two after—for a while it seemed the Worldcons were going to grow at such a rate that before long they would take more days each year than there *were* in each year. But they seem to have stabilized at a basic seventy-two-hour configuration, from dinnertime Friday to dinnertime Monday.

You walk in the door, and you find yourself at a registration desk. Here fan volunteers relieve you of a few dollars and give you in return a program, an envelope full of miscellaneous magazines, posters, invitations and leaflets and a badge. Don't lose the badge. Without it you can't get into some of the events.

If you are there for the opening event, it is usually a keynote speech by a famous writer of science fiction, followed by a master of ceremonies who goes around the room introducing all the celebrities present. Most of them are writers, or otherwise professionally involved in science fiction. Not all; over the years a number of fans have been so energetic and assiduous in their attendance that they have become celebrities themselves.

So far, all is simple enough. After that, it begins to get confused.

After that opening session the problem is not finding something to do, it is deciding which among several competing events you want to be involved in. The formal program itself may have different panels going on in different places. Even if it is monolithic, the "official" program is only a part of what is happening. Other groups have schedules of their own, actually cons-within-the-con: First Fandom (the doddering dinosaurs of fanactivity—to get in you have to have been reading sf more than a quarter of a century); the Burroughs Bibliophiles (their main interest is the ochre sands of Barsoom); SFWA (otherwise known as the Science Fiction Writers of America, the pros' trade union); Star Trekkies; Perry Rhodan freaks; etc. Sometimes there are special meetings for individual writers, where you can sit at the feet of the master or help pay for his eggs Benedict brunch. There are autograph parties, and informal gatherings in coffee shops, lobby and hallways. And there are bidding parties. These are particularly attractive if you are new, because they are free, and because you are very much wanted. The bidding parties are sponsored by groups from other cities who would like to have the next convention there. (Actually, the next but one; the events have become so complex that it takes two years' lead time to put one on.) Each convention votes at its business meeting on the site of the two-year-subsequent one. There is a rotation plan which spells out which part of the world should get preference, but within that area, there are usually several groups who would like to have it for themselves. If you are a registered member, you have a vote, and in order to get your vote, they will bribe you with (limited) free drinks and unlimited supplies of leaflets, lapel buttons and campaign promises.

And, in and around everything else, there are the "standing events": the permanent trade fairs, the art shows and the "hucksters."

The art shows are what they say they are: rooms like galleries, lined with paintings, drawings and *objets d'art* in general, on sf themes, offered for your enjoyment. The way you express your enjoyment is to buy some. Nearly all are for sale, and if you don't like the price on the sticker, you may be able to pick your choice up a lot cheaper at the auction that ends the con. Not only art is auctioned. You can also bid on manuscripts by your favorite writer, or even on your favorite writer himself. (Once I was auctioned off, or at least one hour of my time was. The man who bought me spent the whole hour asking about how to write, what to say to editors, what kinds of stories were salable, and so on. He paid forty dollars, and he got his money's worth; he is now one of the leading sf writers of his area.)

The hucksters are fans who rent tables, spread them with old magazines, comic books or whatever, and sell them to whoever wants to buy. You can pick up a Volume I Number I *Amazing Stories* there (provided you have a good enough credit rating to pay for it), or a coverless last-month's paperback for a dime. The hucksters are open for business nearly all day long, and browsing is encouraged. They know what they're doing. If you look long enough, sooner or later you'll buy.

The program itself?

Mostly it is talk. Single talks, panels, sometimes slide talks. The speakers are generally well-known writers, or persons who have some special knowledge. A lot of scientists are science-fiction fans, and many of them, including some world-famous ones, have come to sf conventions to share their excitement about what is happening in some area of science. I remember a talk by a man who was actually designing an interstellar spaceship—I don't mean drawing plans in his basement, I mean he was *paid* by a major aerospace corporation to do it. Another by a person who proposed to solve the energy crisis by orbiting solar-power generators and beaming microwave power down to earth. Another on robots, by one of the world's greatest computer authorities. Another on the powers of the mind, by *the* world's greatest authority on the physical basis of mind.

What the writers talk about is usually themselves, or what they write, or what they think of other writers. What the fans usually talk about is fandom: slide shows of old conventions, fanzine publishing, feuds.

Whatever the subject and whoever is speaking, in the long run it usually turns into a good, old-fashioned rap session, with questions, discussions and the odd insult from the floor.

All this is true of Worldcons and of most of the larger local events. Smaller ones are—well, smaller. Less organized. Fewer people. But not less fun. A nice thing about the smaller ones is that you don't have to bother with the program at all. Especially in warm weather, you can count on seeing everyone you really care about seeing sooner or later lounging around the hotel pool.

And at almost every convention there is a banquet.

In a sense, the banquet is the core of every convention. It is the place where the honors are paid.

The Worldcons have developed a whole jungly undergrowth of honors: the Big Heart award, the First Fandom award and up to almost a dozen Hugos for various kinds of excellence in the field, all in an atmosphere of enormous tension and embalmed smiles on the faces of every contender. (It is marvelous to be awarded one of these trophies, but not quite as much fun to be a nominee. At last year's convention I sat at a table with Ben Bova and Isaac Asimov. All three of us were in the running for Hugos—fortunately, for three different categories, or actually four, since I was nominated for two. You would not believe the nervous tension among us old pros as the envelopes were opened and the names of the winners read out. Fortunately, we all came away with a Hugo, otherwise some fine old friendships might have died a sudden death that night.)

But all this is only an entr'acte to the star turn of the convention: the banquet speech by the Guest of Honor. I have listened to about a score of these at Worldcons, and given one myself. I can testify that for both the speaker and the audience, they are the emotional highspots of any world convention.

The Worldcon Guests of Honor are the most respected names in science fiction. And this is their book.

—Frederik Pohl
GoH, Los Angeles, 1972

The Science Fiction
Roll of Honor

KINGS WHO DIE

Poul Anderson

DETROIT, 1959

In Toronto's Worldcon of 1948, where I first met Poul Anderson, he was a young fan who had just begun to write science fiction for publication. He did it so prolifically and well that just over a decade later he was Guest of Honor in Detroit.

Since then he has won both Hugos and Nebulas and served a term as president of the sf writers' trade union, the Science Fiction Writers of America. Janus-like, Anderson's gaze goes both ways. During working hours he peers into the future to write science-fiction stories, but in his leisure time he returns to the past. One of the leading spirits behind the Society for Creative Anachronism, Anderson et famille get together wherever there is a greensward, whenever opportunity presents, dress in medieval costume and conduct tourneys, with fullest adherence to the complex and rewarding codes of chivalry in vogue before Agincourt.

With his wife, Karen (like Poul, a science-fiction fan who became a professional writer), Anderson lives just north of San Francisco in the hills inhabited by Jack Vance, Robert Silverberg and a dozen other major science-fiction writers.

LUCKILY, Diaz was facing the other way when the missile exploded. It was too far off to blind him permanently, but the retinal burns would have taken a week or more to heal. He saw the glare reflected in his view lenses. As a ground soldier he would have hit the rock and tried to claw himself a hole. But there was no ground here, no up or down, concealment or shelter, on a slice of spaceship orbiting through the darkness beyond Mars.

Diaz went loose in his armor. Countdown: brow, jaw, neck, shoulders, back, chest, belly . . . No blast came, to slam him against the end of his lifeline and break any bones whose muscles were not relaxed. So it had not been a shaped-charge shell, firing a cone of atomic-powered concussion through space. Or if it was, he had not been caught in the danger zone. As for radiation, he needn't worry much about that. Whatever particles and gamma photons he got at this distance should not be too big a dose for the anti-X in his body to handle the effects.

He was alive.

He drew a breath which was a good deal shakier than the Academy satorist would have approved of. ("If your nerves twitch, cadet-san, then you know yourself alive and they need not twitch. Correct?" To hell with that, except as a technique.) Slowly, he hauled himself in until his boots made magnetic contact and he stood, so to speak, upon his raft.

Then he turned about for a look.

"Nombre de Dios," he murmured, a hollow noise in the helmet. Forgotten habit came back, with a moment's recollection of his mother's face. He crossed himself.

Against blackness and a million wintry stars, a gas cloud expanded. It glowed in many soft hues, the center still bright, edges fading into vacuum. Shaped explosions did not behave like that, thought the calculator part of Diaz; this had been a standard fireball type. But the cloud was nonspherical. Hence a ship had been hit. A big ship. But whose?

Most of him stood in wonder. A few years ago he'd spent a furlough at Antarctic Lodge. He and some girl had taken a snowcat out to watch the aurora, thinking it would make a romantic background. But then they saw the sky and forgot about each other for a long time. There was only the aurora.

The same awesome silence was here, as that incandescence which had been a ship and her crew swelled and vanished into space.

The calculator in his head proceeded with its business. Of those American vessels near the *Argonne* when first contact was made with the enemy, only the *Washington* was sufficiently massive to go out in a blast of yonder size and shape. If that was what had happened, Captain Martin Diaz of the United States Astromilitary Corps was a dead man. The other ships of the line were too distant, traveling on vectors too unlike his own, for their scoutboats to come anywhere close to where he was.

On the other hand, it might well have been a Unasian battlewagon. Diaz had small information on the dispositions of the enemy fleet. He'd had his brain full just directing the torp launchers under his immediate command. If that had indeed been a hostile dreadnaught which got clobbered, surely none but the *Washington* could have delivered the blow, and its boats would be near—

There!

For half a second Diaz was too stiffened by the sight to react. The boat ran black across waning clouds, accelerating on a streak of its own fire. The wings and sharp shape that were needed in atmosphere made him think of a marlin he had once hooked off Florida, blue lightning under the sun . . . Then a flare was in his hand, he squeezed the igniter and radiance blossomed.

Just an attention-getting device, he thought, and laughed unevenly as he and Bernie Sternthal had done, acting out the standard irreverences of high school students toward the psych course. But Bernie had left his bones on Ganymede, three years ago, and in this hour Diaz's throat was constricted and his nostrils full of his own stench.

He skyhooked the flare and hunkered in its harsh illumination by his radio transmitter. Clumsy in their gauntlets, his fingers adjusted controls, set the revolving beams on SOS. If he had been noticed, and if it was physically possible to make the velocity changes required, a boat would come for him. The Corps looked after its own.

Presently the flare guttered out. The pyre cloud faded to nothing.

The raft deck was between Diaz and the shrunken sun, but the stars that crowded on every side gave ample soft light. He allowed his gullet, which felt like sandpaper, a suck from his one water flask. Otherwise he had several air bottles, an oxygen reclaim unit and a ridiculously large box of Q rations. His raft was a section of inner plating, torn off when the *Argonne* encountered the ball storm. She was only a pursuit cruiser, unarmored against such weapons. At thirty miles per second, relative, the little steel spheres tossed in her path by some Unasian gun had not left much but junk and corpses. Diaz had found no other survivors. He'd lashed what he could salvage onto this raft, including a shaped torp charge that rocketed him clear of the ruins. This far spaceward, he didn't need screen fields against solar-particle radiation. So he had had a small hope of rescue. Maybe bigger than small, now.

Unless an enemy craft spotted him first.

His scalp crawled with that thought. His right arm, where the thing lay buried which he might use in the event of capture, began to itch.

But no, he told himself, don't be sillier than regulations require. That scoutboat was positively American. The probability of a hostile vessel being in detection range of his flare and radio—or able to change vectors fast enough—or giving a damn about him in any event—approached so close to zero as made no difference.

"Wish I'd found our bottle in the wreckage," he said aloud. He was talking to Carl Bailey, who'd helped him smuggle the Scotch aboard at Shepard Field when the fleet was alerted for departure. The steel balls had chewed Carl to pieces, some of which Diaz had seen. "It gripes me not to empty that bottle. On behalf of us both, I mean. Maybe," his voice wandered on, "a million years hence, it'll drift into another planetary system and owl-eyed critters will pick it up in boneless fingers, eh, Carl, and put it in a museum."

He realized what he was doing and snapped his mouth shut. But his mind continued. *The trouble is, those critters won't know about Carl Bailey, who collected antique jazz tapes, and played a rough game of poker, and had a D.S.M. and a gimpy leg from rescuing three boys whose patroller crashed on Venus, and went on the town with Martin Diaz one evening not so long ago when— What did happen that evening, anyhow?*

He dreamed . . .

There was a joint down in the Mexican section of San Diego which Diaz remembered was fun. So they caught a giro outside the Hotel Kennedy, where the spacemen were staying— they could afford swank, and felt they owed it to the Corps—and where they had bought their girls dinner. Diaz punched the cantina's name. The autopilot searched its directory and swung the cab onto the Embarcadero-Balboa skyrail.

Sharon sighed and snuggled into the curve of his arm. "How beautiful," she said. "How nice of you to show me this." He felt she meant a little more than polite banality. The view through the bubble really was great tonight. The city winked and blazed, a god's hoard of jewels, from horizon to horizon. Only in one direction was there anything but light: westward, where the ocean lay aglow. A nearly full moon stood high in the sky. He pointed out a tiny distant glitter on its dark edge.

"Vladimir Base."

"Ugh," said Sharon. "Unasians." She stiffened a trifle.

"Oh, they're decent fellows," Bailey said from the rear seat.

"How do you know?" asked his own date, Naomi, a serious-looking girl and quick on the uptake.

"I've been there a time or two." He shrugged.

"What?" Sharon exclaimed. "When we're at *war*?"

"Why not?" Diaz said. "The Ambassador of United Asia gave a party for our President just yesterday. I watched on the news screen. Big social event."

"But that's different," Sharon protested. "The war goes on in space, not on Earth, and—"

"We don't blow up each other's lunar bases either," Bailey said. "Too close to home. So once in a while we have occasion to, uh, parley is the official word. Actually, the last time I went over—couple years ago now—it was to return a craterbug we'd borrowed and bring some algablight antibiotic they needed. They poured me full of very excellent vodka."

"I'm surprised you admit this so openly," said Naomi.

"No secret, my dear," purred Diaz in his best grandee manner, twirling an imaginary mustache. "The news screens simply don't mention it. Wouldn't be popular, I suppose."

"Oh, people wouldn't care, seeing it was the Corps," Sharon said.

"That's right," Naomi smiled. "The Corps can do no wrong."

"Why, thankee kindly." Diaz grinned at Sharon, chucked her under the chin and kissed her. She held back an instant, having met him only this afternoon. But of course she knew what a date with a Corpsman usually meant, and he knew she knew, and she knew he knew, so before long she relaxed and enjoyed it.

The giro stopped those proceedings by descending to the street and rolling three blocks to the cantina. They entered a low, noisy room hung with bullfight posters and dense with smoke. Diaz threw a glance around and wrinkled his nose. *"Sanabiche!"* he muttered. "The tourists have discovered this place."

"Uh-huh," Bailey answered in the same disappointed *sotto voce*. "Loud tunics, lard faces, 3V and a juke wall. But let's have a couple drinks, at least, seeing we're here."

"That's the trouble with being in space two or three years at a time," Diaz said. "You lose track. Well—" They found a booth.

The waiter recognized him, even after so long a lapse, and called the proprietor. The old man bowed nearly to the floor and begged they accept tequila from his private stock. *"No, no, Señor Capitan, conserva el dinero, por favor."* The girls were delighted. Picturesqueness seemed harder to come by each time Diaz made Earthfall. The evening was off to a good start in spite of everything.

But then someone paid the juke.

The wall came awake with a scrawny blond fourteen-year-old, the latest fashion in sex queens, wearing a grass skirt and three times life size:

Bingle-jingle-jungle-bang-POW!
Bingle-jingle-jangle-bang-UGH!
Uh'm uh red-hot Congo gal an' Uh'm lookin' fuh a pal
Tuh share muh bingle-jingle-bangle-jungle-ugh-YOW!

"What did you say?" Sharon called through the saxophones.

"Never mind," Diaz grunted. "They wouldn't've included it in your school Spanish anyway."

"Those things make me almost wish World War Four would start," Naomi said bitterly.

Bailey's mouth tightened. "Don't talk like that," he said. "Wasn't Number Three close enough call for the race? Without even accomplishing its aims, for either side. I've seen . . . Any war is too big."

Lest they become serious, Diaz said thoughtfully above the racket: "You know, it should be possible to do something about those Kallikak walls. Like, maybe, an oscillator. They've got oscillators these days which'll even goof a solid-state apparatus at close range."

"The F.C.C. wouldn't allow that," Bailey said. "Especially since it'd interfere with local 3V reception."

"That's bad? Besides, you could miniaturize the oscillator so it'd be hard to find. Make it small enough to carry in your pocket. Or even in your body, if you could locate a doctor who'd, uh, perform an illegal operation. I've seen uplousing units no bigger than—"

"You could strew 'em around town," Bailey said, getting interested. "Hide 'em in obscure corners and—"

"Ugga-wugga-wugga, hugga me, do!"

"I *wish* it would stop," Naomi said. "I came here to get to know you, Carl, not that thing."

Bailey sat straight. One hand, lying on the table, shaped a fist. "Why not?" he said.

"Eh?" Diaz asked.

Bailey rose. "Excuse me a minute." He bowed to the girls and made his way through the dancers to the wall control. There he switched the record off.

Silence fell like a meteor. For a moment, voices were stilled too. Then a large tourist came barreling off his bar stool and yelled, "Hey, wha' d'you think you're—"

"I'll refund your money, sir," Bailey said mildly. "But the noise bothers the lady I'm with."

"Huh? Hey, who d'yuh think yuh are, you—"

The proprietor came from around the bar. "If the lady weeshes it off," he declared, "off it stays."

"What kinda discrimination is this?" roared the tourist. Several other people growled with him.

Diaz prepared to go help, in case things got rough. But his companion pulled up the sleeve of his mufti tunic. The ID bracelet gleamed into view. "First Lieutenant Carl H. Bailey, United States Astromilitary Corps, at your service," he said; and a circular wave of quietness expanded around him. "Please forgive my action. I'll gladly stand the house a round."

But that wasn't necessary. The tourist fell all over himself apologizing and begged to buy the drinks. Then someone else bought them, and someone after him. Nobody ventured near the booth, where the spacemen obviously wanted privacy. But from time to time, when Diaz glanced out, he got many smiles and a few shy waves. It was almost embarrassing.

"I was afraid for a minute we'd have a fight," he said.

"N-no," Bailey answered. "I've watched our prestige develop exponentially, being Stateside while my leg healed. I doubt if there's an American alive who'd lift a finger against a Corpsman these days. But I admit I was afraid of a scene. That wouldn't've done the name of the Corps any good. As things worked out, though—"

"We came off too bloody well," Diaz finished. "Now there's not even any pseudolife in this place. Let's haul mass. We can catch the transpolar shuttle to Paris if we hurry."

But at that moment the proprietor's friends and relations, who also remembered him, began to arrive. They must have been phoned the great news. Pablo was there, Manuel, Carmen with her castanets, Juan with his guitar, Tío Rico waving a bottle in each enormous fist; and they welcomed Diaz back with embraces, and soon there was song and dancing, and the fiesta ended in the rear courtyard watching the moon set before dawn, and everything was just like the old days, for Señor Capitan Diaz's sake.

That had been a hell of a good furlough . . .

II

Another jet splashed fire across the Milky Way. Closer this time, and obviously reducing relative speed.

Diaz croaked out a cheer. He had spent weary hours waiting. The hugeness and aloneness had eaten further into his defenses than he wished to realize. He had begun to understand what some people told him, that it disturbed them to see the stars on a clear mountain night. (Where wind went soughing through pines whose bark smelled like vanilla if you laid your head close, and a river flowed cold and loud over stones—oh, Christ, how beautiful Earth was!) He shoved such matters aside and reactivated his transmitter.

The streak winked out and the stars crowded back into his eyes. But that was all right. It meant the boat had decelerated as much as necessary, and soon there would be a scooter homing on his beam, and water and food and sleep, and a new ship and eventually certain letters to write. That would be the worst part. But not for months or years yet, not till one side or the other conceded the present phase of the war. Diaz found himself wishing most for a cigarette.

He hadn't seen the boat's hull this time, of course; there had been no rosy cloud to silhouette its blackness. Nor did he see the scooter until it was almost upon him. That jet was very thin, since it need only drive a few hundred pounds of mass on which two spacesuited men sat. They were little more than a highlight and a shadow. Diaz's pulse filled the silence. "Hallo!" he called in his helmet mike. "Hallo, there!"

They didn't answer. The scooter matched velocities a few yards off. One man tossed a line with a luminous bulb at the end. Diaz caught it and made fast. The line was drawn taut. Scooter and raft bumped together and began gently rotating.

Diaz recognized those helmets.

He snatched for a sidearm he didn't have. A Unasian sprang to one side, lifeline unreeling. His companion stayed mounted, a chucker gun cradled in his arms. The sun rose blindingly over the raft edge.

There was nothing to be done. Yet. Diaz fought down a physical nausea of defeat, "raised" his hands and let them hang free. The other man came behind him and deftly wired his wrists together. Both Unasians spent a few minutes inspecting the raft. The man with the gun tuned in on the American band.

"You make very clever salvage, sir," he said.

"Thank you," Diaz whispered, helpless and stunned.

"Come, please." He was lashed to the carrier rack. Weight tugged at him as the scooter accelerated.

They took an hour or more to rendezvous. Diaz had time to adjust his emotions. The first horror passed into numbness; then there was a sneaking relief, that he would get a reasonably comfortable vacation from war until the next prisoner exchange; and then he remembered the new doctrine, which applied to all commissioned officers whom there had been time to operate on.

I may never get the chance, he thought frantically. *They told me not to waste myself on anything less than a cruiser; my chromosomes and several million dollars spent in training me make me that valuable to the country, at least. I may go straight to Pallas, or wherever their handiest prison base is, in a lousy scoutboat or cargo ship.*

But I may get a chance to strike a blow that'll hurt. Have I got the guts? I hope so. No, I don't even know if I hope it. This is a cold place to die.

The feeling passed. Emotional control, drilled into him at the Academy and practiced at every refresher course, took over. It was essentially psychosomatic, a matter of using conditioned reflexes to bring muscles and nerves and glands back toward normal. If the fear symptoms—tension, tachycardia, sweat, decreased salivation and the rest—were alleviated, then fear itself was. Far down under the surface, a four-year-old named Martin woke from nightmare and screamed for his mother, who did not come; but Diaz grew able to ignore him.

The boat became visible, black across star clouds. No, not a boat. A small ship . . . abnormally large jets and light guns, a modified *Panyushkin* . . . what had the enemy been up to in his asteroid shipyards? Some kind of courier vessel, maybe. Recognition signals must be flashing back and forth. The scooter passed smoothly through a lock that closed again behind. Air was pumped in. Diaz went blind as frost condensed on his helmet. Several men assisted him out of the armor. They hadn't quite finished when an alarm rang, engines droned and weight came back. The ship was starting off at about half a gee.

Short bodies in green uniforms surrounded Diaz. Their immaculate appearance reminded him of his own unshaven filthiness, how much he ached and how sandy his brain felt. "Well," he mumbled, "where's your interrogation officer?"

"You go more high, Captain," answered a man with colonel's insignia. "Forgive us we do not attend your needs at once, but he says very important."

Diaz bowed to the courtesy, remembering what had been planted in his arm and feeling rather a bastard. Though it looked as if he wouldn't have occasion to use the thing. Dazed by relief and weariness, he let himself be escorted along corridors and tubes, until he stood before a door marked with great black Cyrillic warnings and guarded by two soldiers. Which was almost unheard of aboard a spaceship, he thought joltingly.

There was a teleye above the door. Diaz barely glanced at it. Whoever sat within the cabin must be staring through it, at him. He tried to straighten his shoulders. "Martin Diaz," he husked, "Captain, U.S.A.C., serial number—"

Someone yelled from the loudspeaker beside the pickup. Diaz half understood. He whirled about. His will gathered itself and surged. He began to think the impulses that would destroy the ship. A guard tackled him. A rifle butt came down on his head. And that was that.

They told him forty-eight hours passed while he was in sickbay. "I wouldn't know," he said dully. "Nor care." But he was again in good physical shape. Only a bandage sheathing his lower right arm, beneath the insigneless uniform given him, revealed that surgeons had been at work. His mind was sharply aware of its environment—muscle play beneath his own skin, pastel bulkheads and cold fluorescence, faint machine-quiver underfoot, gusts from ventilator grilles, odors of foreign cooking. And always the men, with alien faces and carefully expressionless voices, who had caught him.

At least there was no abuse. They might have been justified in resenting his attempt to kill them. Some would call it treacherous. But they gave him the treatment due an officer and, except for supplying his needs, left him alone in his tiny bunk cubicle. Which in some respects was worse than punishment. Diaz was actually glad when he was at last summoned for an interview.

They brought him to the guarded door and gestured him through. It closed behind him.

For a moment Diaz noticed only the suite itself. Even a fleet commander didn't get this much space and comfort. The ship had long ceased accelerating, but spin provided a reasonable weight. The suite was constructed within a rotatable shell, so that the same deck was "down" as when the jets were in operation. Diaz stood on a Persian carpet, looking past low-legged furniture to a pair of arched doorways. One revealed a bedroom, lined with microspools—ye gods, there must be ten thousand volumes! The other showed part of an office, a desk and a great enigmatic control panel and—

The man seated beneath the Monet reproduction got up and made a slight bow. He was tall for a Unasian, with a lean mobile face whose eyes were startlingly blue against a skin as white as a Swedish girl's. His undress uniform was neat but carelessly worn. No rank insignia were visible, for a gray hood, almost a coif, covered his head and fell over the shoulders.

"Good day, Captain Diaz," he said, speaking English with little accent. "Permit me to introduce myself: General Leo Ilyitch Rostock, Cosmonautical Service of the People of United Asia."

Diaz went through the rituals automatically. Most of him was preoccupied with how quiet this place was. How very quiet. But the layout was serene. Rostock must be fantastically important if his comfort rated this much mass. Diaz's gaze flickered to the other man's waist. Rostock bore a sidearm. More to the point, though, one loud holler would doubtless be picked up by the teleye mike and bring in the guards outside.

Diaz tried to relax. *If they haven't kicked my teeth in so far, they don't plan to. I'm going to live.* But he couldn't believe that. Not here, in the presence of this hooded man. Even more so, in his drawing room. Its existence beyond Mars was too eerie. "No, sir, I have no complaints," he heard himself saying. "You run a good ship. My compliments."

"Thank you." Rostock had a charming, almost boyish smile. "Although this is not my ship, actually. Colonel Sumoro commands the *Ho Chi Minh.* I shall convey your appreciation to him."

"You may not be called the captain," Diaz said bluntly, "but the vessel is obviously your instrument."

Rostock shrugged. "Will you not sit down?" he invited, and resumed his own place on the couch. Diaz took a chair across the table from him, feeling knobby and awkward. Rostock pushed a box forward. "Cigarettes?"

"Thank you." Diaz struck and inhaled hungrily.

"I hope your arm does not bother you."

Diaz's belly muscles tightened. "No. It's all right."

"The surgeons left the metal ulnar bone in place, as well as its nervous and muscular connections. Complete replacement would have required more hospital equipment than a spaceship can readily carry. We did not want to cripple you by removing the bone. After all, we were only interested in the cartridge."

Diaz gathered courage and snapped: "The more I see of you, General, the sorrier I am that it didn't work. You're big game."

Rostock chuckled. "Perhaps. I wonder, though, if you are as sorry as you would like to feel you are. You would have died too, you realize."

"Uh-huh."

"Do you know what the weapon embedded in you was?"

"Yes. *We* tell our people such things. A charge of isotopic explosive, with a trigger activated by a particular series of motor nerve pulses. Equivalent to about ten tons of TNT." Diaz gripped the chair arms, leaned forward and said harshly: "I'm not blabbing anything you don't now know. I daresay you consider it a violation of the customs of war. Not me! I gave no parole—"

"Certainly, certainly." Rostock waved a deprecating hand. "There are—what is your idiom?—no hard feelings. The device was ingenious. We have already dispatched a warning to our Central, whence the word can go out through the fleet, so your effort, the entire project, has gone for nothing. But it was a rather gallant attempt."

He leaned back, crossed one leg over the other, and regarded the American candidly. "Of course, as you implied, we would have proceeded somewhat differently," he said. "Our men would not have known what they carried, and the explosion would have been triggered posthypnotically, by some given class of situations, rather than consciously. In that way, there would be less chance of betrayal."

"How did you know, anyway?" Diaz sighed.

Rostock gave him an impish grin. "As the villain of this particular little drama, I shall only say that I have my methods." Suddenly he was grave. "One reason we made such an effort to pick you up before your own rescue party arrived, was to gather data on what you have been doing, you people. You know how comparatively rare it is to get a prisoner in space warfare; and how hard to get spies into an organization of high morale which maintains its own laboratories and factories off Earth. Divergent developments can go far these days, before the other side is aware of them. The miniaturization involved in your own weapon, for example, astonished our engineers."

"I can't tell you anything else," Diaz said.

"Oh, you could," Rostock answered gently. "You know as well as I what can be done with a shot of babble juice. Not to mention other techniques—nothing melodramatic, nothing painful or disabling, merely applied neurology—in which I believe Unasia is ahead of the Western countries. But don't worry, Captain. I shall not permit any such breach of military custom.

"However, I do want you to understand how much trouble we went to, to get you. When combat began, I reasoned that the ships auxiliary to a dreadnaught would be the likeliest to suffer destruction of the type which leaves a few survivors. From the pattern of action in the first day, I deduced the approximate orbits and positions of several American capital ships. Unasian tactics throughout the second day were developed with two purposes: to inflict damage, of course, but also to get the *Ho* so placed that we would be likely to detect any distress signals. This cost us the *Genghis*—a calculated risk which did not pay off— I am not omniscient. But we did hear your call.

"You are quite right about the importance of this ship here. My superiors will be horrified at my action. But of necessity, they have given me *carte blanche*. And since the *Ho* itself takes no direct part in any engagement, if we can avoid it, the probability of our being detected and attacked was small."

Rostock's eyes held Diaz's. He tapped the table, softly and repeatedly, with one fingernail. "Do you appreciate what all this means, Captain?" he asked. "Do you see how badly you were wanted?"

Diaz could only wet his lips and nod.

"Partly," Rostock said, smiling again, "there was the desire I have mentioned, to—er—check up on American activities during the last cease-fire period. But partly, too, there was a wish to bring you up to date on what we have been doing."

"*Huh?*" Diaz half scrambled from his chair, sagged back and gaped.

"The choice is yours, Captain," Rostock said. "You can be transferred to a cargo ship when we can arrange it, and so to an asteroid camp, and in general receive the normal treatment of a war prisoner. Or you may elect to hear what I would like to discuss with you. In the latter event, I can guarantee nothing. Obviously I can't let you go home in a routine prisoner exchange with a prime military secret of ours. You will have to wait until it is no longer a secret. Until American intelligence has learned the truth, and we know that they have. That may take years. It may take forever: because I have some hope that the knowledge will change certain of your own attitudes.

"No, no, don't answer now. Think it over. I will see you again tomorrow. In twenty-four hours, that is to say."

Rostock's eyes shifted past Diaz, as if to look through the bulkheads. His tone dropped suddenly to a whisper. "Have you ever wondered, like me, why we carry Earth's rotation period to space with us? Habit; practicality; but is there not also an element of magical thinking? A hope that somehow we can create our own sunrises? The sky is very black out there. We need all the magic we can invent. Do we not?"

III

Some hours later, alarms sounded, voices barked over the intercoms, spin was halted but weight came quickly back as the ship accelerated.

Diaz knew just enough Mandarin to understand from what he overheard that radar contact had been made with American units and combat would soon resume. The guard who brought him dinner in his cubicle confirmed it, with many a bow and hissing smile. Diaz had gained enormous face by his audience with the man in the suite.

He couldn't sleep, though the racket soon settled down to a purposeful murmur with few loud interruptions. Restless in his bunk harness, he tried to reconstruct a total picture from what clues he had. The primary American objective was the asteroid base system of the enemy. But astromilitary tactics were too complicated for one brain to grasp. A battle might go on for months, flaring up whenever hostile units came near enough in their enormous orbitings to exchange fire. Eventually, Diaz knew, if everything went well—that is, didn't go too badly haywire— Americans would land on the Unasian worldlets. That would be the rough part. He remembered ground operations on Mars and Ganymede much too well.

As for the immediate situation, though, he could only make an educated guess. The leisurely pace at which the engagement was developing indicated that ships of dreadnaught mass were in- volved. Therefore no mere squadron was out there, but an important segment of the American fleet, perhaps the task force headed by the *Alaska*. But if this was true, then the *Ho Chi Minh* must be directing a flotilla of comparable size.

Which wasn't possible! Flotillas and subfleets were bossed from dreadnaughts. A combat computer and its human staff were just too big and delicate to be housed in anything less. And the *Ho* was not even as large as the *Argonne* had been.

Yet what the hell was this but a command ship? Rostock had hinted as much. The activity aboard was characteristic, the repeated sound of courier boats coming and going, intercom calls, technicians hurrying along the corridors, but no shooting.

Nevertheless—

Voices jabbered beyond the cell door. Their note was triumphant. Probably they related a hit on an American vessel. Diaz recalled brushing aside chunks of space-frozen meat that had been his Corps brothers. Sammy Yoshida was in the *Utah Beach*, which was with the *Alaska*—Sammy who'd covered for him back at the Academy when he crawled in dead drunk hours after taps, and some years later had dragged him from a shell-struck foxhole on Mars and shared oxygen till a rescue squad happened by. Had the *Utah Beach* been hit? Was that what they were giggling about out there?

Prisoner exchange, in a year or two or three, will get me back for the next round of the war, Diaz thought in darkness. *But I'm only one man. And I've goofed somehow, spilled a scheme which might've cost the Unies several ships before they tumbled. It's hardly conceivable I could smuggle out whatever information Rostock wants to give me. But there'd be some tiny probability that I could, somehow, sometime. Wouldn't there?*

I don't want to. Dios mio, how I don't want! Let me rest a while, and then be swapped, and go back for a long furlough on Earth, where anything I ask for is mine and mainly I ask for sunlight and ocean and flowering trees. But Carl liked those things too, didn't he? Liked them and lost them forever.

There came a lull in the battle. The fleets had passed each other, decelerating as they fired. They would take many hours to turn around and get back within combat range. A great quietness descended on the *Ho*. Walking down the passageways, which thrummed with rockblast, Diaz saw how the technicians slumped at their posts. The demands on them were as hard as those on a pilot or gunner or missile chief. Evolution designed men to fight with their hands, not with computations and pushbuttons. Maybe ground combat wasn't the worst kind.

The sentries admitted Diaz through the door of the warning. Rostock sat at the table again. His coifed features looked equally drained, and his smile was automatic. A samovar and two teacups stood before him.

"Be seated, Captain," he said tonelessly. "Pardon me if I do not rise. This has been an exhausting time."

Diaz accepted a chair and a cup. Rostock drank noisily, eyes closed and forehead puckered. There might have been an extra stimulant in his tea, for before long he appeared more human. He refilled the cups, passed out cigarettes and leaned back on his couch with a sigh.

"You may be pleased to know," he said, "that the third pass will be the final one. We shall refuse further combat and proceed instead to join forces with another flotilla near Pallas."

"Because that suits your purposes better," Diaz said.

"Well, naturally. I compute a higher likelihood of ultimate success if we follow a strategy of— No matter now."

Diaz leaned forward. His heart slammed. "So this *is* a command ship," he exclaimed. "I thought so."

The blue eyes weighed him with care. "If I give you any further information," Rostock said—softly, but the muscles tightened along his jaw—"you must accept the conditions I set forth."

"I do," Diaz got out.

"I realize that you do so in the hope of passing on the secret to your countrymen," Rostock said. "You may as well forget about that. You won't get the chance."

"Then why do you want to tell me? You won't make a Unie out of me, General." The words sounded too stuck up, Diaz decided. "That is, I respect your people and, and so forth, but, uh, my loyalties lie elsewhere."

"Agreed. I don't hope or plan to change them. At least, not in an easterly direction." Rostock drew hard on his cigarette, let smoke stream from his nostrils and squinted through it. "The microphone is turned down," he remarked. "We cannot be overheard unless we shout. I must warn you, if you make any attempt to reveal what I am about to say to you to any of my own people, I shall not only deny it but order you sent out the airlock. It is that important."

Diaz rubbed his hands on his trousers. The palms were wet. "Okay," he said.

"Not that I mean to browbeat you, Captain," said Rostock hastily. "What I offer is friendship. In the end, maybe, peace." He sat a while longer looking at the wall, before his glance shifted back to Diaz's. "Suppose you begin the discussion. Ask me what you like."

"Uh—" Diaz floundered about, as if he'd been leaning on a door that was thrown open. "Uh . . . well, was I right? Is this a command ship?"

"Yes. It performs every function of a flag dreadnaught, except that it seldom engages in direct combat. The tactical advantages are obvious. A smaller, lighter vessel can get about much more readily, hence be a correspondingly more effective directrix. Furthermore, if due caution is exercised, we are not likely to be detected and fired at. The massive armament of a dreadnaught is chiefly to stave off the missiles which can annihilate the command post within. Ships of this class avoid that whole problem by avoiding attack in the first place."

"But your computer! You, uh, you must have developed a combat computer as . . . small and rugged as an autopilot—I thought miniaturization was our specialty."

Rostock laughed.

"And you'd still need a large human staff," Diaz protested. "Bigger than the whole crew of this ship!

"Wouldn't you?" he finished weakly.

Rostock shook his head. "No." His smile faded. "Not under this new system. I am the computer."

"What?"

"Look." Rostock pulled off his hood.

The head beneath was hairless, not shaved but depilated. A dozen silvery plates were set into it, flush with the scalp; there were outlets in them. Rostock pointed toward the office. "The rest of me is in there," he said. "I need only plug the jacks into the appropriate points of myself, and I become—no, not part of the computer. It becomes part of me."

He fell silent again, gazing now at the floor. Diaz hardly dared move, until his cigarette burned his fingers and he must stub it out. The ship pulsed around them. Monet's picture of sunlight caught in young leaves was like something seen at the far end of a tunnel.

"Consider the problem," Rostock said at last, low. "In spite of much loose talk about giant brains, computers do not think, except perhaps on an idiot level. They merely perform logical operations, symbol-shuffling, according to instructions given them. It was shown long ago that there are infinite classes of problems which no computer can solve: the classes dealt with in Godel's theorem, that can only be solved by the nonlogical process of creating a metalanguage. Creativity is not logical and computers do not create.

"In addition, as you know, the larger a computer becomes, the more staff it requires, to perform such operations as data coding, programming, retranslation of the solutions into practical terms, and adjustment of the artificial answer to the actual problem. Yet your own brain does this sort of thing constantly . . . because it is creative. Moreover, the advanced computers are heavy, bulky, fragile things. They use cryogenics and all the other tricks, but that involves elaborate ancillary apparatus. Your brain weighs a kilogram or so, is very adequately protected in the skull and needs less than a hundred kilos of outside equipment—your body.

"I am not being mystical. There is no reason why creativity cannot someday be duplicated in an artificial structure. But I think that structure will look very much like a living organism; will, indeed, be one. Life has had a billion years to develop these techniques.

"Now if the brain has so many advantages, why use a computer at all? Obviously, to do the uncreative work, for which the brain is not specifically designed. The brain visualizes a problem of say, orbits, masses and tactics, and formulates it as a set of matrix equations. Then the computer goes swiftly through the millions of idiot counting operations needed to produce a numerical solution.

What we have developed here, we Unasians, is nothing but a direct approach. We eliminate the middle man, as you Americans would say.

"In yonder office is a highly specialized computer. It is built from solid-state units, analogous to neurones, but in spite of being able to treat astromilitary problems, it is a comparatively small, simple and sturdy device. Why? Because it is used in connection with my brain, which directs it. The normal computer must have its operational patterns built in. Mine develops synapse pathways as needed, just as a man's lower brain can develop skills under the direction of the cerebral cortex. And these pathways are modifiable by experience; the system is continually restructuring itself. The normal computer must have elaborate failure detection systems and arrangements for re-routing. I in the hookup here sense any trouble directly, and am no more disturbed by the temporary disability of some region than you are disturbed by the fact that most of your brain cells at any given time are resting.

"The human staff becomes superfluous here. My technicians bring me the data, which need not be reduced to standardized format. I link myself to the machine and—think about it—there are no words. The answer is worked out in no more time than any other computer would require. But it comes to my consciousness not as a set of figures, but in practical terms, decisions about what to do. Furthermore, the solution is modified by my human awareness of those factors too complex to go into physical condition of men and equipment, morale, long-range questions of logistics and strategy and ultimate goals. You might say this is a computer system with common sense. Do you understand, Captain?"

Diaz sat still for a long time before he said, "Yes. I think I do."

Rostock had gotten a little hoarse. He poured himself a fresh cup of tea and drank half, struck another cigarette and said earnestly: "The military value is obvious. Were that all, I would never have revealed this much to you. But something else developed as I practiced and increased my command of the system. Something quite unforseen. I wonder if you will comprehend." He finished his cup. "That repeated experience changed me. I am no longer human. Not really."

IV

The ship whispered, driving through darkness.

"I suppose a hookup like that would affect the emotions," Diaz ventured. "How does it feel?"

"There are no words," Rostock repeated, "except those I have made for myself." He rose and walked restlessly across the subdued rainbows in the carpet, hands behind his back, eyes focused on nothing Diaz could see. "As a matter of fact, the only emotional effect may be a simple intensification. Although . . . there are myths about mortals who became gods. How did it feel to them? I think they hardly noticed the palaces and music and feasting on Olympus. What mattered was how, piece by piece, as he mastered his new capacities, the new god won a god's understanding. His perception, involvement, detachment, total-ness . . . there *are* no words."

Back and forth he paced, feet noiseless but metal and energies humming beneath his low and somehow troubled voice. "My cerebrum directs the computer," he said, "and the relationship becomes reciprocal. True, the computer part has no creativity of its own but it endows mine with a speed and sureness you cannot imagine. After all, a great part of original thought consists merely in proposing trial solutions. The scientist hypothesizes, the artist draws a charcoal line, the poet scribbles a phrase. Then they test them to see if they work. By now, to me, this mechanical aspect of imagination is back down on the subconscious level where it belongs. What my awareness senses is the final answer, springing to life almost simultaneously with the question, and yet with a felt reality to it such as comes only from having pondered and tested the issue for thousands of times.

"Also, the amount of sense data I can handle is fantastic. Oh, I am blind and deaf and numb away from my machine half! So you will realize that over the months I have tended to spend more and more time in the linked state. When there was no immediate command problem to solve, I would sit and savor it."

In a practical tone: "That is how I perceived that you were about to sabotage us, Captain. Your posture alone betrayed you. I guessed the means at once and ordered the guards to knock you unconscious. I think, also, that I detected in you the potential I need. But that demands closer examination. Which is easily given. When I am linked, you cannot lie to me. The least insincerity is written across your whole organism."

He paused, to stand a little slumped, looking at the bulkhead. For a moment Diaz's legs tensed. *Three jumps and I can be there and get his gun!* But no, Rostock wasn't any brain-heavy dwarf. The body in that green uniform was young and trained. Diaz took another cigarette. "Okay," he said. "What do you propose?"

"First," Rostock said, turning about—and his eyes kindled— "I want you to understand what you and I are. What the spacemen of both factions are."

"Professional soldiers," Diaz grunted uneasily. Rostock waited. Diaz puffed hard and plowed on, since he was plainly expected to: "The only soldiers left. You can't count those ornamental regiments on Earth, nor the guys sitting by the big missiles. Those missiles will never be fired. World War Three was a large enough dose of nucleonics. Civilization was lucky to survive. Terrestrial life would be lucky to survive, next time around. So war has moved into space. Uh . . . professionalism . . . the old traditions of mutual respect and so forth have naturally revived." He made himself look up. "What more clichés need I repeat?"

"Suppose your side completely annihilated our ships," Rostock said. "What would happen?"

"Why . . . that's been discussed theoretically . . . by damn near every political scientist, hasn't it? The total command of space would not mean total command of Earth. We could destroy the whole eastern hemisphere without being touched. But we wouldn't because Unasia would fire its cobalt weapons while dying, and there'd be no western hemisphere to come home to either. Not that that situation will ever arise. Space is too big. There are too many ships and fortresses scattered around; combat is too slow a process. Neither fleet can wipe out the other."

"Since we have this perpetual stalemate, then," Rostock pursued, "why is there perpetual war?"

"Well, uh, partial victories are possible. Like our capture of Mars, or your destruction of three dreadnaughts in one month, on different occasions. The balance of power shifts. Rather than let its strength continue being whittled down, the side which is losing asks for a parley. There are negotiations, which end to the relative advantage of the stronger side. Meanwhile the arms race continues. Pretty soon a new dispute arises, the cease-fire ends, and maybe the other side is lucky that time."

"Is this situation expected to be eternal?"

"No!" Diaz stopped, thought a minute, and grinned with one corner of his mouth. "That is, they keep talking about an effective international organization. Trouble is, the two cultures are too far apart by now. They can't live together."

"I used to believe that myself," Rostock said. "Lately I have not been sure. A world federalism could be devised which would let both civilizations keep their identities. There have in fact been many such proposals, as you know. None has gotten beyond the talking stage. None ever will. Because you see, what maintains the war is not the difference between our two cultures, but their similarity."

"Whoa, there!" Diaz bristled. "I resent that."

"Please," Rostock said. "I pass no moral judgments. For the sake of argument, at least, I can concede you the moral superiority, remarking only in parenthesis that Earth holds billions of people who not only fail to comprehend what you mean by freedom but would not like it if you gave it to them. The similarity I am talking about is technological. Both civilizations are based on the machine, with all the high organization and dynamism which this implies."

"So?"

"So war is a necessity— Wait! I am not talking about 'merchants of death,' or 'dictators needing an outside enemy,' or whatever the current propaganda lines are. I mean that conflict is built into the culture. There *must* be an outlet for the destructive emotions generated in the mass of the people by the type of life they lead. A type of life for which evolution never designed them.

"Have you ever heard about L. F. Richardson? No? He was an Englishman in the last century, a Quaker, who hated war but, being a scientist, realized the phenomenon must be understood clinically before it can be eliminated. He performed some brilliant theoretical and statistical analyses which showed, for example, that the rate of deadly quarrels was very nearly constant over the decades. There could be many small clashes or a few major ones, but the result was the same. Why were the United States and the Chinese Empire so peaceful during the nineteenth century? The answer is that they were not. They had their Civil War and Taiping Rebellion, which devastated them as much as required. I need not multiply examples. We can discuss this later in detail. I have carried Richardson's work a good deal further and more rigorously. I say to you now only that civilized societies must have a certain rate of immolations."

Diaz listened to silence for a minute before he said: "Well, I've sometimes thought the same. I suppose you mean we spacemen are the goats these days?"

"Exactly. War fought out here does not menace the planet. By our deaths we keep Earth alive."

Rostock sighed. His mouth drooped. "Magic works, you know," he said, "works on the emotions of the people who practice it. If a primitive witch doctor told a storm to go away, the storm did not hear, but the tribe did and took heart. The ancient analogy to us, though, is the sacrificial king in the early agricultural societies: a god in mortal form, who was regularly slain that the fields might bear fruit. This was not mere superstition. You must realize that. It worked—on the people. The rite was essential to the operation of their culture, to their sanity and hence to their survival.

"Today the machine age has developed its own sacrificial kings. We are the chosen of the race. The best it can offer. None gainsays us. We may have what we choose, pleasure, luxury, women, adulation—only not the simple pleasures of wife and child and home, for we must die that the people may live."

Again silence, until: "Do you seriously mean that's why the war goes on?" Diaz breathed.

Rostock nodded.

"But nobody—I mean, people wouldn't—"

"They do not reason these things out, of course. Traditions develop blindly. The ancient peasant did not elaborate logical reasons why the king must die. He merely knew this was so, and left the syllogism for modern anthropologists to expound. I did not see the process going on today until I had had the chance to . . . to become more perceptive than I had been," Rostock said humbly.

Diaz couldn't endure sitting down any longer. He jumped to his feet. "Assuming you're right," he snapped, "and you may be, what of it? What can be done?"

"Much," Rostock said. Calm descended on his face like a mask. "I am not being mystical about this, either. The sacrificial king has reappeared as the end product of a long chain of cause and effect. There is no reason inherent in natural law why this must be. Richardson was right in his basic hope, that when war becomes understood, as a phenomenon, it can be eliminated. This would naturally involve restructuring the entire terrestrial culture. Gradually, subtly. Remember—" His hand shot out, seized Diaz's shoulder and gripped painfully hard. "There is a new element in history today. Us. The kings. We are not like those who spend their lives under Earth's sky. In some ways we are more, in other ways less, but always we are different. You and I are more akin to each other than to our planet-dwelling countrymen. Are we not?

"In the time and loneliness granted me, I have used all my new powers to think about this. Not only think; this is so much more than cold reason. I have tried to feel. To love what is, as the Buddhists say. I believe a nucleus of spacemen like us, slowly and secretly gathered, wishing the good of everyone on Earth and the harm of none, gifted with powers and insights they cannot really imagine at home—I believe we may accomplish something. If not us, then our sons. Men ought not to kill each other, when the stars are waiting."

He let go, turned away and looked at the deck. "Of course," he mumbled, "I, in my peculiar situation, must first destroy a number of your brothers."

They had given Diaz a whole pack of cigarettes, an enormous treasure out here, before they locked him into his cubicle for the duration of the second engagement. He lay in harness, hearing clang and shout and engine roar through the vibrating bulkheads, stared at blackness and smoked until his tongue was foul. Sometimes the *Ho* accelerated, mostly it ran free and he floated. Once a tremor went through the entire hull, near miss by a shaped charge. Doubtless gamma rays, ignoring the magnetic force screens, sleeted through the men and knocked another several months off their life expectancies. Not that that mattered. Spacemen rarely lived long enough to worry about degenerative diseases. Diaz hardly noticed.

He's not lying, Rostock. Why should he? What could he gain? He may be a nut, of course. But he doesn't act like a nut either. He wants me to study his statistics and equations, satisfy myself that he's right. And he must be damn sure I will be convinced, to tell me as much as he has.

How many are there like him? Only a very few, I'm sure. The man-machine symbiosis is obviously new, or we'd've had some inkling ourselves. This is the first field trial of the system. I wonder if the others have reached the same conclusions as Rostock. No, he said he doubts that. Their psychology impressed him as being more deeply channeled than his. He's a lucky accident.

Lucky? Now how can I tell? I'm only a man. I've never experienced an IQ of 1,000, or whatever the figure may be. A god's purposes aren't necessarily what a man would elect.

The eventual end to war? Well, other institutions had been ended, at least in the Western countries; judicial torture, chattel slavery, human sacrifice— No, wait, according to Rostock human sacrifice had been revived.

"But is our casualty rate high enough to fit your equations?" Diaz had argued. "Space forces aren't as big as old-time armies. No country could afford that."

"Other elements than death must be taken into account," Rostock answered. "The enormous expense is one factor. Taxpaying is a form of symbolic self-mutilation. It also tends to direct civilian resentments and aggressions against their own governments, thus taking some pressure off international relations.

"Chiefly, though, there is the matter of emotional intensity. A spaceman not only dies, he usually dies horribly; and that moment is the culmination of a long period under grisly conditions. His groundling brothers, administrative and service personnel, suffer vicariously: 'sweat it out,' as your idiom so well expresses the feeling. His kinfolk, friends, women, are likewise racked. When Adonis dies—or Osiris, Tammuz, Baldur, Christ, Tlaloc, whichever of his hundred names you choose—the people must in some degree share his agony. That is part of the sacrifice."

Diaz had never thought about it just that way. Like most Corpsmen, he had held the average civilian in thinly disguised contempt. But . . . from time to time, he remembered, he'd been glad his mother died before he enlisted. And why did his sister hit the bottle so hard? Then there had been Lois, she of the fire-colored hair and violet eyes, who wept as if she would never stop weeping when he left for duty. He'd promised to get in touch with her on his return, but of course he knew better.

Which did not erase memories of men whose breath and blood came exploding from burst helmets; who shuddered and vomited and defecated in the last stages of radiation sickness; who stared without immediate comprehension at a red spurt which a second ago had been an arm or a leg; who went insane and must be gassed because psychoneurosis is catching on a six months' orbit beyond Saturn; who— Yeah, Carl had been lucky.

You could talk as much as you wished about Corps brotherhood, honor, tradition, and gallantry. It remained sentimental guff . . .

No, that was unjust. The Corps had saved the people, their lives and liberties. There could be no higher achievement—for the Corps. But knighthood had once been a noble thing, too. Then, lingering after its day, it became a yoke and eventually a farce. The warrior virtues were not ends in themselves. If the warrior could be made obsolete—

Could he? How much could one man, even powered by a machine, hope to do? How much could he even hope to understand?

The moment came upon Diaz. He lay as if blinded by shellburst radiance.

As consciousness returned, he knew first, irrelevantly, what it meant to get religion.

"By God," he told the universe, "we're going to try!"

V

The battle would resume very shortly. At any moment, in fact, some scoutship leading the American force might fire a missile. But when Diaz told his guard he wanted to speak with General Rostock, he was taken there within minutes.

The door closed behind him. The living room lay empty, altogether still except for the machine throb, which was not loud since the *Ho* was running free. Because acceleration might be needful on short notice, there was no spin. Diaz hung weightless as fog. And the Monet flung into his eyes all Earth's sunlight and summer forests.

"Rostock?" he called uncertainly.

"Come," said a voice, almost too low to hear. Diaz gave a shove with his foot and flew toward the office.

He stopped himself by grasping the doorjamb. A semicircular room lay before him, the entire side taken up by controls and meters. Lights blinked, needles wavered on dials, buttons and switches and knobs reached across black paneling. But none of that was important. Only the man at the desk mattered, who free-sat with wires running from his head to the wall.

Rostock seemed to have lost weight. Or was that an illusion? The skin was drawn taut across his high cheekbones and gone a dead, glistening white. His nostrils were flared and the colorless lips held tense. Diaz looked into his eyes, once, and then away again. He could not meet them. He could not even think about them. He drew a shaken breath and waited.

"You made your decision quickly," Rostock whispered. "I had not awaited you until after the engagement."

"I . . . I didn't think you would see me till then."

"This is more important." Diaz felt as if he were being probed with knives. He could not altogether believe it was his imagination. He stared desperately at the paneled instruments. Their nonhumanness was like a comforting hand. *They must only be for the benefit of maintenance techs,* he thought in a very distant part of himself. *The brain doesn't need them.*

"You are convinced," Rostock said in frank surprise.

"Yes," Diaz answered.

"I had not expected that. I only hoped for your reluctant agreement to study my work." Rostock regarded him for a still century. "You were ripe for a new faith," he decided. "I had not taken you for the type. But then, the mind can only use what data are given it, and I have hitherto had little opportunity to meet

Americans. Never since I became what I am. You have another psyche from ours."

"I need to understand your findings, sir," Diaz said. "Right now I can only believe. That isn't enough, is it?"

Slowly, Rostock's mouth drew into a smile of quite human warmth. "Correct. But given the faith, intellectual comprehension should be swift."

"I . . . I shouldn't be taking your time . . . now, sir," Diaz stammered. "How should I begin? Should I take some books back with me?"

"No." Acceptance had been reached. Rostock spoke resonantly, a master to his trusted servant. "I need your help here. Strap into yonder harness. Our first necessity is to survive the battle upon us. You realize that this means sacrificing many of your comrades. I know how much that will hurt you. Afterward we shall spend our lives repaying our people—both our peoples. But today I shall ask you questions about your fleet. Any information is valuable, especially details of construction and armament which our intelligence has not been able to learn."

Doña mía. Diaz let go the door, covered his face and fell free, endlessly. *Help me.*

"It is not betrayal," said the superman. "It is the ultimate loyalty you can offer."

Diaz made himself look at the cabin again. He shoved against the bulkhead and stopped by the harness near the desk.

"You cannot lie to me," said Rostock. "Do not deny how much pain I am giving you." Diaz glimpsed his fists clamping together. "Each time I look at you, I share what you feel."

Diaz clung to his harness. There went an explosion through him.

NO, BY GOD!

Rostock screamed.

"Don't," Diaz sobbed. "I don't want—" But wave after wave ripped outward. Rostock flopped about in his harness and shrieked. The scene came back, ramming home like a bayonet.

.　　.　　.

"We like to put an extra string on our bow," the psych officer said. Lunar sunlight, scarcely softened by the dome, blazed off his bronze eagles, wings and beaks. "You know that your right ulna will be replaced with a metal section in which there is a nerve-triggered nuclear cartridge. But that may not be all, gentlemen."

He bridged his fingers. The young men seated on the other side of his desk stirred uneasily. "In this country," the psych officer said, "we don't believe humans should be turned into puppets. Therefore you will have voluntary control of your bombs; no posthypnosis, Pavlov reflex or any such insult. However, those of you who are willing will receive a rather special extra treatment, and that fact will be buried from the consciousness of all of you.

"Our reasoning is that if and when the Unasians learn about the prisoner weapon, they'll remove the cartridge by surgery but leave the prosthetic bone in place. And they will, we hope, not examine it in microscopic detail. Therefore they won't know that it contains an oscillator, integrated with the crystal structure. Nor will you; because what you don't know, you can't babble under anesthesia.

"The opportunity may come, if you are captured and lose your bomb, to inflict damage by this reserve means. You may find yourself near a crucial electronic device, for example a spaceship's autopilot. At short range, the oscillator will do an excellent job of bollixing it. Which will at least discomfit the enemy, and may even give you a chance to escape.

"The posthypnotic command will be such that you'll remember about this oscillator when conditions seem right for using it. Not before. Of course, the human mind is a damned queer thing, that twists and turns and bites its own tail. In order to make an opportunity to strike this blow, your subconscious may lead you down strange paths. It may even have you seriously contemplating treason, if treason seems the only way of getting access to what you can wreck. Don't let that bother you afterward, gentlemen. Your superiors will know what happened.

"Nevertheless, the experience may be painful. And posthypnosis is, at best, humiliating to a free man. So this aspect of the program is strictly volunteer. Does anybody want to go for broke?"

The door flung open. The guards burst in. Diaz was already behind the desk, next to Rostock. He yanked out the general's sidearm and fired at the soldiers. Free fall recoil sent him back against the computer panel. He braced himself, fired again and used his left elbow to smash the nearest meter face.

Rostock clawed at the wires in his head. For a moment Diaz guessed what it must be like to have random oscillations in your brain, amplified by an electronic engine that was part of you. He laid the pistol to the screaming man's temple and fired once more.

Now to get out! He shoved hard, arrowing past the sentries, who rolled through the air in a crimson galaxy of blood globules. Confusion boiled in the corridor beyond. Someone snatched at him. He knocked the fellow aside and dove along a tubeway. Somewhere hereabouts should be a scooter locker—there, and nobody around!

He didn't have time to get on a spacesuit, even if a Unasian one would have fitted, but he slipped on an air dome over the scooter. That, with the heater unit and oxy reclaim, would serve. He didn't want to get off anywhere en route; not before he'd steered the machine through an American hatch.

With luck, he'd do that. Their command computer gone, the enemy were going to get smeared. American ships would close in as the slaughter progressed. Eventually one should come within range of the scooter's little radio.

He set the minilock controls, mounted the saddle, dogged the air dome and waited for ejection. It came none too soon. Three soldiers had just appeared down the passageway. Diaz applied full thrust and jetted away from the *Ho.* Its blackness was soon lost among the star clouds.

Battle commenced. The first Unasian ship to be destroyed must have been less than fifty miles distant. Luckily, Diaz was facing the other way when the missile exploded.

THE LAST QUESTION

Isaac Asimov

In Brooklyn, New York, in the late 1930s, a group called
*The Futurian Society came to be. We were all fans and, almost
without exception, we all desperately wanted to be writers. Some
of us—C. M. Kornbluth, Richard Wilson and half a dozen
others—made it; others (like Donald Wollheim and Robert
Lowndes) wandered into the adjacent area of being editors; a few
(Damon Knight and myself) did both. But of us all, none realized
the paramount goal more fully and brilliantly than the diffident
young college student and candy-store worker from the far end of
Prospect Park, Isaac Asimov. I don't know how many books
Asimov has published—something over a hundred; how much
over, I don't want to hear—but I do know that in addition to any
quantity of science fiction, he has also written his own concord-
ances to Shakespeare and the Bible, dozens of books on science,*

*several mystery books, a joke collection and a number of juveniles.
(He has not as yet published either a cookbook or a slim volume of
verse—but who knows what the future will bring?)*

*Nevertheless, what Asimov is primarily and best is a science-
fiction writer, and it is only fitting that he is the first former-fan to
have been a Guest of Honor—and that he is included in this
volume.*

THE last question was asked for the first time, half in jest,
on May 21, 2061, at a time when humanity first stepped into the
light. The question came about as a result of a five-dollar bet over
highballs, and it happened this way:

Alexander Adell and Bertram Lupov were two of the faithful
attendants of Multivac. As well as any human beings could, they
knew what lay behind the cold, clicking, flashing face—miles and
miles of face—of that giant computer. They had at least a vague
notion of the general plan of relays and circuits that had long
since grown past the point where any single human could possibly
have a firm grasp of the whole.

Multivac was self-adjusting and self-correcting. It had to be, for
nothing human could adjust and correct it quickly enough or even
adequately enough. So Adell and Lupov attended the monstrous
giant only lightly and superficially, yet as well as any men could.
They fed it data, adjusted questions to its needs and translated the
answers that were issued. Certainly they, and all others like them,
were fully entitled to share in the glory that was Multivac's.

For decades, Multivac had helped design the ships and plot the
trajectories that enabled man to reach the Moon, Mars, and
Venus, but past that, Earth's poor resources could not support the
ships. Too much energy was needed for the long trips. Earth
exploited its coal and uranium with increasing efficiency, but
there was only so much of both.

But slowly Multivac learned enough to answer deeper questions
more fundamentally, and on May 14, 2061, what had been theory,
became fact.

The energy of the sun was stored, converted, and utilized

directly on a planet-wide scale. All Earth turned off its burning coal, its fissioning uranium, and flipped the switch that connected all of it to a small station, one mile in diameter, circling the Earth at half the distance of the Moon. All Earth ran by invisible beams of sunpower.

Seven days had not sufficed to dim the glory of it and Adell and Lupov finally managed to escape from the public function, and to meet in quiet where no one would think of looking for them, in the deserted underground chambers, where portions of the mighty buried body of Multivac showed. Unattended, idling, sorting data with contented lazy clickings, Multivac, too, had earned its vacation and the boys appreciated that. They had no intention, originally, of disturbing it.

They had brought a bottle with them, and their only concern at the moment was to relax in the company of each other and the bottle.

"It's amazing when you think of it," said Adell. His broad face had lines of weariness in it, and he stirred his drink slowly with a glass rod, watching the cubes of ice slur clumsily about. "All the energy we can possibly ever use for free. Enough energy, if we wanted to draw on it, to melt all Earth into a big drop of impure liquid iron, and still never miss the energy so used. All the energy we could ever use, forever and forever and forever."

Lupov cocked his head sideways. He had a trick of doing that when he wanted to be contrary, and he wanted to be contrary now, partly because he had had to carry the ice and glassware. "Not forever," he said.

"Oh, hell, just about forever. Till the sun runs down, Bert."

"That's not forever."

"All right, then. Billions and billions of years. Twenty billion, maybe. Are you satisfied?"

Lupov put his fingers through his thinning hair as though to reassure himself that some was still left and sipped gently at his own drink. "Twenty billion years isn't forever."

"Well, it will last our time, won't it?"

"So would the coal and uranium."

"All right, but now we can hook up each individual spaceship to the Solar Station, and it can go to Pluto and back a million times without ever worrying about fuel. You can't do *that* on coal and uranium. Ask Multivac, if you don't believe me."

"I don't have to ask Multivac. I know that."

"Then stop running down what Multivac's done for us," said Adell, blazing up. "It did all right."

"Who says it didn't? What I say is that a sun won't last forever. That's all I'm saying. We're safe for twenty billion years, but then what?" Lupov pointed a slightly shaky finger at the other. "And don't say we'll switch to another sun."

There was silence for a while. Adell put his glass to his lips only occasionally, and Lupov's eyes slowly closed. They rested.

Then Lupov's eyes snapped open. "You're thinking we'll switch to another sun when ours is done, aren't you?"

"I'm not thinking."

"Sure you are. You're weak on logic, that's the trouble with you. You're like the guy in the story who was caught in a sudden shower and who ran to a grove of trees and got under one. He wasn't worried, you see, because he figured when one tree got wet through, he would just get under another one."

"I get it," said Adell. "Don't shout. When the sun is done, the other stars will be gone, too."

"Darn right they will," muttered Lupov. "It all had a beginning in the original cosmic explosion, whatever that was, and it'll all have an end when all the stars run down. Some run down faster than others. Hell, the giants won't last a hundred million years. The sun will last twenty billion years and maybe the dwarfs will last a hundred billion for all the good they are. But just give us a trillion years and everything will be dark. Entropy has to increase to maximum, that's all."

"I know all about entropy," said Adell, standing on his dignity.

"The hell you do."

"I know as much as you do."

"Then you know everything's got to run down someday."

"All right. Who says they won't?"

"You did, you poor sap. You said we had all the energy we needed, forever. You said 'forever.' "

It was Adell's turn to be contrary. "Maybe we can build things up again someday," he said.

"Never."

"Why not? Someday."

"Never."

"Ask Multivac."

"*You* ask Multivac. I dare you. Five dollars says it can't be done."

Adell was just drunk enough to try, just sober enough to be able to phrase the necessary symbols and operations into a question which, in words, might have corresponded to this: Will mankind one day without the net expenditure of energy be able to restore the sun to its full youthfulness even after it had died of old age?

Or maybe it could be put more simply like this: How can the net amount of entropy of the universe be massively decreased?

Multivac fell dead and silent. The slow flashing of lights ceased, the distant sounds of clicking relays ended.

Then, just as the frightened technicians felt they could hold their breath no longer, there was a sudden springing to life of the teletype attached to that portion of Multivac. Five words were printed: INSUFFICIENT DATA FOR MEANINGFUL ANSWER.

"No bet," whispered Lupov. They left hurriedly.

By next morning, the two, plagued with throbbing head and cottony mouth, had forgotten the incident.

Jerrodd, Jerrodine, and Jerrodette I and II watched the starry picture in the visiplate change as the passage through hyperspace was completed in its non-time lapse. At once, the even powdering of stars gave way to the predominance of a single bright marble-disk, centered.

"That's X-23," said Jerrodd confidently. His thin hands clamped tightly behind his back and the knuckles whitened.

The little Jerrodettes, both girls, had experienced the hyperspace passage for the first time in their lives and were self-conscious over the momentary sensation of inside-outness. They buried their giggles and chased one another wildly about their mother, screaming, "We've reached X-23—we've reached X-23—we've—"

"Quiet, children," said Jerrodine sharply. "Are you sure, Jerrodd?"

"What is there to be but sure?" asked Jerrodd, glancing up at the bulge of featureless metal just under the ceiling. It ran the length of the room, disappearing through the wall at either end. It was as long as the ship.

Jerrodd scarcely knew a thing about the thick rod of metal except that it was called a Microvac, that one asked it questions if one wished; that if one did not it still had its task of guiding the ship to a preordered destination; of feeding on energies from the various Sub-galactic Power Stations; of computing the equations for the hyperspacial jumps.

Jerrodd and his family had only to wait and live in the comfortable residence quarters of the ship.

Someone had once told Jerrodd that the "ac" at the end of "Microvac" stood for "analog computer" in ancient English, but he was on the edge of forgetting even that.

Jerrodine's eyes were moist as she watched the visiplate. "I can't help it. I feel funny about leaving Earth."

"Why, for Pete's sake?" demanded Jerrodd. "We had nothing there. We'll have everything on X-23. You won't be alone. You won't be a pioneer. There are over a million people on the planet already. Good Lord, our great-grandchildren will be looking for new worlds because X-23 will be overcrowded." Then, after a reflective pause, "I tell you, it's a lucky thing the computers worked out interstellar travel the way the race is growing."

"I know, I know," said Jerrodine miserably.

Jerrodette I said promptly, "Our Microvac is the best Microvac in the world."

"I think so, too," said Jerrodd, tousling her hair.

It *was* a nice feeling to have a Microvac of your own and Jerrodd was glad he was part of his generation and no other. In his father's youth, the only computers had been tremendous machines taking up a hundred square miles of land. There was only one to a planet. Planetary ACs they were called. They had been growing in size steadily for a thousand years and then, all at once, came refinement. In place of transistors had come molecular valves, so that even the largest Planetary AC could be put into a space only half the volume of a spaceship.

Jerrodd felt uplifted, as he always did when he thought that his own personal Microvac was many times more complicated than the ancient and primitive Multivac that had first tamed the Sun, and almost as complicated as Earth's Planetary AC (the largest) that had first solved the problem of hyperspatial travel and had made trips to the stars possible.

"So many stars, so many planets," sighed Jerrodine, busy with her own thoughts. "I suppose families will be going out to new planets forever, the way we are now."

"Not forever," said Jerrodd, with a smile. "It will all stop someday, but not for billions of years. Many billions. Even the stars run down, you know. Entropy must increase."

"What's entropy, daddy?" shrilled Jerrodette II.

"Entropy, little sweet, is just a word which means the amount of running-down of the universe. Everything runs down, you know, like your little walkie-talkie robot, remember?"

"Can't you just put in a new power-unit, like with my robot?"

"The stars *are* the power-units, dear. Once they're gone, there are no power-units."

Jerrodette I at once set up a howl. "Don't let them, daddy. Don't let the stars run down."

"Now look what you've done," whispered Jerrodine, exasperated.

"How was I to know it would frighten them?" Jerrodd whispered back.

"Ask the Microvac," wailed Jerrodette I. "Ask him how to turn the stars on again."

"Go ahead," said Jerrodine. "It will quiet them down." (Jerrodette II was beginning to cry, also.)

Jerrodd shrugged. "Now, now, honeys. I'll ask Microvac. Don't worry, he'll tell us."

He asked the Microvac, adding quickly, "Print the answer."

Jerrodd cupped the strip of thin cellufilm and said cheerfully, "See now, the Microvac says it will take care of everything when the time comes so don't worry."

Jerrodine said, "And now, children, it's time for bed. We'll be in our new home soon."

Jerrodd read the words on the cellufilm again before destroying it: INSUFFICIENT DATA FOR MEANINGFUL ANSWER.

He shrugged and looked at the visiplate. X-23 was just ahead.

VJ-23X of Lameth stared into the black depths of the three-dimensional, small-scale map of the Galaxy and said, "Are we ridiculous, I wonder, in being so concerned about the matter?"

MQ-17J of Nicron shook his head. "I think not. You know the Galaxy will be filled in five years at the present rate of expansion."

Both seemed in their early twenties, both were tall and perfectly formed.

"Still," said VJ-23X, "I hesitate to submit a pessimistic report to the Galactic Council."

"I wouldn't consider any other kind of report. Stir them up a bit. We've got to stir them up."

VJ-23X sighed. "Space is infinite. A hundred billion Galaxies are there for the taking. More."

"A hundred billion is *not* infinite and it's getting less infinite all the time. Consider! Twenty thousand years ago, mankind first solved the problem of utilizing stellar energy, and a few centuries later, interstellar travel became possible. It took mankind a million years to fill one small world and then only fifteen thousand years to fill the rest of the Galaxy. Now the population doubles every ten years—"

VJ-23X interrupted. "We can thank immortality for that."

"Very well. Immortality exists and we have to take it into account. I admit it has its seamy side, this immortality. The Galactic AC has solved many problems for us, but in solving the problem of preventing old age and death, it has undone all its other solutions."

"Yet you wouldn't want to abandon life, I suppose."

"Not at all," snapped MQ-17J, softening it at once to, "Not yet. I'm by no means old enough. How old are you?"

"Two hundred twenty-three. And you?"

"I'm still under two hundred. But to get back to my point.

Population doubles every ten years. Once this Galaxy is filled, we'll have filled another in ten years. Another ten years and we'll have filled two more. Another decade, four more. In a hundred years, we'll have filled a thousand Galaxies. In a thousand years, a million Galaxies. In ten thousand years, the entire known Universe. Then what?"

VJ-23X said, "As a side issue, there's a problem of transportation. I wonder how many sunpower units it will take to move Galaxies of individuals from one Galaxy to the next."

"A very good point. Already, mankind consumes two sunpower units per year."

"Most of it's wasted. After all, our own Galaxy alone pours out a thousand sunpower units a year and we only use two of those."

"Granted, but even with a hundred per cent efficiency, we only stave off the end. Our energy requirements are going up in a geometric progression even faster than our population. We'll run out of energy even sooner than we run out of Galaxies. A good point. A very good point."

"We'll just have to build new stars out of interstellar gas."

"Or out of dissipated heat?" asked MQ-17J, sarcastically.

"There may be some way to reverse entropy. We ought to ask the Galactic AC."

VJ-23X was not really serious, but MQ-17J pulled out his AC-contact from his pocket and placed it on the table before him.

"I've half a mind to," he said. "It's something the human race will have to face someday."

He stared somberly at his small AC-contact. It was only two inches cubed and nothing in itself, but it was connected through hyperspace with the great Galactic AC that served all mankind. Hyperspace considered, it was an integral part of the Galactic AC.

MQ-17J paused to wonder if someday in his immortal life he would get to see the Galactic AC. It was a little world of its own, a spider webbing of force-beams holding the matter within which surges of sub-mesons took the place of the old clumsy molecular valves. Yet despite its sub-etheric workings, the Galactic AC was known to be a full thousand feet across.

MQ-17J asked suddenly of his AC-contact, "Can entropy ever be reversed?"

VJ-23X looked startled and said at once, "Oh, say, I didn't really mean to have you ask that."

"Why not?"

"We both know entropy can't be reversed. You can't turn smoke and ash back into a tree."

"Do you have trees on your world?" asked MQ-17J.

The sound of the Galactic AC startled them into silence. Its voice came thin and beautiful out of the small AC-contact on the desk. It said: THERE IS INSUFFICIENT DATA FOR A MEANINGFUL ANSWER.

VJ-23X said, "See!"

The two men thereupon returned to the question of the report they were to make to the Galactic Council.

Zee Prime's mind spanned the new Galaxy with a faint interest in the countless twists of stars that powdered it. He had never seen this one before. Would he ever see them all? So many of them, each with its load of humanity. But a load that was almost a dead weight. More and more, the real essence of men was to be found out here, in space.

Minds, not bodies! The immortal bodies remained back on the planets, in suspension over the eons. Sometimes they roused for material activity but that was growing rarer. Few new individuals were coming into existence to join the incredibly mighty throng, but what matter? There was little room in the Universe for new individuals.

Zee Prime was roused out of his reverie upon coming across the wispy tendrils of another mind.

"I am Zee Prime," said Zee Prime. "And you?"

"I am Dee Sub Wun. Your Galaxy?"

"We call it only the Galaxy. And you?"

"We call ours the same. All men call their Galaxy their Galaxy and nothing more. Why not?"

"True. Since all Galaxies are the same."

"Not all Galaxies. On one particular Galaxy the race of man must have originated. That makes it different."

Zee Prime said, "On which one?"

"I cannot say. The Universal AC would know."

"Shall we ask him? I am suddenly curious."

Zee Prime's perceptions broadened until the Galaxies themselves shrank and became a new, more diffuse powdering on a much larger background. So many hundreds of billions of them, all with their immortal beings, all carrying their load of intelligences with minds that drifted freely through space. And yet one of them was unique among them all in being the original Galaxy. One of them had, in its vague and distant past, a period when it was the only Galaxy populated by man.

Zee Prime was consumed with curiosity to see this Galaxy and he called out: "Universal AC! On which Galaxy did mankind originate?"

The Universal AC heard, for on every world and throughout space, it had its receptors ready, and each receptor led through hyperspace to some unknown point where the Universal AC kept itself aloof.

Zee Prime knew of only one man whose thoughts had penetrated within sensing distance of Universal AC, and he reported only a shining globe, two feet across, difficult to see.

"But how can that be all of Universal AC?" Zee Prime had asked.

"Most of it," had been the answer, "is in hyperspace. In what form it is there I cannot imagine."

Nor could anyone, for the day had long sinced passed, Zee Prime knew, when any man had any part of the making of a Universal AC. Each Universal AC designed and constructed its successor. Each, during its existence of a million years or more accumulated the necessary data to build a better and more intricate, more capable successor in which its own store of data and individuality would be submerged.

The Universal AC interrupted Zee Prime's wandering thoughts, not with words, but with guidance. Zee Prime's mentality was guided into the dim sea of Galaxies and one in particular enlarged into stars.

A thought came, infinitely distant, but infinitely clear. "THIS IS THE ORIGINAL GALAXY OF MAN."

But it was the same after all, the same as any other, and Zee Prime stifled his disappointment.

Dee Sub Wun, whose mind had accompanied the other, said suddenly, "And is one of these stars the original star of Man?"

The Universal AC said, "MAN'S ORIGINAL STAR HAS GONE NOVA. IT IS A WHITE DWARF."

"Did the men upon it die?" asked Zee Prime, startled and without thinking.

The Universal AC said, "A NEW WORLD, AS IN SUCH CASES, WAS CONSTRUCTED FOR THEIR PHYSICAL BODIES IN TIME."

"Yes, of course," said Zee Prime, but a sense of loss overwhelmed him even so. His mind released its hold on the original Galaxy of Man, let it spring back and lose itself among the blurred pinpoints. He never wanted to see it again.

Dee Sub Wun said, "What is wrong?"

"The stars are dying. The original star is dead."

"They must all die. Why not?"

"But when all energy is gone, our bodies will finally die, and you and I with them."

"It will take billions of years."

"I do not wish it to happen even after billions of years. Universal AC! How may stars be kept from dying?"

Dee Sub Wun said in amusement, "You're asking how entropy might be reversed in direction."

And the Universal AC answered: "THERE IS AS YET INSUFFICIENT DATA FOR A MEANINGFUL ANSWER."

Zee Prime's thoughts fled back to his own Galaxy. He gave no further thought to Dee Sub Wun, whose body might be waiting on a Galaxy a trillion light-years away, or on the star next to Zee Prime's own. It didn't matter.

Unhappily, Zee Prime began collecting interstellar hydrogen out of which to build a small star of his own. If the stars must someday die, at least some could yet be built.

Man considered with himself, for in a way, Man, mentally, was one. He consisted of a trillion, trillion, trillion ageless bodies, each in its place, each resting quiet and incorruptible, each cared for by perfect automatons, equally incorruptible, while the minds of all the bodies freely melted one into the other, indistinguishable.

Man said, "The Universe is dying."

Man looked about at the dimming Galaxies. The giant stars, spendthrifts, were gone long ago, back in the dimmest of the dim far past. Almost all stars were white dwarfs, fading to the end.

New stars had been built of the dust between the stars, some by natural processes, some by Man himself, and those were going, too. White dwarfs might yet be crashed together and of the mighty forces so released, new stars built, but only one star for every thousand white dwarfs destroyed, and those would come to an end, too.

Man said, "Carefully husbanded, as directed by the Cosmic AC, the energy that is even yet left in all the Universe will last for billions of years."

"But even so," said Man, "eventually it will all come to an end. However it may be husbanded, however stretched out, the energy once expended is gone and cannot be restored. Entropy must increase forever to the maximum."

Man said, "Can entropy not be reversed? Let us ask the Cosmic AC."

The Cosmic AC surrounded them but not in space. Not a fragment of it was in space. It was in hyperspace and made of something that was neither matter nor energy. The question of its size and nature no longer had meaning in any terms that Man could comprehend.

"Cosmic AC," said Man, "how may entropy be reversed?"

The Cosmic AC said, "THERE IS YET INSUFFICIENT DATA FOR A MEANINGFUL ANSWER."

Man said, "Collect additional data."

The Cosmic AC said, "I WILL DO SO. I HAVE BEEN DOING SO FOR A HUNDRED BILLION YEARS. MY PREDECESSORS AND I HAVE BEEN ASKED THIS QUESTION MANY TIMES. ALL THE DATA I HAVE REMAINS INSUFFICIENT."

"Will there come a time," said Man, "when data will be sufficient or is the problem insoluble in all conceivable circumstances?"

The Cosmic AC said, "NO PROBLEM IS INSOLUBLE IN ALL CONCEIVABLE CIRCUMSTANCES."

Man said, "When will you have enough data to answer the question?"

The Cosmic AC said, "THERE IS AS YET INSUFFICIENT DATA FOR A MEANINGFUL ANSWER."

"Will you keep working on it?" asked Man.

The Cosmic AC said, "I WILL."

Man said, "We shall wait."

The stars and Galaxies died and snuffed out, and space grew black after ten trillion years of running down.

One by one Man fused with AC, each physical body losing its mental identity in a manner that was somehow not a loss but a gain.

Man's last mind paused before fusion, looking over a space that included nothing but the dregs of one last dark star and nothing besides but incredibly thin matter, agitated randomly by the tag ends of heat wearing out, asymptotically, to the absolute zero.

Man said, "AC, is this the end? Can this chaos not be reversed into the Universe once more? Can that not be done?"

AC said, "THERE IS AS YET INSUFFICIENT DATA FOR A MEANINGFUL ANSWER."

Man's last mind fused and only AC existed—and that in hyperspace.

Matter and energy had ended and with it space and time. Even AC existed only for the sake of the one last question that it had never answered from the time a half-drunken computer operator ten trillion years before had asked the question of a computer that was to AC far less than was a man to Man.

All other questions had been answered, and until this last question was answered also, AC might not release his consciousness.

All collected data had come to a final end. Nothing was left to be collected.

But all collected data had yet to be completely correlated and put together in all possible relationships.

A timeless interval was spent in doing that.

And it came to pass that AC learned how to reverse the direction of entropy.

But there was now no man to whom AC might give the answer of the last question. No matter. The answer—by demonstration—would take care of that, too.

For another timeless interval, AC thought how best to do this. Carefully, AC organized the program.

The consciousness of AC encompassed all of what had once been a Universe and brooded over what was now Chaos. Step by step, it must be done.

And AC said, "LET THERE BE LIGHT!"

And there was light—

HOW BEAUTIFUL WITH BANNERS

James Blish

Around the time of the first (non-world) convention of all, in 1936, the motion picture Things to Come *opened in New York, and local fans invited some fans from the surrounding suburbs to join in a theater party to see the wondrous new science-fiction film. (Actually, it was wondrous—for that time, at least, the best sf film ever made.) Among those who made the trek in was young James Blish. He had already been active in fandom, mainly by publishing a fanzine (i.e., an amateur magazine devoted to science fiction, generally mimeographed). Not long after he began writing professionally, and began the steady climb upward which brought him to the upper reaches of the profession in time to be Guest of Honor in Pittsburgh in 1960.*

*Blish's works include some of the most memorable novels in the field (*A Case of Conscience, *for one; the "Cities in Flight" series* *for a few more), but perhaps he is most widely known as the chronicler of the cruises of the* Starship Enterprise. *Blish himself did not write any of the Star Trek episodes, but he has taken on the task of transforming all of them into fiction—at last count, ten volumes of Star Trek already in print, and two more at least on the way.*

In recent years Blish has made his home near Oxford, in England, where he continues his writing and serves as director of the English branch of the Milford SF Writers' Workshop.

I

FEELING as naked as a peppermint soldier in her transparent film wrap, Dr. Ulla Hillström watched a flying cloak swirl away toward the black horizon with a certain consequent irony. Although nearly transparent itself in the distant dim arc-light flame that was Titan's sun, the fluttering creature looked warmer than what she was wearing, for all that reason said it was at the same minus 316° F. as the thin methane it flew in. Despite the virus space-bubble's warranted and eerie efficiency, she found its vigilance—itself probably as nearly alive as the flying cloak was—rather difficult to believe in, let alone to trust.

The machine—as Ulla much preferred to think of it—was inarguably an improvement on the old-fashioned pressure suit. Made (or more accurately, cultured) of a single colossal protein molecule, the vanishingly thin sheet of life-stuff processed gases, maintained pressure, monitored radiation through almost the whole of the electromagnetic spectrum, and above all did not get in the way. Also, it could not be cut, punctured or indeed sustain any damage short of total destruction; macroscopically it was a single, primary unit, with all the physical integrity of a crystal of salt or steel.

If it did not actually think, Ulla was grateful; often it almost seemed to, which was sufficient. Its primary drawback for her was that much of the time it did not really seem to be there.

Still, it seemed to be functioning; otherwise Ulla would in fact have been as solid as a stick of candy, toppled forever across the confectionery whiteness that frosted the knife-edged stones of this cruel moon, layer upon layer. Outside—only a perilous few inches from the lightly clothed warmth of her skin—the brief gust the cloak had been soaring on died, leaving behind a silence so cataleptic that she could hear the snow creaking in a mockery of motion. Impossible though it was to comprehend, it was getting still colder out there. Titan was swinging out across Saturn's orbit toward eclipse, and the apparently fixed sun was secretly going down, its descent sensed by the snows no matter what her Earthly sight, accustomed to the nervousness of living skies, tried to tell her. In another two Earth days it would be gone, for an eternal week.

At the thought, Ulla turned to look back the way she had come that morning. The virus bubble flowed smoothly with the motion and the stars became brighter as it compensated for the fact that the sun was now at her back. She still could not see the base camp, of course. She had strayed too far for that, and in any event, except for a few wiry palps, it was wholly underground.

Now there was no sound but the creaking of the methane snow, and nothing to see but a blunt, faint spearhead of hazy light, deceptively like an Earthly aurora or the corona of the sun, pushing its way from below the edge of the cold into the indifferent company of the stars. Saturn's rings were rising, very slightly awaver in the dark blue air, like the banners of a spectral army. The idiot face of the gas giant planet itself, faintly striped with meaningless storms, would be glaring down at her before she could get home if she did not get herself in motion soon. Obscurely disturbed, Dr. Hillström faced front and began to unload her sled.

The touch and clink of the sampling gear cheered her, a little, even in this ultimate loneliness. She was efficient—many years, and a good many suppressed impulses, had seen to that; it was too late for temblors, especially so far out from the sun that had warmed her Stockholm streets and her silly friendships. All those null adventures were gone now like a sickness. The phantom embrace of the virus suit was perhaps less satisfying—only perhaps—but it was much more reliable. Much more reliable; she could depend on that.

Then, as she bent to thrust the spike of a thermocouple into the wedding-cake soil, the second flying cloak (or was it the same one?) hit her in the small of the back and tumbled her into nightmare.

II

With the sudden darkness there came a profound, ambiguous emotional blow—ambiguous, yet with something shockingly familiar about it. Instantly exhausted, she felt herself go flaccid and unstrung, and her mind, adrift in nowhere, blurred and spun downward too into trance.

The long fall slowed just short of unconsciousness, lodged precariously upon a shelf of dream, a mental buttress founded four years in the past—a long distance, when one recalls that in a four-dimensional plenum every second of time is 186,000 miles of space. The memory was curiously inconsequential to have arrested her, let alone supported her: not of her home, of her few triumphs or even of her aborted marriage, but of a sordid little encounter with a reporter that she had talked herself into at the Madrid genetics conference, when she herself was already an associate professor, a Swedish government delegate, a twenty-five-year-old divorcée, and altogether a woman who should have known better.

But better than what? The life of science even in those days had been almost by definition the life of the eternal campus exile. There was so much to learn—or, at least, to show competence in—that people who wanted to be involved in the ordinary, vivid concerns of human beings could not stay with it long, indeed often could not even be recruited. They turned aside from the prospect with a shudder or even a snort of scorn. To prepare for the sciences had become a career in indefinitely protracted adolescence, from which one awakened fitfully to find one's adult self in the body of a stranger. It had given her no pride, no self-love, no defenses of any sort; only a queer kind of virgin numbness, highly dependent upon familiar surroundings and unvalued habits, and easily breached by any normally confident siege in print, in person, anywhere—and remaining just as numb as before when the spasm of fashion, politics or romanticism had swept by and left her stranded, too easy a recruit to have been allowed into the center of things or even considered for it.

Curious, most curious that in her present remote terror she should find even a moment's rest upon so wobbly a pivot. The Madrid incident had not been important; she had been through with it almost at once. Of course, as she had often told herself, she had never been promiscuous, and had often described the affair, defiantly, as that single (or at worst, second) test of the joys of impulse which any woman is entitled to have in her history. Nor had it really been that joyous. She could not now recall the boy's face, and remembered how he had felt primarily because he had been in so casual and contemptuous a hurry.

But now that she came to dream of it, she saw with a bloodless, lightless eye that all her life, in this way and in that, she had been repeatedly seduced by the inconsequential. She had nothing else to remember even in this hour of her presumptive death. Acts have consequences, a thought told her, but not ours; we have done, but never felt. We are no more alone on Titan, you and I, than we have ever been. *Basta, per carita!*—so much for Ulla.

Awakening in the same darkness as before, Ulla felt the virus bubble snuggling closer to her blind skin, and recognized the shock that had so regressed her—a shock of recognition, but recognition of something she had never felt herself. Alone in a Titanic snowfield, she had eavesdropped on an . . .

No. Not possible. Sniffling, and still blind, she pushed the cozy bubble away from her breasts and tried to stand up. Light flushed briefly around her, as though the bubble had cleared just above her forehead and then clouded again. She was still alive, but everything else was utterly problematical. What had happened to her? She simply did not know.

Therefore, she thought, begin with ignorance. No one begins anywhere else . . . but I did not know even that, once upon a time.

Hence:

III

Though the virus bubble ordinarily regulated itself, there was a control box on her hip—actually an ultra-short-range microwave transmitter—by which it could be modulated against more special environments than the bubble itself could cope with alone. She had never had to use it before, but she tried it now.

The fogged bubble cleared patchily, but it would not stay cleared. Crazy moirés and herringbone patterns swept over it, changing direction repeatedly, and, outside, the snowy landscape kept changing color like a delirium. She found, however, that by continuously working the frequency knob on her box—at random, for the responses seemed to bear no relation to the Braille calibrations on the dial—she could maintain outside vision of a sort in pulses of two or three seconds each.

This was enough to show her, finally, what had happened. There was a flying cloak around her. This in itself was unprecedented; the cloaks had never attacked a man before, or indeed paid any of them the least attention during their brief previous forays. On the other hand, this was the first time anyone had ventured more than five or ten minutes outdoors in a virus suit.

It occurred to her suddenly that insofar as anything was known about the nature of the cloaks, they were in some respect much like the bubbles. It was almost as though the one were a wild species of the other.

It was an alarming notion and possibly only a metaphor, containing as little truth as most poetry. Annoyingly, she found herself wondering if, once she got out of this mess, the men at the base camp would take to referring to it as "the cloak and suit business."

The snowfield began to turn brighter; Saturn was rising. For a moment the drifts were a pale straw color, the normal hue of Saturn light through an atmosphere; then it turned a raving Kelly green. Muttering, Ulla twisted the potentiometer dial, and was rewarded with a brief flash of normal illumination which was promptly overridden by a torrent of crimson lake, as though she were seeing everything through a series of photographic color separations.

Since she could not help this, she clenched her teeth and ignored it. It was much more important to find out what the flying cloak had done to her bubble, if she were to have any hope of shucking the thing.

There was no clear separation between the bubble and the Titanian creature. They seemed to have blended into a mélange which was neither one nor the other, but a sort of coarse burlesque of both. Yet the total surface area of the integument about her did not seem to be any greater—only more ill-fitting, less responsive to her own needs. Not much less; after all, she was still alive, and any really gross insensitivity to the demands and cues of her body would have been instantly fatal. But there was no way to guess how long the bubble would stay even that obedient. At the moment the wild thing that had enslaved it was perhaps dangerous to the wearer only if she panicked, but the change might well be progressive, pointed ultimately toward some saturnine equivalent of the shirt of Nessus.

And that might be happening very rapidly. She might not be allowed the time to think her way out of this fix by herself. Little though she wanted any help from the men at the base camp, and useless though she was sure they would prove, she had damn well better ask for it now, just in case.

But the bubble was not allowing any radio transmission through its roiling unicell wall today. The earphone was dead; not even the hiss of the stars came through it—only an occasional pop of noise that was born of entropy loss in the circuits themselves.

She was cut off. *Nun denn, allein!*

With the thought, the bubble cloak shifted again around her. A sudden pressure at her lower abdomen made her stumble forward over the crisp snow, four or five steps. Then it was motionless once more, except within itself.

That it should be able to do this was not surprising, for the cloaks had to be able to flex voluntarily at least a little to catch the thermals they rode, and the bubble had to be able to vary its dimensions and surface tension over a wide range to withstand pressure changes, outside and in, and do it automatically. No, of course the combination would be able to move by itself. What was disquieting was that it should want to.

Another stir of movement in the middle distance caught her eye: a free cloak, seemingly riding an updraft over a fixed point. For a moment she wondered what on that ground could be warm enough to produce so localized a thermal. Then, abruptly, she realized that she was shaking with hatred, and fought furiously to drive the spasm down, her fingernails slicing into her naked palms.

A raster of jagged black lines, like a television interference pattern, broke across her view and brought her attention fully back to the minutely solipsistic confines of her dilemma. The wave of emotion, nevertheless, would not quite go away, and she had a vague but persistent impression that it was being imposed from outside, at least in part—a cold passion she was interpreting as fury because its real nature, whatever it was, had no necessary relevance to her own imprisoned soul. For all that it was her own life and no other that was in peril, she felt guilty, as though she were eavesdropping, and as angry with herself as with what she was overhearing, yet burning as helplessly as the forbidden lamp in the bedchamber of Psyche and Eros.

Another metaphor—but was it after all so far-fetched? She was a mortal present at the mating of inhuman essences; mountain-ously far from home; borne here like invisible lovers upon the arms of the wind; empalaced by a whole virgin-white world, over which flew the banners of a high god and a father of gods and, equally appropriately, Venus was very far away from whatever love was being celebrated here.

What ancient and coincidental nonsense! Next she would be thinking herself degraded at the foot of some cross.

Yet the impression, of an eerie tempest going on just slightly outside any possibility of understanding what it was, would not pass away. Still worse, it seemed to mean something, to be important, to mock her with subtle clues to matters of great moment, of which her own present trap was only the first and not necessarily the most significant.

And suppose that all these impressions were in fact not extraneous or irrelevant, but did have some import—not just as an abstract puzzle, but to that morsel of displaced life that was Ulla Hillström? No matter how frozen her present world, she could not escape the fact that from the moment the cloak had captured her she had been simultaneously gripped by a Sabbat of specifically erotic memories, images, notions, analogies, myths, symbols and frank physical sensations, all the more obtrusive because they were both inappropriate and disconnected. It might well have to be faced that a season of love can fall due in the heaviest weather—and never mind what terrors flow in with it or what deep damnations. At the very least, it was possible that somewhere in all this was the clue that would help her to divorce herself at last even from this violent embrace.

But the concept was preposterous enough to defer consideration of it if there were any other avenues open, and at least one seemed to be: the source of the thermal. The virus bubble, like many of the Terrestrial microorganisms to which it was analogous, could survive temperatures well above boiling, but it seemed reasonable to assume that the flying cloaks, evolved on a world where even words congealed, might be sensitive to a relatively slight amount of heat.

Now, could she move of her own volition inside this shroud? She tried a step. The sensation was tacky, as though she were plowing in thin honey, but it did not impede her except for a slight imposed clumsiness which experience ought to obviate. She was able to mount the sled with no trouble.

The cogs bit into the snow with a dry, almost inaudible squeaking and the sled inched forward. Ulla held it to as slow a crawl as possible, because of her interrupted vision.

The free cloak was still in sight, approximately where it had been before, insofar as she could judge against this featureless snowscape; which was fortunate, since it might well be her only flag for the source of the thermal, whatever it was.

A peculiar fluttering in her surroundings—a whisper of sound, of motion, of flickering in the light—distracted her. It was as though her compound sheath were trembling slightly. The impression grew slowly more pronounced as the sled continued to lurch forward. As usual there seemed to be nothing she could do about it, except, possibly, to retreat; but she could not do that either, now; she was committed. Outside, she began to hear the soft soughing of a steady wind.

The cause of the thermal, when she finally reached it, was almost bathetic—a pool of liquid. Placid and deep blue, it lay inside a fissure in a low, heart-shaped hummock, rimmed with feathery snow. It looked like nothing more or less than a spring, though she did not for a moment suppose that the liquid could be water. She could not see the bottom of it; evidently it was welling up from a fair depth. The spring analogy was probably completely false; the existence of anything in a liquid state on this world had to be thought of as a form of vulcanism. Certainly the column of heat rising from it was considerable; despite the thinness of the air, the wind here nearly howled. The free cloak floated up and down, about a hundred feet above her, like the last leaf of a long, cruel autumn. Nearer home, the bubble cloak shook with something comically like subdued fury.

Now, what to do? Should she push boldly into that cleft, hoping that the alien part of the bubble cloak would be unable to bear the heat? Close up, that course now seemed foolish, as long as she was ignorant of the real nature of the magma down there. And besides, any effective immersion would probably have to surround at least half of the total surface area of the bubble, which was not practicable—the well was not big enough to accommodate it, even supposing that the compromised virus suit did not fight back, as in the pure state it had been obligated to do. On the whole she was reluctantly glad that the experiment was impossible, for the mere notion of risking a new immolation in that problematical well horrified her.

Yet the time left for decision was obviously now very short, even supposing—as she had no right to do—that the environment-maintaining functions of the suit were still in perfect order. The quivering of the bubble was close to being explosive, and even were it to remain intact, it might shut her off from the outside world at any second.

The free cloak dipped lower, as if in curiosity. That only made the trembling worse. She wondered why.

Was it possible—was it possible that the thing embracing her companion was jealous?

IV

There was no time left to examine the notion, no time even to sneer at it. Act—act! Forcing her way off the sled, she stumbled to the well and looked frantically for some way of stopping it up. If she could shut off the thermal, bring the free cloak still closer—but how?

Throw rocks. But were there any? Yes, there, there were two, not very big, but at least she could move them. She bent stiffly and tumbled them into the crater.

The liquid froze around them with soundless speed. In seconds, the snow rimming the pool had drawn completely over it, like lips closing, leaving behind only a faint dimpled streak of shadow on a white ground.

The wind moaned and died, and the free cloak, its hems outspread to the uttermost, sank down as if to wrap her in still another deadly swath. Shadow spread around her; the falling cloak, its color deepening, blotted Saturn from the sky, and then was sprawling over the beautiful banners of the rings—

The virus bubble convulsed and turned black, throwing her to the frozen ground beside the hummock like a bead doll. A blast of wind squalled over her.

Terrified, she tried to curl into a ball. The suit puffed up around her.

Then at last, with a searing invisible wrench at its contained kernel of space-time which burned out the control box instantly, the single creature that was the bubble cloak tore itself free of Ulla and rose to join its incomplete fellow.

In the single second before she froze forever into the livid backdrop of Titan, she failed even to find time to regret what she had never felt, for she had never known it, and only died as she had lived, an artifact of successful calculation. She never saw the cloaks go flapping away downwind—nor could it ever have occurred to her that she had brought anything new to Titan, thus beginning that long evolution the end of which, sixty millions of years away, no human being would see.

No, her last thought was for the virus bubble, and it was only two words long:

You philanderer—

Almost on the horizon, the two cloaks, the two Titanians, flailed and tore at each other, becoming smaller and smaller with distance. Bits and pieces of them flaked off and fell down the sky like ragged tears. Ungainly though the cloaks normally were, they courted even more clumsily.

Beside Ulla, the well was gone; it might never have existed. Overhead, the banners of the rings flew changelessly, as though they too had seen nothing—or perhaps, as though in the last six billion years they had seen everything, siftings upon siftings in oblivion, until nothing remained but the banners of their own mirrored beauty.

DAYBROKE

Robert Bloch

TORONTO, 1948

For almost a decade now the Worldcons had been rolling along, and it was becoming rather painfully obvious that there was a certain amount of fraud in their name. New York, Chicago, Denver, Los Angeles and Philadelphia were all certainly important cities, but wasn't it a fact that when you came right down to it, they all happened to be cities of a single country, the U.S.A.?

They were; and right-thinking fans did something about it: in 1948 they held the first Worldcon outside the borders of the United States. Not far outside, to be sure. Toronto is only an hour's drive from the U.S. boundary. But still, at last fans could speak of a "world" convention without stammering in shame. (It would be nine more years before the next convention turned up outside the U.S.—and more than twenty years until a non-English-speaking country could boast of hosting one.)

Toronto's choice for Guest of Honor was a marvelously bright and witty young fellow who had, he said, the heart of a small boy. ("I keep it in my bureau drawer," he would then add.) A little later he would go on to write the novel (which later still became the motion picture) Psycho, and so achieve instant fame far outside the field of science fiction. But his labors inside the field entitled him to honor, and an example of those well-rewarded labors is his story Daybroke.

UP IN the sky the warheads whirled, and the thunder of their passing shook the mountain.

Deep in his vaulted sanctuary he sat, godlike and inscrutable, marking neither the sparrow's nor the missile's fall. There was no need to leave his shelter to stare down at the city.

He knew what was happening—had known ever since early in the evening when the television flickered and died. An announcer in the holy white garb of the healing arts had been delivering an important message about the world's most popular laxative—the one most people preferred, the one four out of five doctors used themselves. Midway in his praise of this amazing new medical discovery he had paused and advised the audience to stand by for a special bulletin.

But the bulletin never came; instead the screen went blank and the thunder boomed.

All night long the mountain trembled, and the seated man trembled too; not with anticipation but with realization. He had expected this, of course, and that was why he was here. Others had talked about it for years; there had been wild rumors and solemn warnings and much muttering in taverns. But the rumor-mongers and the warning-sounders and the tavern-mutterers had made no move. They had stayed in the city and he alone had fled.

Some of them, he knew, had stayed to stave off the inevitable end as best they could, and these he saluted for their courage. Others had attempted to ignore the future, and these he detested for their blindness. And all of them he pitied.

For he had realized, long ago, that courage was not enough and that ignorance was no salvation. Wise words and foolish words are one—they will not halt the storm. And when the storm approaches, it is best to flee.

So he prepared for himself this mountain retreat, high over the city, and here he was safe; would be safe for years to come. Other men of equal wealth could have done the same, but they were too wise or too foolish to face reality. So while they spread their rumors and sounded their warnings and muttered in their cups, he built his sanctuary; lead-guarded, amply provisioned, and stocked with every need for years to come, including even a generous supply of the world's most popular laxative.

Dawn came at last and the echoes of the thunder died, and he went to a special, shielded place where he could sight his spyglass at the city. He stared and he squinted, but there was nothing to be seen—nothing but swirling clouds that billowed blackly and rolled redly across the hazed horizon.

Then he knew that he must go down to the city if he wanted to find out, and made due preparations.

There was a special suit to wear, a cunning seamless garment of insulated cloth and lead, difficult and costly to obtain. It was a top secret suit; the kind only Pentagon generals possess. They cannot procure them for their wives, and they must steal them for their mistresses. But he had one. He donned it now.

An elevated platform aided his descent to the base of the mountain, and there his car was waiting. He drove out, the shielded doors closing automatically behind him, and started for the city. Through the eyepiece of his insulated helmet he stared out at a yellowish fog, and he drove slowly, even though he encountered no traffic nor any sign of life.

After a time the fog lifted, and he could see the countryside. Yellow trees and yellow grass stood stiffly silhouetted against a yellow sky in which great clouds writhed and whirled.

Van Gogh's work, he told himself, knowing it was a lie. For no artist's hand had smashed the windows of the farmhouses, peeled the paint from the sides of the barns, or squeezed the warm breath from the herds huddling in the fields, standing fright-frozen but dead.

He drove along to the broad arterial leading to the city; an arterial which ordinarily swarmed with the multicolored corpuscles of motor vehicles. But there were no cars moving today, not in this artery.

Not until he neared the suburbs did he see them, and then he rounded a curve and was halfway upon the vanguard before he panicked and halted in a ditch.

The roadway ahead was packed with automobiles as far as the eye could see—a solid mass, bumper to bumper, ready to descend upon him with whirring wheels.

But the wheels were not turning.

The cars were dead. The further stretches of the highway were an automobile graveyard. He approached the spot on foot, treading with proper reverence past the Cadillac-corpses, the cadavers of Chevrolets, the bodies of Buicks. Close at hand he could see the evidence of violent ends: the shattered glass, the smashed fenders, the battered bumpers and twisted hoods.

The signs of struggle were often pitiable to observe; here was a tiny Volkswagen, trapped and crushed between two looming Lincolns; there an MG had died beneath the wheels of a charging Chrysler. But all were still now. The Dodges dodged no longer, the Hornets had ceased their buzzing, and the Ramblers would never ramble again.

It was hard for him to realize with equal clarity the tragedy that had overtaken the people inside these cars—they were dead, too, of course, but somehow their passing seemed insignificant. Maybe his thinking had been affected by the attitude of the age, in which a man tended to be less and less identified as an individual and more and more regarded on the basis of the symbolic status of the car he drove. When a stranger rode down the street, one seldom thought of him as a person; one's only immediate reaction was "There goes a Ford—there goes a Pontiac—there goes one of those big goddam Imperials." And men bragged about their cars instead of their characters. So somehow the death of the automobiles seemed more important than the death of their owners. It didn't seem as though human beings had perished in this panic-stricken effort to escape from the city; it was the cars which had made a dash for final freedom and then failed.

He skirted the road and now continued along the ditch until he came to the first sidewalks of the suburbs. Here the evidence of destruction was accentuated. Explosion and implosion had done their work. In the country, paint had been peeled from the walls, but in the suburbs walls had been peeled from the buildings. Not every home was leveled. There were still plenty of ranchhouses standing, though no sign of a rancher in a gray flannel suit. In some of the picturesquely modern white houses, with their light lines and heavy mortgages, the glass side walls remained unshattered, but there was no sign of happy, busy suburban life within—the television sets were dead.

Now he found his progress impeded by an increasing litter. Apparently a blast had swept through this area; his way was blocked by a clutter of the miscellaneous debris of Exurbia.

He waded through or stepped around:

Boxes of Kleenex, artificial shrunken heads which had once dangled in the windows of station-wagons, crumpled shopping-lists and scribbled notices of appointments with psychiatrists.

He stepped on an Ivy League cap, nearly tripped over a twisted barbecue grille, got his feet tangled in the straps of foam-rubber falsies. The gutters were choked with the glut from a bombed-out drugstore; bobbie-pins, nylon bobby-socks, a spate of pocket-books, a carton of tranquilizers, a mass of suntan lotion, suppositories, deodorants, and a big cardboard cutout of Harry Belafonte obscured by a spilled can of hot fudge.

He shuffled on, through a welter of women's electric shavers, Book-of-the-Month-Club bonus selections, Presley records, false teeth, and treatises of Existentialism. Now he was actually approaching the city proper. Signs of devastation multiplied. Trudging past the campus of the university he noted, with a start of horror, that the huge football stadium was no more. Nestled next to it was the tiny Fine Arts building, and at first he thought that it too had been razed. Upon closer inspection, however, he realized it was untouched, save for the natural evidence of neglect and decay.

He found it difficult to maintain a regular course, now, for the streets were choked with wrecked vehicles and the sidewalks often blocked by beams or the entire toppled fronts of buildings. Whole structures had been ripped apart, and here and there were freakish variations where a roof had fallen in or a single room smashed to expose its contents. Apparently the blow had come instantly, and without forewarning, for there were a few bodies on the streets and those he glimpsed inside the opened buildings gave indication that death had found them in the midst of their natural occupations.

Here, in a gutted basement, a fat man sprawled over the table of his home workshop, his sightless eyes fixed upon the familiar calendar exhibiting entirely the charms of Marilyn Monroe. Two flights above him, through the empty frame of a bathroom window, one could see his wife, dead in the tub, her hand still clutching a movie magazine with a Rock Hudson portrait on the cover. And up in the attic, open to the sky, two young lovers stretched on a brass bed, locked naked in headless ecstasy.

He turned away, and as his progress continued he deliberately avoided looking at the bodies. But he could not avoid seeing them now, and with familiarity the revulsion softened to the merest twinge. It then gave way to curiosity.

Passing a school playground he was pleased to see that the end had come without grotesque or unnatural violence. Probably a wave of paralyzing gas had swept through this area. Most of the figures were frozen upright in normal postures. Here were all of the aspects of ordinary childhood—the big kid punching the little kid, both leaning up against a fence where the blast had found them; a group of six youngsters in uniform black leather jackets piled upon the body of a child wearing a white leather jacket.

Beyond the playground loomed the center of the city. From a distance the mass of shattered masonry looked like a crazy garden-patch turned by a mad plowman. Here and there were tiny blossoms of flame sprouting forth from the interstices of huge clods, and at intervals he could see lopped, stemlike formations, the lower stories of skyscrapers from which the tops had been sheared by the swish of a thermonuclear scythe.

He hesitated, wondering if it was practical to venture into this weird welter. Then he caught sight of the hillside beyond, and of the imposing structure which was the new Federal Building. It stood there, somehow miraculously untouched by the blast, and in the haze he could see the flag still fluttering from its roof. There would be life here, and he knew he would not be content until he reached it.

But long before he attained his objective, he found other evidences of continued existence. Moving delicately and deliberately through the debris, he became aware that he was not entirely alone here in the central chaos.

Wherever the flames flared and flickered, there were furtive figures moving against the fire. To his horror, he realized that they were actually kindling the blazes; burning away barricades that could not otherwise be removed, as they entered shops and stores to loot. Some of the scavengers were silent and ashamed, others were boisterous and drunken; all were doomed.

It was this knowledge which kept him from interfering. Let them plunder and pilfer at will, let them quarrel over the spoils in the shattered streets; in a few hours or a few days, radiation and fallout would take inevitable toll.

No one interfered with his passage; perhaps the helmet and protective garment resembled an official uniform. He went his way unhindered and saw:

A barefooted man wearing a mink coat, dashing through the door of a cocktail lounge and passing bottles out to a bucket-brigade of four small children—

An old woman standing in a bombed-out bank vault, sweeping stacks of bills into the street with her broom. Over in one corner lay the body of a white-haired man, his futile arms outstretched to embrace a heap of coins. Impatiently, the old woman nudged him with her broom. His head lolled, and a silver dollar popped out of his open mouth—

A soldier and a woman wearing the armband of the Red Cross, carrying a stretcher to the blocked entrance of a partially-razed church. Unable to enter, they bore the stretcher around to the side, and the soldier kicked in one of the stained-glass windows—

An artist's basement studio, open to the sky; its walls still intact and covered with abstract paintings. In the center of the room stood the easel, but the artist was gone. What was left of him was smeared across the canvas in a dripping mass, as though the artist had finally succeeded in putting something of himself into his picture—

A welter of glassware that had once been a chemical laboratory, and in the center of it a smocked figure slumped over a microscope. On the slide was a single cell which the scientists had been intently observing when the world crashed about his ears— A woman with the face of a *Vogue* model, spread-eagled in the street. Apparently she had been struck down while answering the call of duty, for one slim, aristocratic hand still gripped the strap of her hatbox. Otherwise, due to some prank of explosion, the blast had stripped her quite naked; she lay there with all her expensive loveliness exposed—

A thin man, emerging from a pawnshop and carrying an enormous tuba. He disappeared momentarily into a meat market, next door, then came out again, the bell of his tuba stuffed with sausages—

A broadcasting studio, completely demolished, its once immaculate sound stage littered with the crumpled cartons of fifteen different varieties of America's Favorite Cigarette and the broken bottles of twenty brands of America's Favorite Beer. Protruding from the wreckage was the head of America's Favorite Quizmaster, eyes staring glassily at a sealed booth in the corner which now served as the coffin for a nine-year-old boy who had known the batting-averages of every team in the American and National Leagues since 1882—

A wild-eyed woman sitting in the street, crying and crooning over a kitten cradled in her arms—

A broker caught at his desk, his body mummified in coils of ticker-tape—

A motor-bus, smashed into a brick wall; its passengers still jamming the aisles; standees clutching straps in *rigor mortis*—

The hindquarters of a stone lion before what had once been the Public Library; before it, on the steps, the corpse of an elderly lady whose shopping-bag had spewed its contents over the street—two murder-mysteries, a rental copy of *Peyton Place*, and the latest issue of the *Reader's Digest*—

A small boy wearing a cowboy hat, who leveled a toy pistol at his little sister and shouted, "Bang! You're dead!"

(She was.)

He walked slowly now, his pace impeded by obstacles both physical and of the spirit. He approached the building on the hillside by a circuitous route; avoiding repugnance, overcoming morbid curiosity, shunning pity, recoiling from horror, surmounting shock.

He knew there were others about him here in the city's core, some bent on acts of mercy, some on heroic rescue. But he ignored them all, for they were dead. Mercy had no meaning in this mist, and there was no rescue from radiation. Some of those who passed called out to him, but he went his way unheeding, knowing their words were mere death-rattles.

But suddenly, as he climbed the hillside, he was crying. The salty warmth ran down his cheeks and blurred the inner surface of his helmet so that he no longer saw anything clearly. And it was thus he emerged from the inner circle; the inner circle of the city, the inner circle of Dante's hell.

His tears ceased to flow and his vision cleared. Ahead of him was the proud outline of the Federal Building, shining and intact—or almost so.

As he neared the imposing steps and gazed up at the façade, he noted that there were a few hints of crumbling and corrosion on the surface of the structure. The freakish blast had done outright damage only to the sculptured figures surmounting the great arched doorway; the symbolic statuary had been partially shattered so that the frontal surface had fallen away. He blinked at the empty outlines of the three figures; somehow he never had realized that Faith, Hope and Charity were hollow.

Then he walked inside the building. There were tired soldiers guarding the doorway, but they made no move to stop him, probably because he wore a protective garment even more intricate and impressive than their own.

Inside the structure a small army of low clerks and high brass moved antlike in the corridors; marching grim-faced up and down the stairs. There were no elevators, of course—they'd ceased functioning when the electricity gave out. But he could climb.

He wanted to climb now, for that was why he had come here. He wanted to gaze out over the city. In his gray insulation he resembled an automaton, and like an automaton he plodded stiffly up the stairways until he reached the topmost floor.

But there were no windows here, only walled-in offices. He walked down a long corridor until he came to the very end. Here, a single large cubicle glowed with gray light from the glass wall beyond.

A man sat at a desk, jiggling the receiver of a field telephone and cursing softly. He glanced curiously at the intruder, noted the insulating uniform, and returned to his abuse of the instrument in his hand.

So it was possible to walk over to the big window and look down.

It was possible to see the city, or the crater where the city had been.

Night was mingling with the haze on the horizon, but there was no darkness. The little incendiary blazes had been spreading, apparently, as the wind moved in, and now he gazed down upon a growing sea of flame. The crumbling spires and gutted structures were drowning in red waves. As he watched, the tears came again, but he knew there would not be enough tears to put the fires out.

So he turned back to the man at the desk, noting for the first time that he wore one of the very special uniforms reserved for generals.

This must be the commander, then. Yes, he was certain of it now, because the floor around the desk was littered with scraps of paper. Maybe they were obsolete maps, maybe they were obsolete treaties. It didn't matter now.

There was another map on the wall behind the desk, and this one mattered very much. It was studded with black and red pins, and it took but a moment to decipher their meaning. The red pins signified destruction, for there was one affixed to the name of this city. And there was one for New York, one for Chicago, Detroit, Los Angeles—every important center had been pierced.

He looked at the general, and finally the words came.

"It must be awful," he said.

"Yes, awful," the general echoed.

"Millions upon millions dead."

"Dead."

"The cities destroyed, the air polluted, and no escape. No escape anywhere in the world."

"No escape."

He turned away and stared out the window once more, stared down at Inferno. Thinking, *this is what it has come to, this is the way the world ends.*

He glanced at the general again, and then sighed. "To think of our being beaten," he whispered.

The red glare mounted, and in its light he saw the general's face, gleeful and exultant.

"What do you mean, man?" the general said proudly, the flames rising. "We won!"

WHO GOES THERE?

John W. Campbell

PHILADELPHIA, 1947
SAN FRANCISCO, 1954
LONDON, 1957

When people ask, "What is science fiction good for?"—
one answer, at least, is that it gives its readers a chance to survey
any number of possible alternate futures, choose among them the
ones they like and spend their efforts trying to bend events to make
the desirable futures come true. John Campbell was the living
proof that such a thing can happen. Campbell was a fascinating,
opinionated, obstinate man who generated a vision in his mind of
what science fiction could be . . . and made it happen, just as he
had planned.

No one else has ever done anything like that. Maybe H. G.
Wells and Hugo Gernsback, for two, came close; but Campbell
alone calculatedly threw a switch and changed the course of all sf

writing. How did he do it? For openers, he sacrificed his own first-rate writing career to it. When he became editor of Astounding *he wrote a few stories to show others how, then stopped cold. He continued to develop exciting ideas for stories. He didn't write them; he gave them to other writers, and out of them came some of the finest stories he published. Half the writers in this volume got their start in Campbell's* Astounding, *or had their careers shaped and developed by his criticisms, suggestions and constant prodding to write better and different.*

The John W. Campbell (as Don A. Stuart) story that follows is the longest in this volume, as it should be; in fact, it should be three stories, because he was Guest of Honor for three separate Worldcons. No one else ever achieved that record; and no one was ever more fully entitled to it.

THE place stank. A queer, mingled stench that only the ice-buried cabins of an Antarctic camp know, compounded of reeking human sweat, and the heavy, fish-oil stench of melted seal blubber. An overtone of liniment combated the musty smell of sweat-and-snow-drenched furs. The acrid odor of burnt cooking fat, and the animal, not-unpleasant smell of dogs, diluted by time, hung in the air.

Lingering odors of machine oil contrasted sharply with the taint of harness dressing and leather. Yet, somehow, through all that reek of human beings and their associates—dogs, machines and cooking—came another taint. It was a queer, neck-ruffling thing, a faintest suggestion of an odor alien among the smells of industry and life. And it was a life-smell. But it came from the thing that lay bound with cord and tarpaulin on the table, dripping slowly, methodically onto the heavy planks, dank and gaunt under the unshielded glare of the electric light.

Blair, the little bald-pated biologist of the expedition, twitched nervously at the wrappings, exposing clear, dark ice beneath and then pulling the tarpaulin back into place restlessly. His little birdlike motions of suppressed eagerness danced his shadow across the fringe of dingy gray underwear hanging from the low ceiling, the equatorial fringe of stiff, graying hair around his naked skull a comical halo about the shadow's head.

Commander Garry brushed aside the lax legs of a suit of underwear, and stepped toward the table. Slowly his eyes traced around the rings of men sardined into the Administration Building. His tall, stiff body straightened finally, and he nodded. "Thirty-seven. All here." His voice was low, yet carried the clear authority of the commander by nature, as well as by title.

"You know the outline of the story back of that find of the Secondary Pole Expedition. I have been conferring with Second-in-Command McReady, and Norris, as well as Blair and Dr. Copper. There is a difference of opinion, and because it involves the entire group, it is only just that the entire Expedition personnel act on it.

"I am going to ask McReady to give you the details of the story, because each of you has been too busy with his own work to follow closely the endeavors of the others. McReady?"

Moving from the smoke-blued background, McReady was a figure from some forgotten myth, a looming, bronze statue that held life, and walked. Six-feet-four inches he stood as he halted beside the table, and, with a characteristic glance upward to assure himself of room under the low ceiling beams, straightened. His rough, clashingly orange windproof jacket he still had on, yet on his huge frame it did not seem misplaced. Even here, four feet beneath the drift-wind that droned across the Antarctic waste above the ceiling, the cold of the frozen continent leaked in, and gave meaning to the harshness of the man. And he was bronze—his great red-bronze beard, the heavy hair that matched it. The gnarled, corded hands gripping, relaxing, gripping and relaxing on the table planks were bronze. Even the deep-sunken eyes beneath heavy brows were bronzed.

Age-resisting endurance of the metal spoke in the cragged heavy outlines of his face, and the mellow tones of the heavy voice. "Norris and Blair agree on one thing; that animal we found was not—terrestrial in origin. Norris fears there may be danger in that; Blair says there is none.

"But I'll go back to how, and why, we found it. To all that was known before we came here, it appeared that this point was exactly over the South Magnetic Pole of Earth. The compass does point straight down here, as you all know. The more delicate instruments of the physicists, instruments especially designed for this expedition and its study of the magnetic pole, detected a secondary effect, a secondary, less powerful magnetic influence about 80 miles southwest of here.

"The Secondary Magnetic Expedition went out to investigate it. There is no need for details. We found it, but it was not the huge meteorite or magnetic mountain Norris had expected to find. Iron ore is magnetic, of course, iron more so—and certain special steels even more magnetic. From the surface indications, the secondary pole we found was small, so small that the magnetic effect it had was preposterous. No magnetic material conceivable could have that effect. Soundings through the ice indicated it was within one hundred feet of the glacier surface.

"I think you should know the structure of the place. There is a broad plateau, a level sweep that runs more than 150 miles due south from the Secondary Station, Van Wall says. He didn't have time or fuel to fly farther, but it was running smoothly due south then. Right there, where that buried thing was, there is an ice-drowned mountain ridge, a granite wall of unshakable strength that has dammed back the ice creeping from the south.

"And four hundred miles due south is the South Polar Plateau. You have asked me at various times why it gets warmer here when the wind rises, and most of you know. As a meteorologist I'd have staked my word that no wind could blow at − 70 degrees—that no more than a five-mile wind could blow at − 50—without causing warming due to friction with ground, snow and ice and the air itself.

"We camped there on the lip of that ice-drowned mountain range for twelve days. We dug our camp into the blue ice that formed the surface, and escaped most of it. But for twelve consecutive days the wind blew at 45 miles an hour. It went as high as 48, and fell to 41 at times. The temperature was − 63 degrees. It rose to − 60 and fell to − 68. It was meteorologically impossible, and it went on uninterruptedly for twelve days and twelve nights.

"Somewhere to the south, the frozen air of South Polar Plateau slides down from that 18,000-foot bowl, down a mountain pass, over a glacier, and starts north. There must be a funneling mountain chain that directs it, and sweeps it away for four hundred miles to hit that bald plateau where we found the secondary pole, and 350 miles farther north reaches the Antarctic Ocean.

"It's been frozen there since Antarctica froze twenty million years ago. There never has been a thaw there.

"Twenty million years ago Antarctica was beginning to freeze. We've investigated, thought and built speculations. What we believe happened was about like this.

"Something came down out of space, a ship. We saw it there in the blue ice, a thing like a submarine without a conning tower or directive vanes, 280 feet long and 45 feet in diameter at its thickest.

"Eh, Van Wall? Space? Yes, but I'll explain that better later." McReady's steady voice went on.

"It came down from space, driven and lifted by forces men haven't discovered yet, and somehow—perhaps something went wrong then—it tangled with Earth's magnetic field. It came south here, out of control probably, circling the magnetic pole. That's a savage country there, but when Antarctica was still freezing it must have been a thousand times more savage. There must have been blizzard snow, as well as drift, new snow falling as the continent glaciated. The swirl there must have been particularly bad, the wind hurling a solid blanket of white over the lip of that now-buried mountain.

"The ship struck solid granite head-on, and cracked up. Not every one of the passengers in it was killed, but the ship must have been ruined, her driving mechanism locked. It tangled with Earth's field, Norris believes. No thing made by intelligent beings can tangle with the dead immensity of a planet's natural forces and survive.

"One of its passengers stepped out. The wind we saw there never fell below 41, and the temperature never rose above −60. Then—the wind must have been stronger. And there was drift falling in a solid sheet. The *thing* was lost completely in ten paces." He paused for a moment, the deep, steady voice giving way to the drone of wind overhead, and the uneasy, malicious gurgling in the pipe of the galley stove.

Drift—a drift-wind was sweeping by overhead. Right now the snow picked up by the mumbling wind fled in level, blinding lines across the face of the buried camp. If a man stepped out of the tunnels that connected each of the camp buildings beneath the surface, he'd be lost in ten paces. Out there, the slim, black finger of the radio mast lifted 300 feet into the air, and at its peak was the clear night sky. A sky of thin, whining wind rushing steadily from beyond to another beyond under the licking, curling mantle of the aurora. And off north, the horizon flamed with queer, angry colors of the midnight twilight. That was spring 300 feet above Antarctica.

At the surface—it was white death. Death of a needle-fingered cold driven before the wind, sucking heat from any warm thing. Cold—and white mist of endless, everlasting drift, the fine, fine particles of licking snow that obscured all things.

Kinner, the little, scar-faced cook, winced. Five days ago he had stepped out to the surface to reach a cache of frozen beef. He had reached it, started back—and the drift-wind leapt out of the south. Cold, white death that streamed across the ground blinded him in twenty seconds. He stumbled on wildly in circles. It was half an hour before rope-guided men from below found him in the impenetrable murk.

It was easy for man—or *thing*—to get lost in ten paces.

"And the drift-wind then was probably more impenetrable than we know." McReady's voice snapped Kinner's mind back. Back to welcome, dank warmth of the Ad Building. "The passenger of the ship wasn't prepared either, it appears. It froze within ten feet of the ship.

"We dug down to find the ship, and our tunnel happened to find the frozen—animal. Barclay's ice-ax struck its skull.

"When we saw what it was, Barclay went back to the tractor, started the fire up and when the steam pressure built, sent a call for Blair and Dr. Copper. Barclay himself was sick then. Stayed sick for three days, as a matter of fact.

"When Blair and Copper came, we cut out the animal in a

block of ice, as you see, wrapped it and loaded it on the tractor for return here. We wanted to get into that ship.

"We reached the side and found the metal was something we didn't know. Our beryllium-bronze, non-magnetic tools wouldn't touch it. Barclay had some tool-steel on the tractor, and that wouldn't scratch it either. We made reasonable tests—even tried some acid from the batteries with no results.

"They must have had a passivating process to make magnesium metal resist acid that way, and the alloy must have been at least 95 per cent magnesium. But we had no way of guessing that, so when we spotted the barely opened lock door, we cut around it. There was clear, hard ice insde the lock, where we couldn't reach it. Through the little crack we could look in and see that only metal and tools were in there, so we decided to loosen the ice with a bomb.

"We had decanite bombs and thermite. Thermite is the ice-softener; decanite might have shattered valuable things, where the thermite's heat would just loosen the ice. Dr. Copper, Norris and I placed a 25-pound thermite bomb, wired it, and took the connector up the tunnel to the surface, where Blair had the steam tractor waiting. A hundred yards the other side of that granite wall we set off the thermite bomb.

"The magnesium metal of the ship caught, of course. The glow of the bomb flared and died, then it began to flare again. We ran back to the tractor, and gradually the glare built up. From where we were we could see the whole ice-field illuminated from beneath with an unbearable light; the ship's shadow was a great, dark cone reaching off toward the north, where the twilight was just about gone. For a moment it lasted, and we counted three other shadow-things that might have been other—passengers— frozen there. Then the ice was crashing down and against the ship.

"That's why I told you about that place. The wind sweeping down from the Pole was at our backs. Steam and hydrogen flame were torn away in white ice-fog; the flaming heat under the ice there was yanked away toward the Antarctic Ocean before it touched us. Otherwise we wouldn't have come back, even with the shelter of that granite ridge that stopped the light.

"Somehow in the blinding inferno we could see great hunched things, black bulks glowing, even so. They shed even the furious incandescence of the magnesium for a time. Those must have been the engines, we knew. Secrets going in blazing glory—secrets that might have given Man the planets. Mysterious things that could lift and hurl that ship—and had soaked in the force of the Earth's magnetic field. I saw Norris' mouth move, and ducked. I couldn't hear him.

"Insulation—something—gave way. All Earth's field they'd soaked up twenty million years before broke loose. The aurora in the sky above licked down, and the whole plateau there was bathed in cold fire that blanketed vision. The ice-ax in my hand got red hot, and hissed on the ice. Metal buttons on my clothes burned into me. And a flash of electric blue seared upward from beyond the granite wall.

"Then the walls of ice crashed down on it. For an instant it squealed the way dry-ice does when it's pressed between metal.

"We were blind and groping in the dark for hours while our eyes recovered. We found every coil within a mile was fused rubbish, the dynamo and every radio set, the earphones and speakers. If we hadn't had the steam tractor, we wouldn't have gotten over to the Secondary Camp.

"Van Wall flew in from Big Magnet at sun-up, as you know. We came home as soon as possible. That is the history of—that." McReady's great bronze beard gestured toward the thing on the table.

II

Blair stirred uneasily, his little, bony fingers wriggling under the harsh light. Little brown freckles on his knuckles slid back and forth as the tendons under the skin twitched. He pulled aside a bit of the tarpaulin and looked impatiently at the dark ice-bound thing inside.

McReady's big body straightened somewhat. He'd ridden the rocking, jarring steam tractor forty miles that day, pushing on to Big Magnet here. Even his calm will had been pressed by the anxiety to mix again with humans. It was lone and quiet out there in Secondary Camp, where a wolf-wind howled down from the Pole. Wolf-wind howling in his sleep—winds droning and the evil, unspeakable face of that monster leering up as he'd first seen it through clear, blue ice, with a bronze ice-ax buried in its skull.

The giant meteorologist spoke again. "The problem is this. Blair wants to examine the thing. Thaw it out and make micro slides of its tissues and so forth. Norris doesn't believe that is safe, and Blair does. Dr. Copper agrees pretty much with Blair. Norris is a physicist, of course, not a biologist. But he makes a point I think we should all hear. Blair has described the microscopic life-forms biologists find living, even in this cold and inhospitable place. They freeze every winter, and thaw every summer—for three months—and live.

"The point Norris makes is—they thaw, and live again. There must have been microscopic life associated with this creature. There is with every living thing we know. And Norris is afraid that we may release a plague—some germ disease unknown to Earth—if we thaw those microscopic things that have been frozen there for twenty million years.

"Blair admits that such micro-life might retain the power of living. Such unorganized things as individual cells can retain life for unknown periods, when solidly frozen. The beast itself is as dead as those frozen mammoths they find in Siberia. Organized, highly developed life-forms can't stand that treatment.

"But micro-life could. Norris suggests that we may release some disease-form that man, never having met it before, will be utterly defenseless against.

"Blair's answer is that there may be such still-living germs, but that Norris has the case reversed. They are utterly non-immune to man. Our life-chemistry probably—"

"Probably!" The little biologist's head lifted in a quick, birdlike motion. The halo of gray hair about his bald head ruffled as though angry. "Heh. One look—"

"I know," McReady acknowledged. "The thing is not Earthly. It does not seem likely that it can have a life-chemistry sufficiently like ours to make cross-infection remotely possible. I would say that there is no danger."

McReady looked toward Dr. Copper. The physician shook his

head slowly. "None whatever," he asserted confidently. "Man cannot infect or be infected by germs that live in such comparatively close relatives as the snakes. And they are, I assure you," his clean-shaven face grimaced uneasily, "*much* nearer to us than—*that.*"

Vance Norris moved angrily. He was comparatively short in this gathering of big men, some five-feet-eight, and his stocky, powerful build tended to make him seem shorter. His black hair was crisp and hard, like short, steel wires, and his eyes were the gray of fractured steel. If McReady was a man of bronze, Norris was all steel. His movements, his thoughts, his whole bearing had the quick, hard impulse of steel spring. His nerves were steel—hard, quick-acting—swift corroding.

He was decided on his point now, and he lashed out in its defense with a characteristic quick, clipped flow of words. "Different chemistry be damned. That thing may be dead—or, by God, it may not—but I don't like it. Damn it, Blair, let them see the monstrosity you are petting over there. Let them see the foul thing and decide for themselves whether they want that thing thawed out in this camp.

"Thawed out, by the way. That's got to be thawed out in one of the shacks tonight, if it is thawed out. Somebody—who's watchman tonight? Magnetic—oh, Connant. Cosmic rays tonight. Well, you get to sit up with that twenty-million-year-old mummy of his.

"Unwrap it, Blair. How the hell can they tell what they are buying if they can't see it? It may have a different chemistry. I don't know what else it has, but I know it has something I don't want. If you can judge by the look on its face—it isn't human so maybe you can't—it was annoyed when it froze. Annoyed, in fact, is just about as close an approximation of the way it felt as crazy, mad, insane hatred. Neither one touches the subject.

"How the hell can these birds tell what they are voting on? They haven't seen those three red eyes, and that blue hair like crawling worms. Crawling—damn, it's crawling there in the ice right now!

"Nothing Earth ever spawned had the unutterable sublimation of devastating wrath that thing let loose in its face when it looked around this frozen desolation twenty million years ago. Mad? It was mad clear through—searing, blistering mad!

"Hell, I've had bad dreams ever since I looked at those three red eyes. Nightmares. Dreaming the thing thawed out and came to life—that it wasn't dead, or even wholly unconscious all those twenty million years, but just slowed, waiting—waiting. You'll dream, too, while that damned thing that Earth wouldn't own is dripping, dripping in the Cosmos House tonight.

"And, Connant," Norris whipped toward the cosmic ray specialist, "won't you have fun sitting up all night in the quiet. Wind whining above—and that thing dripping—" He stopped for a moment, and looked around.

"I know. That's not science. But this is, it's psychology. You'll have nightmares for a year to come. Every night since I looked at that thing I've had 'em. That's why I hate it—sure I do—and don't want it around. Put it back where it came from and let it freeze for another twenty million years. I had some swell nightmares—that it wasn't made like we are—which is obvious—but of a different kind of flesh that it can really control. That it can change its shape, and look like a man—and wait to kill and eat—

"That's not a logical argument. I know it isn't. The thing isn't Earth-logic anyway.

"Maybe it has an alien body-chemistry, and maybe its bugs do have a different body-chemistry. A germ might not stand that, but, Blair and Copper, how about a virus? That's just an enzyme molecule, you've said. That wouldn't need anything but a protein molecule of any body to work on.

"And how are you so sure that, of the million varieties of microscopic life it may have, *none* of them are dangerous? How about diseases like hydrophobia—rabies—that attacks any warm-blooded creature, whatever its body-chemistry may be? And parrot fever? Have you a body like a parrot, Blair? And plain rot—gangrene—necrosis, do you want? *That* isn't choosy about body-chemistry!"

Blair looked up from his puttering long enough to meet Norris' angry, gray eyes for an instant. "So far the only thing you have said this thing gave off that was catching was dreams. I'll go so far as to admit that." An impish, slightly malignant grin crossed the little man's seamed face. "I had some, too. So. It's dream-infectious. No doubt an exceedingly dangerous malady.

"So far as your other things go, you have a badly mistaken idea about viruses. In the first place, nobody has shown that the enzyme-molecule theory, and that alone, explains them. And in the second place, when you catch tobacco mosaic or wheat rust, let me know. A wheat plant is a lot nearer your body-chemistry than this other-world creature is.

"And your rabies is limited, strictly limited. You can't get it from, nor give it to, a wheat plant or a fish—which is a collateral descendant of a common ancestor of yours. Which this, Norris, is not." Blair nodded pleasantly toward the tarpaulined bulk on the table.

"Well, thaw the damned thing in a tub of formalin if you must thaw it. I've suggested that—"

"And I've said there would be no sense in it. You can't compromise. Why did you and Commander Garry come down here to study magnetism? Why weren't you content to stay at home? There's magnetic force enough in New York. I could no more study the life this thing once had from a formalin-pickled sample than you could get the information you wanted back in New York. And—if this one is so treated, never in all time to come can there be a duplicate! The race it came from must have passed away in the twenty million years it lay frozen, so that even if it came from Mars then, we'd never find its like. And—the ship is gone.

"There's only one way to do this—and that is the best possible way. It must be thawed slowly, carefully, and not in formalin."

Commander Garry stood forward again, and Norris stepped back, muttering angrily. "I think Blair is right, gentlemen. What do you say?"

Connant grunted. "It sounds right to us, I think—only perhaps he ought to stand watch over it while it's thawing." He grinned ruefully, brushing a stray lock of ripe-cherry hair back from his forehead. "Swell idea, in fact—if he sits up with his jolly little corpse."

Garry smiled slightly. A general chuckle of agreement rippled over the group. "I should think any ghost it may have had would have starved to death if it hung around here that long, Connant," Garry suggested. "And you look capable of taking care of it. 'Ironman' Connant ought to be able to take out any opposing players, still."

Connant shook himself uneasily. "I'm not worrying about ghosts. Let's see that thing. I—"

Eagerly Blair was stripping back the ropes. A single throw of the tarpaulin revealed the thing. The ice had melted somewhat in the heat of the room, and it was clear and blue as thick, good glass. It shone wet and sleek under the harsh light of the unshielded globe above.

The room stiffened abruptly. It was face up there on the plain, greasy planks of the table. The broken half of the bronze ice-ax was still buried in the queer skull. Three mad, hate-filled eyes blazed up with a living fire, bright as fresh-spilled blood, from a face ringed with a writhing, loathsome nest of worms, blue, mobile worms that crawled where hair should grow—

Van Wall, six feet and 200 pounds of ice-nerved pilot, gave a queer, strangled gasp and butted, stumbled his way out to the corridor. Half the company broke for the doors. The others stumbled away from the table.

McReady stood at one end of the table watching them, his great body planted solid on his powerful legs. Norris from the opposite end glowered at the thing with smouldering hate. Outside the door, Garry was talking with half a dozen of the men at once.

Blair had a tack hammer. The ice that cased the thing *schluffed* crisply under its steel claw as it peeled from the thing it had cased for twenty thousand thousand years—

III

"I know you don't like the thing, Connant, but it just has to be thawed out right. You say leave it as it is till we get back to civilization. All right, I'll admit your argument that we could do a better and more complete job there is sound. But—how are we going to get this across the Line? We have to take this through one temperate zone, the equatorial zone, and half way through the other temperate zone before we get it to New York. You don't want to sit with it one night, but you suggest, then, that I hang its corpse in the freezer with the beef?" Blair looked up from his cautious chipping, his bald, freckled skull nodding triumphantly.

Kinner, the stocky, scar-faced cook, saved Connant the trouble of answering. "Hey, you listen, mister. You put that thing in the box with the meat, and by all the gods there ever were, I'll put you in to keep it company. You birds have brought everything movable in this camp in onto my mess tables here already, and I had to stand for that. But you go putting things like that in my meat box or even my meat cache here, and you cook your own damn grub."

"But, Kinner, this is the only table in Big Magnet that's big enough to work on," Blair objected. "Everybody's explained that."

"Yeah, and everybody's brought everything in here. Clark brings his dogs every time there's a fight and sews them up on that table. Ralsen brings in his sledges. Hell, the only thing you haven't had on that table is the Boeing. And you'd 'a' had that in if you coulda figured a way to get it through the tunnels."

Commander Garry chuckled and grinned at Van Wall, the huge Chief Pilot. Van Wall's great blond beard twitched suspiciously as he nodded gravely to Kinner. "You're right, Kinner. The aviation department is the only one that treats you right."

"It does get crowded, Kinner," Garry acknowledged. "But I'm afraid we all find it that way at times. Not much privacy in an Antarctic camp."

"Privacy? What the hell's that? You know, the thing that really made me weep, was when I saw Barclay marchin' through here chantin' 'The last lumber in the camp! The last lumber in the camp!' and carryin' it out to build that house on his tractor. Damn it, I missed that moon cut in the door he carried out more'n I missed the sun when it set. That wasn't just the last lumber Barclay was walkin' off with. He was carryin' off the last bit of privacy in this blasted place."

A grin rode even on Connant's heavy face as Kinner's perennial good-natured grouch came up again. But it died away quickly as his dark, deep-set eyes turned again to the red-eyed thing Blair was chipping from its cocoon of ice. A big hand ruffed his shoulder-length hair, and tugged at a twisted lock that fell behind his ear in a familiar gesture. "I know that cosmic ray shack's going to be too crowded if I have to sit up with that thing," he growled. "Why can't you go on chipping the ice away from around it—you can do that without anybody butting in, I assure you—and then hang the thing up over the power-plant boiler? That's warm enough. It'll thaw out a chicken, even a whole side of beef, in a few hours."

"I know," Blair protested, dropping the tack hammer to gesture more effectively with his bony, freckled fingers, his small body tense with eagerness, "but this is too important to take any chances. There never was a find like this; there never can be again. It's the only chance men will ever have, and it has to be done exactly right.

"Look, you know how the fish we caught down near the Ross Sea would freeze almost as soon as we got them on deck, and come to life again if we thawed them gently? Low forms of life aren't killed by quick freezing and slow thawing. We have—"

"Hey, for the love of Heaven—you mean that damned thing will come to life!" Connant yelled. "You get the damned thing— Let me at it! That's going to be in so many pieces—"

"NO! No, you fool—" Blair jumped in front of Connant to protect his precious find. "No. Just low forms of life. For Pete's sake, let me finish. You can't thaw higher forms of life and have them come to. Wait a moment now—hold it! A fish can come to after freezing because it's so low a form of life that the individual cells of its body can revive, and that alone is enough to re-establish life. Any higher forms thawed out that way are dead. Though the individual cells revive, they die because there must be organization and cooperative effort to live. That cooperation cannot be re-established. There is a sort of potential life in any uninjured, quick-frozen animal. But it can't—can't under any circumstances—become active life in higher animals. The higher animals are too complex, too delicate. This is an intelligent creature as high in its evolution as we are in ours. Perhaps higher. It is as dead as a frozen man would be."

"How do you know?" demanded Connant, hefting the ice-ax he had seized a moment before.

Commander Garry laid a restraining hand on his heavy shoulder. "'Wait a minute, Connant. I want to get this straight. I agree that there is going to be no thawing of this thing if there is the remotest chance of its revival. I quite agree it is much too unpleasant to have alive, but I had no idea there was the remotest possibility."

Dr. Copper pulled his pipe from between his teeth and heaved his stocky, dark body from the bunk he had been sitting in. "Blair's being technical. That's dead. As dead as the mammoths they find frozen in Siberia. Potential life is like atomic energy—there, but nobody can get it out, and it certainly won't release itself except in rare cases, as rare as radium in the chemical analogy. We have all sorts of proof that things don't live after being frozen—not even fish, generally speaking—and no proof that higher animal life can under any circumstances. What's the point, Blair?"

The little biologist shook himself. The little ruff of hair standing out around his bald pate waved in righteous anger. "The point is," he said in an injured tone, "that the individual cells might show the characteristics they had in life, if it is properly thawed. A man's muscle cells live many hours after he has died. Just because they live, and a few things like hair and fingernail cells still live, you wouldn't accuse a corpse of being a Zombie, or something.

"Now if I thaw this right, I may have a chance to determine what sort of world it's native to. We don't, and can't know by any other means, whether it came from Earth or Mars or Venus or from beyond the stars.

"And just because it looks unlike men, you don't have to accuse it of being evil, or vicious or something. Maybe that expression on its face is its equivalent to a resignation to fate. White is the color of mourning to the Chinese. If men can have different customs, why can't a so-different race have different understandings of facial expressions?"

Connant laughed softly, mirthlessly. "Peaceful resignation! If that is the best it could do in the way of resignation, I should exceedingly dislike seeing it when it was looking mad. That face was never designed to express peace. It just didn't have any philosophical thoughts like peace in its make-up.

"I know it's your pet—but be sane about it. That thing grew up on evil, adolesced slowly roasting alive the local equivalent of kittens, and amused itself through maturity on new and ingenious torture."

"You haven't the slightest right to say that," snapped Blair. "How do you know the first thing about the meaning of a facial expression inherently inhuman? It may well have no human equivalent whatever. That is just a different development of Nature, another example of Nature's wonderful adaptability. Growing on another, perhaps harsher world, it has different form and features. But it is just as much a legitimate child of Nature as you are. You are displaying the childish human weakness of hating the different. On its own world it would probably class you as a fish-belly, white monstrosity with an insufficient number of eyes and a fungoid body pale and bloated with gas.

"Just because its nature is different, you haven't any right to say it's necessarily evil."

Norris burst out a single, explosive "Haw!" He looked down at the thing. "May be that things from other worlds don't *have* to be evil just because they're different. But that thing *was!* Child of Nature, eh? Well, it was a hell of an evil Nature."

"Aw, will you mugs cut crabbing at each other and get the damned thing off my table?" Kinner growled. "And put a canvas over it. It looks indecent."

"Kinner's gone modest," jeered Connant.

Kinner slanted his eyes up to the big physicist. The scarred cheek twisted to join the line of his tight lips in a twisted grin. "All right, big boy, and what were you grousing about a minute ago? We can set the thing in a chair next to you tonight, if you want."

"I'm not afraid of its face," Connant snapped. "I don't like keeping a wake over its corpse particularly, but I'm going to do it."

Kinner's grin spread. "Uh-huh." He went off to the galley stove and shook down ashes vigorously, drowning the brittle chipping of the ice as Blair fell to work again.

IV

"Cluck," reported the cosmic ray counter, *"cluck-brrrp-cluck."* Connant started and dropped his pencil.

"Damnation." The physicist looked toward the far corner, back at the Geiger counter on the table near that corner, and crawled under the desk at which he had been working to retrieve the pencil. He sat down at his work again, trying to make his writing more even. It tended to have jerks and quavers in it, in time with the abrupt proud-hen noises of the Geiger counter. The muted whoosh of the pressure lamp he was using for illumination, the mingled gargles and bugle calls of a dozen men sleeping down the corridor in Paradise House formed the background sounds for the irregular, clucking noises of the counter, the occasional rustle of falling coal in the copper-bellied stove. And a soft, steady *drip-drip-drip* from the thing in the corner.

Connant jerked a pack of cigarettes from his pocket, snapped it so that a cigarette protruded and jabbed the cylinder into his mouth. The lighter failed to function, and he pawed angrily through the pile of papers in search of a match. He scratched the wheel of the lighter several times, dropped it with a curse and got up to pluck a hot coal from the stove with the coal tongs.

The lighter functioned instantly when he tried it on returning to the desk. The counter ripped out a series of chucking guffaws as a burst of cosmic rays struck through to it. Connant turned to glower at it, and tried to concentrate on the interpretation of data collected during the past week. The weekly summary—

He gave up and yielded to curiosity, or nervousness. He lifted the pressure lamp from the desk and carried it over to the table in the corner. Then he returned to the stove and picked up the coal tongs. The beast had been thawing for nearly 18 hours now. He poked at it with an unconscious caution; the flesh was no longer hard as armor plate, but had assumed a rubbery texture. It looked like wet, blue rubber glistening under droplets of water like little round jewels in the glare of the gasoline pressure lantern. Connant felt an unreasoning desire to pour the contents of the lamp's reservoir over the thing in its box and drop the cigarette into it.

The three red eyes glared up at him sightlessly, the ruby eyeballs reflecting murky, smoky rays of light.

He realized vaguely that he had been looking at them for a very long time, even vaguely understood that they were no longer sightless. But it did not seem of importance, of no more importance than the labored, slow motion of the tentacular things that sprouted from the base of the scrawny, slowly pulsing neck.

Connant picked up the pressure lamp and returned to his chair. He sat down, staring at the pages of mathematics before him. The clucking of the counter was strangely less disturbing, the rustle of the coals in the stove no longer distracting.

The creak of the floorboards behind him didn't interrupt his thoughts as he went about his weekly report in an automatic manner, filling in columns of data and making brief, summarizing notes.

The creak of the floorboards sounded nearer.

V

Blair came up from the nightmare-haunted depths of sleep abruptly. Connant's face floated vaguely above him; for a moment it seemed a continuance of the wild horror of the dream. But Connant's face was angry, and a little frightened. "Blair— Blair, you damned log, wake up."

"Uh-eh?" the little biologist rubbed his eyes, his bony, freckled fingers crooked to a mutilated child-fist. From surrounding bunks other faces lifted to stare down at them.

Connant straightened up. "Get up—and get a lift on. Your damned animal's escaped."

"Escaped—what!" Chief Pilot Van Wall's bull voice roared out with a volume that shook the walls. Down the communication tunnels other voices yelled suddenly. The dozen inhabitants of Paradise House tumbled in abruptly, Barclay, stocky and bulbous in long woolen underwear, carrying a fire extinguisher.

"What the hell's the matter?" Barclay demanded.

"Your damned beast got loose. I fell asleep about twenty minutes ago, and when I woke up, the thing was gone. Hey, Doc, the hell you say those things can't come to life. Blair's blasted potential life developed a hell of a lot of potential and walked out on us."

Copper stared blankly. "It wasn't—Earthly," he sighed suddenly. "I—I guess Earthly laws don't apply."

"Well, it applied for leave of absence and took it. We've got to find it and capture it somehow." Connant swore bitterly, his deep-set black eyes sullen and angry. "It's a wonder the hellish creature didn't eat me in my sleep."

Blair stared back, his pale eyes suddenly fear-struck. "Maybe it di—er—uh—we'll have to find it."

"You find it. It's your pet. I've had all I want to do with it, sitting there for seven hours with the counter clucking every few seconds, and you birds in here singing night-music. It's a wonder I got to sleep. I'm going through to the Ad Building."

Commander Garry ducked through the doorway, pulling his belt tight. "You won't have to. Van's roar sounded like the Boeing taking off down wind. So it wasn't dead?"

"I didn't carry it off in my arms, I assure you," Connant snapped. "The last I saw, that split skull was oozing green goo, like a squashed caterpillar. Doc just said our laws don't work—it's unearthly. Well, it's an unearthly monster, with an unearthly disposition, judging by the face, wandering around with a split skull and brains oozing out."

Norris and McReady appeared in the doorway, a doorway filling with other shivering men. "Has anybody seen it coming over here?" Norris asked innocently. "About four feet tall—three red eyes—brains oozing— Hey, has anybody checked to make sure this isn't a cracked idea of humor? If it is, I think we'll unite in tying Blair's pet around Connant's neck like the Ancient Mariner's albatross."

"It's no humor," Connant shivered. "Lord, I wish it were. I'd rather wear—" He stopped. A wild, weird howl shrieked through the corridors. The men stiffened abruptly, and half turned.

"I think it's been located," Connant finished. His dark eyes shifted with a queer unease. He darted back to his bunk in Paradise House, to return almost immediately with a heavy .45 revolver and an ice-ax. He hefted both gently as he started for the corridor toward Dogtown. "It blundered down the wrong corridor—and landed among the huskies. Listen—the dogs have broken their chains—"

The half-terrorized howl of the dog pack changed to a wild hunting melee. The voices of the dogs thundered in the narrow corridors, and through them came a low rippling snarl of distilled hate. A shrill of pain, a dozen snarling yelps.

Connant broke for the door. Close behind him, McReady, then Barclay and Commander Garry came. Other men broke for the Ad Building, and weapons—the sledge house. Pomroy, in charge of Big Magnet's five cows, started down the corridor in the opposite direction—he had a six-foot-handled, long-tined pitchfork in mind.

Barclay slid to a halt, as McReady's giant bulk turned abruptly away from the tunnel leading to Dogtown, and vanished off at an angle. Uncertainly, the mechanician wavered a moment, the fire extinguisher in his hands, hesitating from one side to the other. Then he was racing after Connant's broad back. Whatever McReady had in mind, he could be trusted to make it work.

Connant stopped at the bend in the corridor. His breath hissed suddenly through his throat. "Great God—" The revolver exploded thunderously; three numbing, palpable waves of sound crashed through the confined corridors. Two more. The revolver dropped to the hard-packed snow of the trail, and Barclay saw the ice-ax shift into defensive position. Connant's powerful body blocked his vision, but beyond he heard something mewing, and, insanely, chuckling. The dogs were quieter; there was a deadly seriousness in their low snarls. Taloned feet scratched at hard-packed snow, broken chains were clinking and tangling.

Connant shifted abruptly, and Barclay could see what lay beyond. For a second he stood frozen, then his breath went out in a gusty curse. The Thing launched itself at Connant, the powerful arms of the man swung the ice-ax flatside first at what might have been a hand. It scrunched horribly, and the tattered flesh, ripped by a half-dozen savage huskies, leapt to its feet again. The red eyes blazed with an unearthly hatred, an unearthly, unkillable vitality.

Barclay turned the fire extinguisher on it; the blinding, blistering stream of chemical spray confused it, baffled it, together with the savage attacks of the huskies, not for long afraid of anything that did, or could live, held it at bay.

McReady wedged men out of his way and drove down the narrow corridor packed with men unable to reach the scene. There was a sure fore-planned drive to McReady's attack. One of the giant blow-torches used in warming the plane's engines was in his bronzed hands. It roared gustily as he turned the corner and opened the valve. The mad mewing hissed louder. The dogs scrambled back from the three-foot lance of blue-hot flame.

"Bar, get a power cable, run it in somehow. And a handle. We can electrocute this—monster, if I don't incinerate it." McReady spoke with an authority of planned action. Barclay turned down the long corridor to the power plant, but already before him Norris and Van Wall were racing down.

Barclay found the cable in the electrical cache in the tunnel wall. In a half minute he was hacking at it, walking back. Van Wall's voice rang out in a warning shout of "Power!" as the emergency gasoline-powered dynamo thudded into action. Half a dozen other men were down there now; the coal, kindling were going into the firebox of the steam power plant. Norris, cursing in a low, deadly monotone, was working with quick, sure fingers on the other end of Barclay's cable, splicing in a contactor in one of the power leads.

The dogs had fallen back when Barclay reached the corridor bend, fallen back before a furious monstrosity that glared from baleful red eyes, mewing in trapped hatred. The dogs were a semi-circle of red-dipped muzzles with a fringe of glistening white teeth, whining with a vicious eagerness that near matched the fury of the red eyes. McReady stood confidently alert at the corridor bend, the gustily muttering torch held loose and ready for action in his hands. He stepped aside without moving his eyes from the beast as Barclay came up. There was a slight, tight smile on his lean, bronzed face.

Norris' voice called down the corridor, and Barclay stepped forward. The cable was taped to the long handle of a snow-shovel, the two conductors split, and held eighteen inches apart by a scrap of lumber lashed at right angles across the far end of the handle. Bare copper conductors, charged with 220 volts, glinted in the light of pressure lamps. The Thing mewed and halted and dodged. McReady advanced to Barclay's side. The dogs beyond sensed the plan with the almost-telepathic intelligence of trained huskies. Their whimpering grew shriller, softer, their mincing steps carried them nearer. Abruptly a huge, night-black Alaskan leapt onto the trapped thing. It turned squalling, saber-clawed feet slashing.

Barclay leapt forward and jabbed. A weird, shrill scream rose and choked out. The smell of burnt flesh in the corridor intensified; greasy smoke curled up. The echoing pound of the gas-electric dynamo down the corridor became a slogging thud.

The red eyes clouded over in a stiffening, jerking travesty of a face. Armlike, leglike members quivered and jerked. The dogs leapt forward, and Barclay yanked back his shovel-handled weapon. The thing on the snow did not move as gleaming teeth ripped it open.

VI

Garry looked about the crowded room. Thirty-two men, some tensed nervously standing against the wall, some uneasily relaxed, some sitting, most perforce standing, as intimate as sardines. Thirty-two, plus the five engaged in sewing up wounded dogs, made thirty-seven, the total personnel.

Garry started speaking. "All right, I guess we're here. Some of you—three or four at most—saw what happened. All of you have seen that thing on the table, and can get a general idea. Anyone hasn't, I'll lift—" His hand strayed to the tarpaulin bulking over the thing on the table. There was an acrid odor of singed flesh seeping out of it. The men stirred restlessly, hasty denials.

"It looks rather as though Charnauk isn't going to lead any more teams," Garry went on. "Blair wants to get at this thing, and make some more detailed examination. We want to know what happened, and make sure right now that this is permanently, totally dead. Right?"

Connant grinned. "Anybody that doesn't agree can sit up with it tonight."

"All right then, Blair, what can you say about it? What was it?" Garry turned to the little biologist.

"I wonder if we ever saw its natural form." Blair looked at the covered mass. "It may have been imitating the beings that built that ship—but I don't think it was. I think that was its true form. Those of us who were up near the bend saw the thing in action; the thing on the table is the result. When it got loose, apparently, it started looking around. Antarctica still frozen as it was ages ago when the creature first saw it—and froze. From my observations while it was thawing out, and the bits of tissue I cut and hardened then, I think it was native to a hotter planet than Earth. It couldn't, in its natural form, stand the temperature. There is no life-form on Earth that can live in Antarctica during the winter, but the best compromise is the dog. It found the dogs, and somehow got near enough to Charnauk to get him. The others smelled it—heard it—I don't know—anyway they went wild, and broke chains, and attacked it before it was finished. The thing we found was part Charnauk, queerly only half-dead, part Charnauk half-digested by the jellylike protoplasm of that creature, and part the remains of the thing we originally found, sort of melted down to the basic protoplasm.

"When the dogs attacked it, it turned into the best fighting thing it could think of. Some other-world beast apparently."

"Turned," snapped Garry. "How?"

"Every living thing is made up of jelly—protoplasm and minute, submicroscopic things called nuclei, which control the bulk, the protoplasm. This thing was just a modification of that same worldwide plan of Nature; cells made up of protoplasm, controlled by infinitely tinier nuclei. You physicists might compare it—an individual cell of any living thing—with an atom; the bulk of the atom, the space-filling part, is made up of the electron orbits, but the character of the thing is determined by the atomic nucleus.

"This isn't wildly beyond what we already know. It's just a modification we haven't seen before. It's as natural, as logical, as any other manifestation of life. It obeys exactly the same laws. The cells are made of protoplasm, their character determined by the nucleus.

"Only in this creature, the cell-nuclei can control those cells at *will*. It digested Charnauk, and as it digested, studied every cell of his tissue, and shaped its own cells to imitate them exactly. Parts of it—parts that had time to finish changing—are dog-cells. But they don't have dog-cell nuclei." Blair lifted a fraction of the tarpaulin. A torn dog's leg with stiff gray fur protruded. "That, for instance, isn't dog at all; it's imitation. Some parts I'm uncertain about; the nucleus was hiding itself, covering up with dog-cell imitation nucleus. In time, not even a microscope would have shown the difference."

"Suppose," asked Norris bitterly, "it had had lots of time?"

"Then it would have been a dog. The other dogs would have accepted it. We would have accepted it. I don't think anything would have distinguished it, not microscope, nor X-ray, nor any other means. This is a member of a supremely intelligent race, a race that has learned the deepest secrets of biology, and turned them to its use."

"What was it planning to do?" Barclay looked at the humped tarpaulin.

Blair grinned unpleasantly. The wavering halo of thin hair round his bald pate wavered in the stir of air. "Take over the world, I imagine."

"Take over the world! Just it, all by itself?" Connant gasped. "Set itself up as a lone dictator?"

"No," Blair shook his head. The scalpel he had been fumbling in his bony fingers dropped; he bent to pick it up, so that his face was hidden as he spoke. "It would become the population of the world."

"Become—populate the world? Does it reproduce asexually?"

Blair shook his head and gulped. "It's—it doesn't have to. It weighed eighty-five pounds. Charnauk weighed about ninety. It would have become Charnauk, and had eighty-five pounds left, to become—oh, Jack, for instance, or Chinook. It can imitate anything—that is, become anything. If it had reached the Antarctic Sea, it would have become a seal, maybe two seals. They might have attacked a killer whale, and become either killers, or a herd of seals. Or maybe it would have caught an albatross, or a skua gull, and flown to South America."

Norris cursed softly. "And every time it digested something, and imitated it—"

"It would have had its original bulk left, to start again," Blair finished. "Nothing would kill it. It has no natural enemies, because it becomes whatever it wants to. If a killer whale attacked it, it would become a killer whale. If it was an albatross, and an eagle attacked it, it would become an eagle. Lord, it might become a female eagle. Go back—build a nest and lay eggs!"

"Are you sure that thing from hell is dead?" Dr. Copper asked softly.

"Yes, thank Heaven," the little biologist gasped. "After they drove the dogs off, I stood there poking Bar's electrocution thing into it for five minutes. It's dead and—cooked."

"Then we can only give thanks that this is Antarctica, where there is not one, single, solitary, living thing for it to imitate, except these animals in camp."

"Us," Blair giggled. "It can imitate us. Dogs can't make 400 miles to the sea; there's no food. There aren't any skua gulls to imitate at this season. There aren't any penguins this far inland. There's nothing that can reach the sea from this point—except us. We've got brains. We can do it. Don't you see—*it's got to imitate us—it's got to be one of us—that's the only way it can fly an airplane—fly a plane for two hours, and rule—be—all Earth's inhabitants.* A world for the taking—*if it imitates us!*

"It didn't know yet. It hadn't had a chance to learn. It was rushed—hurried—took the thing nearest its own size. Look—I'm Pandora! I opened the box! And the only hope that can come out is—that nothing can come out. You didn't see me. I did it. I fixed it. I smashed every magneto. Not a plane can fly. Nothing can fly." Blair giggled and lay down on the floor crying.

Chief Pilot Van Wall made a dive for the door. His feet were fading echoes in the corridors as Dr. Copper bent unhurriedly over the little man on the floor. From his office at the end of the room he brought something, and injected a solution into Blair's arm. "He might come out of it when he wakes up," he sighed, rising. McReady helped him lift the biologist onto a near-by bunk. "It all depends on whether we can convince him that thing is dead."

Van Wall ducked into the shack brushing his heavy blond beard absently. "I didn't think a biologist would do a thing like that up thoroughly. He missed the spares in the second cache. It's all right. I smashed them."

Commander Garry nodded. "I was wondering about the radio."

Dr. Copper snorted. "You don't think it can leak out on a radio wave, do you? You'd have five rescue attempts in the next three months if you stop the broadcasts. The thing to do is talk loud and not make a sound. Now I wonder—"

McReady looked speculatively at the doctor. "It might be like an infectious disease. Everything that drank any of its blood—"

Copper shook his head. "Blair missed something. Imitate it may, but it has, to a certain extent, its own body-chemistry, its own metabolism. If it didn't, it would become a dog—and be a dog and nothing more. It has to be an imitation dog. Therefore you can detect it by serum tests. And its chemistry, since it comes from another world, must be so wholly, radically different that a few cells, such as gained by drops of blood, would be treated as disease germs by the dog, or human body."

"Blood—would one of those imitations bleed?" Norris demanded.

"Surely. Nothing mystic about blood. Muscle is about 90 per cent water; blood differs only in having a couple per cent more water, and less connective tissue. They'd bleed all right," Copper assured him.

Blair sat up in his bunk suddenly. "Connant—where's Connant?"

The physicist moved over toward the little biologist. "Here I am. What do you want?"

"Are you?" giggled Blair. He lapsed back into the bunk contorted with silent laughter.

Connant looked at him blankly. "Huh? Am I what?"

"*Are* you there?" Blair burst into gales of laughter. "*Are* you Connant? The beast wanted to be a *man*—not a dog—"

VII

Dr. Copper rose wearily from the bunk, and washed the hypodermic carefully. The little tinkles it made seemed loud in the packed room, now that Blair's gurgling laughter had finally quieted. Copper looked toward Garry and shook his head slowly. "Hopeless, I'm afraid. I don't think we can ever convince him the thing is dead now."

Norris laughed uncertainly. "I'm not sure you can convince me. Oh, damn you, McReady."

"McReady?" Commander Garry turned to look from Norris to McReady curiously.

"The nightmares," Norris explained. "He had a theory about the nightmares we had at the Secondary Station after finding that thing."

"And that was?" Garry looked at McReady levelly.

Norris answered for him, jerkily, uneasily. "That the creature wasn't dead, had a sort of enormously slowed existence, an existence that permitted it, nonetheless, to be vaguely aware of the passing of time, of our coming, after endless years. I had a dream it could imitate things."

"Well," Copper grunted, "it can."

"Don't be an ass," Norris snapped. "That's not what's bothering me. In the dream it could read minds, read thoughts and ideas and mannerisms."

"What's so bad about that? It seems to be worrying you more than the thought of the joy we're going to have with a mad man in an Antarctic camp." Copper nodded toward Blair's sleeping form.

McReady shook his head slowly. "You know that Connant is Connant, because he not merely looks like Connant—which we're beginning to believe that beast might be able to do—but he thinks like Connant, talks like Connant, moves himself around as Connant does. That takes more than merely a body that looks like him; that takes Connant's own mind, and thoughts and mannerisms. Therefore, though you know that the thing might make itself *look* like Connant, you aren't much bothered, because you know it has a mind from another world, a totally unhuman mind, that couldn't possibly react and think and talk like a man we know, and do it so well as to fool us for a moment. The idea of the creature imitating one of us is fascinating, but unreal because it is too completely unhuman to deceive us. It doesn't have a human mind."

"As I said before," Norris repeated, looking steadily at McReady, "you can say the damnedest things at the damnedest times. Will you be so good as to finish that thought—one way or the other?"

Kinner, the scar-faced expedition cook, had been standing near Connant. Suddenly he moved down the length of the crowded room toward his familiar galley. He shook the ashes from the galley stove noisily.

"It would do it no good," said Dr. Copper, softly as though thinking out loud, "to merely look like something it was trying to imitate; it would have to understand its feelings, its reaction. It *is* unhuman; it has powers of imitation beyond any conception of man. A good actor, by training himself, can imitate another man, another man's mannerisms, well enough to fool most people. Of course no actor could imitate so perfectly as to deceive men who had been living with the imitated one in the complete lack of privacy of an Antarctic camp. That would take a super-human skill."

"Oh, you've got the bug too?" Norris cursed softly.

Connant, standing alone at one end of the room, looked about him wildly, his face white. A gentle eddying of the men had crowded them slowly down toward the other end of the room, so that he stood quite alone. "My God, will you two Jeremiahs shut up?" Connant's voice shook. "What am I? Some kind of a microscopic specimen you're dissecting? Some unpleasant worm you're discussing in the third person?"

McReady looked up at him; his slowly twisting hands stopped for a moment. "Having a lovely time. Wish you were here. Signed: Everybody.

"Connant, if you think you're having a hell of a time, just move over on the other end for a while. You've got one thing we haven't; you know what the answer is. I'll tell you this, right now you're the most feared and respected man in Big Magnet."

"Lord, I wish you could see your eyes," Connant gasped. "Stop staring, will you! What the hell are you going to do?"

"Have you any suggestions, Dr. Copper?" Commander Garry asked steadily. "The present situation is impossible."

"Oh, is it?" Connant snapped. "Come over here and look at

that crowd. By Heaven, they look exactly like that gang of huskies around the corridor bend. Benning, will you stop hefting that damned ice-ax?"

The coppery blade rang on the floor as the aviation mechanic nervously dropped it. He bent over and picked it up instantly, hefting it slowly, turning it in his hands, his brown eyes moving jerkily about the room.

Copper sat down on the bunk beside Blair. The wood creaked noisily in the room. Far down a corridor, a dog yelped in pain, and the dog-drivers' tense voices floated softly back. "Microscopic examination," said the doctor thoughtfully, "would be useless, as Blair pointed out. Considerable time has passed. However, serum tests would be definitive."

"Serum tests? What do you mean exactly?" Commander Garry asked.

"If I had a rabbit that had been injected with human blood—a poison to rabbits, of course, as is the blood of any animal save that of another rabbit—and the injections continued in increasing doses for some time, the rabbit would be human-immune. If a small quantity of its blood were drawn off, allowed to separate in a test-tube, and to the clear serum, a bit of human blood were added, there would be a visible reaction, proving the blood was human. If cow, or dog blood were added—or any protein material other than that one thing, human blood—no reaction would take place. That would prove definitely."

"Can you suggest where I might catch a rabbit for you, Doc?" Norris asked. "That is, nearer than Australia; we don't want to waste time going that far."

"I know there aren't any rabbits in Antarctica," Copper nodded, "but that is simply the usual animal. Any animal except man will do. A dog, for instance. But it will take several days, and due to the greater size of the animal, considerable blood. Two of us will have to contribute."

"Would I do?" Garry asked.

"That will make two," Copper nodded. "I'll get to work on it right away."

"What about Connant in the meantime?" Kinner demanded.

"I'm going out that door and head off for the Ross Sea before I cook for him."

"He may be human—" Copper started.

Connant burst out in a flood of curses. "Human! *May* be human, you damned saw-bones! What in hell do you think I am?"

"A monster," Copper snapped sharply. "Now shut up and listen." Connant's face drained of color and he sat down heavily as the indictment was put into words. "Until we know—you know as well as we do that we have reason to question the fact, and only you know how that question is to be answered—we may reasonably be expected to lock you up. If you are—unhuman— you're a lot more dangerous than poor Blair there, and I'm going to see that he's locked up thoroughly. I expect that his next stage will be a violent desire to kill you, all the dogs, and probably all of us. When he wakes, he will be convinced we're all unhuman, and nothing on the planet will ever change his conviction. It would be kinder to let him die, but we can't do that, of course. He's going in one shack, and you can stay in Cosmos House with your cosmic ray apparatus. Which is about what you'd do anyway. I've got to fix up a couple of dogs."

Connant nodded bitterly. "I'm human. Hurry that test. Your eyes—Lord, I wish you could see your eyes staring—"

Commander Garry watched anxiously as Clark, the dog-handler, held the big brown Alaskan husky, while Copper began the injection treatment. The dog was not anxious to cooperate; the needle was painful, and already he'd experienced considerable needle work that morning. Five stitches held closed a slash that ran from his shoulder across the ribs half way down his body. One long fang was broken off short; the missing part was to be found half-buried in the shoulder bone of the monstrous thing on the table in the Ad Building.

"How long will that take?" Garry asked, pressing his arm gently. It was sore from the prick of the needle Dr. Copper had used to withdraw blood.

Copper shrugged. "I don't know, to be frank. I know the general method, I've used it on rabbits. But I haven't experimented with dogs. They're big, clumsy animals to work with;

naturally rabbits are preferable, and serve ordinarily. In civilized places you can buy a stock of human-immune rabbits from suppliers, and not many investigators take the trouble to prepare their own."

"What do they want with them back there?" Clark asked.

"Criminology is one large field. A says he didn't murder B, but that the blood on his shirt came from killing a chicken. The State makes a test, then it's up to A to explain how it is the blood reacts on human-immune rabbits, but not on chicken-immunes."

"What are we going to do with Blair in the meantime?" Garry asked wearily. "It's all right to let him sleep where he is for a while, but when he wakes up—"

"Barclay and Benning are fitting some bolts on the door of Cosmos House," Copper replied grimly. "Connant's acting like a gentleman. I think perhaps the way the other men look at him makes him rather want privacy. Lord knows, heretofore we've all of us individually prayed for a little privacy."

Clark laughed bitterly. "Not any more, thank you. The more the merrier."

"Blair," Copper went on, "will also have to have privacy—and locks. He's going to have a pretty definite plan in mind when he wakes up. Ever hear the old story of how to stop hoof-and-mouth disease in cattle?

"If there isn't any hoof-and-mouth disease, there won't be any hoof-and-mouth disease," Copper explained. "You get rid of it by killing every animal that exhibits it, and every animal that's been near the diseased animal. Blair's a biologist, and knows that story. He's afraid of this thing we loosed. The answer is probably pretty clear in his mind now. Kill everybody and everything in this camp before a skua gull or a wandering albatross coming in with the spring chances out this way and—catches the disease."

Clark's lips curled in a twisted grin. "Sounds logical to me. If things get too bad—maybe we'd better let Blair get loose. It would save us committing suicide. We might also make something of a vow that if things get bad, we see that that does happen."

Copper laughed softly. "The last man alive in Big Magnet—wouldn't be a man," he pointed out. "Somebody's got to kill those—creatures that don't desire to kill themselves, you know.

We don't have enough thermite to do it all at once, and the decanite explosive wouldn't help much. I have an idea that even small pieces of one of those beings would be self-sufficient."

"If," said Garry thoughtfully, "they can modify their protoplasm at will, won't they simply modify themselves to birds and fly away? They can read all about birds, and imitate their structure without even meeting them. Or imitate, perhaps, birds of their home planet."

Copper shook his head, and helped Clark to free the dog. "Man studied birds for centuries, trying to learn how to make a machine to fly like them. He never did do the trick; his final success came when he broke away entirely and tried new methods. Knowing the general idea, and knowing the detailed structure of wing and bone and nerve-tissue is something far, far different. And as for other-world birds, perhaps, in fact very probably, the atmospheric conditions here are so vastly different that their birds couldn't fly. Perhaps, even, the being came from a planet like Mars with such a thin atmosphere that there were no birds."

Barclay came into the building, trailing a length of airplane control cable. "It's finished, Doc. Cosmos House can't be opened from the inside. Now where do we put Blair?"

Copper looked toward Garry. "There wasn't any biology building. I don't know where we can isolate him."

"How about East Cache?" Garry said after a moment's thought. "Will Blair be able to look after himself—or need attention?"

"He'll be capable enough. We'll be the ones to watch out," Copper assured him grimly. "Take a stove, a couple of bags of coal, necessary supplies and a few tools to fix it up. Nobody's been out there since last fall, have they?"

Garry shook his head. "If he gets noisy—I thought that might be a good idea."

Barclay hefted the tools he was carrying and looked up at Garry. "If the muttering he's doing now is any sign, he's going to sing away the night hours. And we won't like his song."

"What's he saying?" Copper asked.

Barclay shook his head. "I didn't care to listen much. You can if you want to. But I gathered that the blasted idiot had all the dreams McReady had, and a few more. He slept beside the thing when we stopped on the trail coming in from Secondary Magnetic, remember. He dreamt the thing was alive, and dreamt more details. And—damn his soul—knew it wasn't all dream, or had reason to. He knew it had telepathic powers that were stirring vaguely, and that it could not only read minds, but project thoughts. They weren't dreams, you see. They were stray thoughts that thing was broadcasting, the way Blair's broadcasting his thoughts now—a sort of telepathic muttering in its sleep. That's why he knew so much about its powers. I guess you and I, Doc, weren't so sensitive—if you want to believe in telepathy."

"I have to," Copper sighed. "Dr. Rhine of Duke University has shown that it exists, shown that some are much more sensitive than others."

"Well, if you want to learn a lot of details, go listen in on Blair's broadcast. He's driven most of the boys out of the Ad Building; Kinner's rattling pans like coal going down a chute. When he can't rattle a pan, he shakes ashes.

"By the way, Commander, what are we going to do this spring, now the planes are out of it?"

Garry sighed. "I'm afraid our expedition is going to be a loss. We cannot divide our strength now."

"It won't be a loss—if we continue to live, and come out of this," Copper promised him. "The find we've made, if we can get it under control, is important enough. The cosmic ray data, magnetic work, and atmospheric work won't be greatly hindered."

Garry laughed mirthlessly. "I was just thinking of the radio broadcasts. Telling half the world about the wonderful results of our exploration flights, trying to fool men like Byrd and Ellsworth back home there that we're doing something."

Copper nodded gravely. "They'll know something's wrong. But men like that have judgment enough to know we wouldn't do tricks without some sort of reason, and will wait for our return to judge us. I think it comes to this: men who know enough to recognize our deception will wait for our return. Men who haven't discretion and faith enough to wait will not have the experience to detect any fraud. We know enough of the conditions here to put through a good bluff."

"Just so they don't send 'rescue' expeditions," Garry prayed. "When—if—we're ever ready to come out, we'll have to send word to Captain Forsythe to bring a stock of magnetos with him when he comes down. But—never mind that."

"You mean if we don't come out?" asked Barclay. "I was wondering if a nice running account of an eruption or an earthquake via radio—with a swell windup by using a stick of decanite under the microphone—would help. Nothing, of course, will entirely keep people out. One of those swell, melodramatic 'last-man-alive-scenes' might make 'em go easy though."

Garry smiled with genuine humor. "Is everybody in camp trying to figure that out too?"

Copper laughed. "What do you think, Garry? We're confident we can win out. But not too easy about it, I guess."

Clark grinned up from the dog he was petting into calmness. "Confident, did you say, Doc?"

VIII

Blair moved restlessly around the small shack. His eyes jerked and quivered in vague, fleeting glances at the four men with him: Barclay, six feet tall and weighing over 190 pounds; McReady, a bronze giant of a man; Dr. Copper, short, squatly powerful; and Benning, five-feet-ten of wiry strength.

Blair was huddled up against the far wall of the East Cache cabin, his gear piled in the middle of the floor beside the heating stove, forming an island between him and the four men. His bony hands clenched and fluttered, terrified. His pale eyes wavered uneasily as his bald, freckled head darted about in birdlike motion.

"I don't want anybody coming here. I'll cook my own food," he snapped nervously. "Kinner may be human now, but I don't believe it. I'm going to get out of here, but I'm not going to eat any food you send me. I want cans. Sealed cans."

"O.K., Blair, we'll bring 'em tonight," Barclay promised. "You've got coal, and the fire's started. I'll make a last—" Barclay started forward.

Blair instantly scurried to the farthest corner. "Get out! Keep away from me, you monster!" the little biologist shrieked, and tried to claw his way through the wall of the shack. "Keep away from me—keep away—I won't be absorbed—I won't be—"

Barclay relaxed and moved back. Dr. Copper shook his head. "Leave him alone, Bar. It's easier for him to fix the thing himself. We'll have to fix the door, I think—"

The four men let themselves out. Efficiently, Benning and Barclay fell to work. There were no locks in Antarctica; there wasn't enough privacy to make them needed. But powerful screws had been driven in each side of the door frame, and the spare aviation control cable, immensely strong, woven steel wire, was rapidly caught between them and drawn taut. Barclay went to work with a drill and a keyhole saw. Presently he had a trap cut in the door through which goods could be passed without unlashing the entrance. Three powerful hinges from a stock-crate, two hasps and a pair of three-inch cotter-pins made it proof against opening from the other side.

Blair moved about restlessly inside. He was dragging something over to the door with panting gasps and muttering, frantic curses. Barclay opened the hatch and glanced in, Dr. Copper peering over his shoulder. Blair had moved the heavy bunk against the door. It could not be opened without his cooperation now.

"Don't know but what the poor man's right at that," McReady sighed. "If he gets loose, it is his avowed intention to kill each and all of us as quickly as possible, which is something we don't agree with. But we've something on our side of that door that is worse than a homicidal maniac. If one or the other has to get loose, I think I'll come up and undo those lashings here."

Barclay grinned. "You let me know, and I'll show you how to get these off fast. Let's go back."

The sun was painting the northern horizon in multi-colored rainbows still, though it was two hours below the horizon. The field of drift swept off to the north, sparkling under its flaming colors in a million reflected glories. Low mounds of rounded white on the northern horizon showed the Magnet Range was barely awash above the sweeping drift. Little eddies of wind-lifted snow swirled away from their skis as they set out toward the main encampment two miles away. The spidery finger of the broadcast radiator lifted a gaunt black needle against the white of the Antarctic continent. The snow under their skis was like fine sand, hard and gritty.

"Spring," said Benning bitterly, "is come. Ain't we got fun! I've been looking forward to getting away from this blasted hole in the ice."

"I wouldn't try it now, if I were you," Barclay grunted. "Guys that set out from here in the next few days are going to be marvelously unpopular."

"How is your dog getting along, Dr. Copper?" McReady asked. "Any results yet?"

"In thirty hours? I wish there were. I gave him an injection of my blood today. But I imagine another five days will be needed. I don't know certainly enough to stop sooner."

"I've been wondering—if Connant were—changed, would he have warned us so soon after the animal escaped? Wouldn't he have waited long enough for it to have a real chance to fix itself? Until we woke up naturally?" McReady asked slowly.

"The thing is selfish. You didn't think it looked as though it were possessed of a store of the higher justices, did you?" Dr. Copper pointed out. "Every part of it is all of it, every part of it is all for itself, I imagine. If Connant were changed, to save his skin, he'd have to—but Connant's feelings aren't changed; they're imitated perfectly, or they're his own. Naturally, the imitation, imitating perfectly Connant's feelings, would do exactly what Connant would do."

"Say, couldn't Norris or Van give Connant some kind of a test? If the thing is brighter than men, it might know more physics than Connant should, and they'd catch it out," Barclay suggested.

Copper shook his head wearily. "Not if it reads minds. You can't plan a trap for it. Van suggested that last night. He hoped it would answer some of the questions of physics he'd like to know answers to."

"This expedition-of-four idea is going to make life happy." Benning looked at his companions. "Each of us with an eye on the others to make sure he doesn't do something—peculiar. Man, aren't we going to be a trusting bunch! Each man eyeing his neighbors with the grandest exhibition of faith and trust—I'm beginning to know what Connant meant by 'I wish you could see your eyes.' Every now and then we all have it, I guess. One of you looks around with a sort of 'I-wonder-if-the-other-*three*-are-look.' Incidentally, I'm not excepting myself."

"So far as we know, the animal is dead, with a slight question as to Connant. No other is suspected," McReady stated slowly. "The 'always-four' order is merely a precautionary measure."

"I'm waiting for Garry to make it four-in-a-bunk," Barclay sighed. "I thought I didn't have any privacy before, but since that order—"

None watched more tensely than Connant. A little sterile glass test-tube, half-filled with straw-colored fluid. One—two—three—four—five drops of the clear solution Dr. Copper had prepared from the drops of blood from Connant's arm. The tube was shaken carefully, then set in a beaker of clear, warm water. The thermometer read blood heat, a little thermostat clicked noisily, and the electric hotplate began to glow as the lights flickered slightly.

Then—little white flecks of precipitation were forming, snowing down in the clear straw-colored fluid. "Lord," said Connant. He dropped heavily into a bunk, crying like a baby. "Six days—" Connant sobbed, "six days in there—wondering if that damned test would lie—"

Garry moved over silently, and slipped his arm across the physicist's back.

"It couldn't lie," Dr. Copper said. "The dog was human-immune—and the serum reacted."

"He's—all right?" Norris gasped. "Then—the animal is dead—dead forever?"

"He is human," Copper spoke definitely, "and the animal is dead."

Kinner burst out laughing, laughing hysterically. McReady turned toward him and slapped his face with a methodical one-two, one-two action. The cook laughed, gulped, cried a moment, and sat up rubbing his cheeks, mumbling his thanks vaguely. "I was scared. Lord, I was scared—"

Norris laughed brittlely. "You think we weren't, you ape? You think maybe Connant wasn't?"

The Ad Building stirred with a sudden rejuvenation. Voices laughed, the men clustering around Connant spoke with unnecessarily loud voices, jittery, nervous voices relievedly friendly again. Somebody called out a suggestion, and a dozen started for their skis. Blair. Blair might recover—Dr. Copper fussed with his test-tubes in nervous relief, trying solutions. The party of relief for Blair's shack started out the door, skis clapping noisily. Down the corridor, the dogs set up a quick yelping howl as the air of excited relief reached them.

Dr. Copper fussed with his tubes. McReady noticed him first, sitting on the edge of the bunk, with two precipitin-whitened test-tubes of straw-colored fluid, his face whiter than the stuff in the tubes, silent tears slipping down from horror-widened eyes.

McReady felt a cold knife of fear pierce through his heart and freeze in his breast. Dr. Copper looked up.

"Garry," he called hoarsely. "Garry, for God's sake, come here."

Commander Garry walked toward him sharply. Silence clapped down on the Ad Building. Connant looked up, rose stiffly from his seat.

"Garry—tissue from the monster—precipitates too. It proves nothing. Nothing but—but the dog was monster-immune too. That one of the two contributing blood—one of us two, you and I, Garry—*one of us is a monster.*"

IX

"Bar, call back those men before they tell Blair," McReady said quietly. Barclay went to the door; faintly his shouts came back to the tensely silent men in the room. Then he was back.

"They're coming," he said. "I didn't tell them why. Just that Dr. Copper said not to go."

"McReady," Garry sighed, "you're in command now. May God help you. I cannot."

The bronzed giant nodded slowly, his deep eyes on Commander Garry.

"I may be the one," Garry added. "I know I'm not, but I cannot prove it to you in any way. Dr. Copper's test has broken down. The fact that he showed it was useless, when it was to the advantage of the monster to have that uselessness not known, would seem to prove he was human."

Copper rocked back and forth slowly on the bunk. "I know I'm human. I can't prove it either. One of us two is a liar, for that test cannot lie, and it says one of us is. I gave proof that the test was wrong, which seems to prove I'm human, and now Garry has given that argument which proves me human—which he, as the monster, should not do. Round and round and round and round and—"

Dr. Copper's head, then his neck and shoulders began circling slowly in time to the words. Suddenly he was lying back on the bunk, roaring with laughter. "It doesn't have to prove one of us is a monster! It doesn't have to prove that at all! Ho-ho. If we're *all* monsters it works the same! We're all monsters—all of us—Connant and Garry and I—and all of you."

"McReady," Van Wall, the blond-bearded Chief Pilot, called softly, "you were on the way to an M.D. when you took up meteorology, weren't you? Can you make some kind of test?"

McReady went over to Copper slowly, took the hypodermic from his hand, and washed it carefully in 95 per cent alcohol. Garry sat on the bunk-edge with wooden face, watching Copper and McReady expressionlessly. "What Copper said is possible," McReady sighed. "Van, will you help here? Thanks." The filled needle jabbed into Copper's thigh. The man's laughter did not stop, but slowly faded into sobs, then sound sleep as the morphia took hold.

McReady turned again. The men who had started for Blair stood at the far end of the room, skis dripping snow, their faces as white as their skis. Connant had a lighted cigarette in each hand; one he was puffing absently, and staring at the floor. The heat of the one in his left hand attracted him and he stared at it, and the one in the other hand stupidly for a moment. He dropped one and crushed it under his heel slowly.

"Dr. Copper," McReady repeated, "could be right. I know I'm human—but of course can't prove it. I'll repeat the test for my own information. Any of you others who wish to may do the same."

Two minutes later, McReady held a test-tube with white precipitin settling slowly from straw-colored serum. "It reacts to human blood too, so they aren't both monsters."

"I didn't think they were," Van Wall sighed. "That wouldn't suit the monster either; we could have destroyed them if we knew. Why hasn't the monster destroyed us, do you suppose? It seems to be loose."

McReady snorted. Then laughed softly. "Elementary, my dear Watson. The monster wants to have life-forms available. It cannot animate a dead body, apparently. It is just waiting—waiting until the best opportunities come. We who remain human, it is holding in reserve."

Kinner shuddered violently. "Hey. Hey, Mac. Mac, would I know if I was a monster? Would I know if the monster had already got me? Oh Lord, I may be a monster already."

"You'd know," McReady answered.

"But we wouldn't," Norris laughed shortly, half-hysterically.

McReady looked at the vial of serum remaining. "There's one thing this damned stuff is good for, at that," he said thoughtfully. "Clark, will you and Van help me? The rest of the gang better stick together here. Keep an eye on each other," he said bitterly. "See that you don't get into mischief, shall we say?"

McReady started down the tunnel toward Dog town, with Clark and Van Wall behind him. "You need more serum?" Clark asked.

McReady shook his head. "Tests. There's four cows and a bull, and nearly seventy dogs down there. This stuff reacts only to human blood and—monsters."

McReady came back to the Ad Building and went silently to the wash stand. Clark and Van Wall joined him a moment later. Clark's lips had developed a tic, jerking into sudden, unexpected sneers.

"What did you do?" Connant exploded suddenly. "More immunizing?"

Clark snickered, and stopped with a hiccough. "Immunizing. Haw! Immune all right."

"That monster," said Van Wall steadily, "is quite logical. Our immune dog was quite all right, and we drew a little more serum for the tests. But we won't make any more."

"Can't—can't you use one man's blood on another dog—" Norris began.

"There aren't," said McReady softly, "any more dogs. Nor cattle, I might add."

"No more dogs?" Benning sat down slowly.

"They're very nasty when they start changing," Van Wall said precisely, "but slow. That electrocution iron you made up, Barclay, is very fast. There is only one dog left—our immune. The monster left that for us, so we could play with our little test. The rest—" He shrugged and dried his hands.

"The cattle—" gulped Kinner.

"Also. Reacted very nicely. They look funny as hell when they start melting. The beast hasn't any quick escape, when it's tied in dog chains, or halters, and it had to be to imitate."

Kinner stood up slowly. His eyes darted around the room, and came to rest horribly quivering on a tin bucket in the galley. Slowly, step by step, he retreated toward the door, his mouth opening and closing silently, like a fish out of water.

"The milk—" he gasped. "I milked 'em an hour ago—" His voice broke into a scream as he dived through the door. He was out on the ice cap without windproof or heavy clothing.

Van Wall looked after him for a moment thoughtfully. "He's probably hopelessly mad," he said at length, "but he might be a monster escaping. He hasn't skis. Take a blow-torch—in case."

The physical motion of the chase helped them; something that needed doing. Three of the other men were quietly being sick. Norris was lying flat on his back, his face greenish, looking steadily at the bottom of the bunk above him.

"Mac, how long have the—cows been not-cows—"

McReady shrugged his shoulders hopelessly. He went over to the milk bucket, and with his little tube of serum went to work on it. The milk clouded it, making certainty difficult. Finally he dropped the test-tube in the stand and shook his head. "It tests negatively. Which means either they were cows then, or that, being perfect imitations, they gave perfectly good milk."

Copper stirred restlessly in his sleep and gave a gurgling cross between a snore and a laugh. Silent eyes fastened on him. "Would morphia—a monster—" somebody started to ask.

"Lord knows," McReady shrugged. "It affects every Earthly animal I know of."

Connant suddenly raised his head. "Mac! The dogs must have swallowed pieces of the monster, and the pieces destroyed them! The dogs were where the monster resided. I was locked up. Doesn't that prove—"

Van Wall shook his head. "Sorry. Proves nothing about what you are, only proves what you didn't do."

"It doesn't do that," McReady sighed. "We are helpless. Because we don't know enough, and so jittery we don't think straight. Locked up! Ever watch a white corpuscle of the blood go through the wall of a blood vessel? No? It sticks out a pseudopod. And there it is—on the far side of the wall."

"Oh," said Van Wall unhappily. "The cattle tried to melt down, didn't they? They could have melted down—become just a thread of stuff and leaked under a door to re-collect on the other side. Ropes—no—no, that wouldn't do it. They couldn't live in a sealed tank or—"

"If," said McReady, "you shoot it through the heart, and it doesn't die, it's a monster. That's the best test I can think of, offhand."

"No dogs," said Garry quietly, "and no cattle. It has to imitate men now. And locking up doesn't do any good. Your test might work, Mac, but I'm afraid it would be hard on the men."

x

Clark looked up from the galley stove as Van Wall, Barclay, McReady and Benning came in, brushing the drift from their clothes. The other men jammed into the Ad Building continued studiously to do as they were doing, playing chess, poker, reading. Ralsen was fixing a sledge on the table; Van and Norris had their heads together over magnetic data, while Harvey read tables in a low voice.

Dr. Copper snored softly on the bunk. Garry was working with

Dutton over a sheaf of radio messages on the corner of Dutton's bunk and a small fraction of the radio table. Connant was using most of the table for Cosmic Ray sheets.

Quite plainly through the corridor, despite two closed doors, they could hear Kinner's voice. Clark banged a kettle onto the galley stove and beckoned McReady silently. The meteorologist went over to him.

"I don't mind the cooking so damn much," Clark said nervously, "but isn't there some way to stop that bird? We all agreed that it would be safe to move him into Cosmos House."

"Kinner?" McReady nodded toward the door. "I'm afraid not. I can dope him, I suppose, but we don't have an unlimited supply of morphia, and he's not in danger of losing his mind. Just hysterical."

"Well, we're in danger of losing ours. You've been out for an hour and a half. That's been going on steadily ever since, and it was going for two hours before. There's a limit, you know."

Garry wandered over slowly, apologetically. For an instant, McReady caught the feral spark of fear—horror—in Clark's eyes, and knew at the same instant it was in his own. Garry—Garry or Copper—was certainly a monster.

"If you could stop that, I think it would be a sound policy, Mac," Garry spoke quietly. "There are—tensions enough in this room. We agreed that it would be safe for Kinner in there, because everyone else in camp is under constant eyeing." Garry shivered slightly. "And try, try in God's name, to find some test that will work."

McReady sighed. "Watched or unwatched, everyone's tense. Blair's jammed the trap so it won't open now. Says he's got food enough, and keeps screaming 'Go away, go away—you're monsters. I won't be absorbed. I won't. I'll tell men when they come. Go away.' So—we went away."

"There's no other test?" Garry pleaded.

McReady shrugged his shoulders. "Copper was perfectly right. The serum test could be absolutely definitive if it hadn't been—contaminated. But that's the only dog left, and he's fixed now."

"Chemicals? Chemical tests?"

McReady shook his head. "Our chemistry isn't that good. I tried the microscope, you know."

Garry nodded. "Monster-dog and real dog were identical. But—you've got to go on. What are we going to do after dinner?"

Van Wall had joined them quietly. "Rotation sleeping. Half the crowd asleep; half awake. I wonder how many of us are monsters? All the dogs were. We thought we were safe, but somehow it got Copper—or you." Van Wall's eyes flashed uneasily. "It may have gotten every one of you—all of you but myself may be wondering, looking. No, that's not possible. You'd just spring then. I'd be helpless. We humans must somehow have the greater numbers now. But—" he stopped.

McReady laughed shortly. "You're doing what Norris complained of in me. Leaving it hanging. 'But if one more is changed—that may shift the balance of power.' It doesn't fight. I don't think it ever fights. It must be a peaceable thing, in its own—inimitable—way. It never had to, because it always gained its end—otherwise."

Van Wall's mouth twisted in a sickly grin. "You're suggesting then, that perhaps it already *has* the greater numbers, but is just waiting—waiting, all of them—all of you, for all I know—waiting till I, the last human, drop my wariness in sleep. Mac, did you notice their eyes, all looking at us?"

Garry sighed. "You haven't been sitting here for four straight hours, while all their eyes silently weighed the information that one of us two, Copper or I, is a monster certainly—perhaps both of us."

Clark repeated his request. "Will you stop that bird's noise? He's driving me nuts. Make him tone down, anyway."

"Still praying?" McReady asked.

"Still praying," Clark groaned. "He hasn't stopped for a second. I don't mind his praying if it relieves him, but he yells, he sings psalms and hymns and shouts prayers. He thinks God can't hear well way down here."

"Maybe He can't," Barclay grunted. "Or He'd have done something about this thing loosed from hell."

"Somebody's going to try that test you mentioned, if you don't stop him," Clark stated grimly. "I think a cleaver in the head would be as positive a test as a bullet in the heart."

"Go ahead with the food. I'll see what I can do. There may be something in the cabinets." McReady moved wearily toward the corner Copper had used as his dispensary. Three tall cabinets of rough boards, two locked, were the repositories of the camp's medical supplies. Twelve years ago McReady had graduated, had started for an internship, and been diverted to meteorology. Copper was a picked man, a man who knew his profession thoroughly and modernly. More than half the drugs available were totally unfamiliar to McReady; many of the others he had forgotten. There was no huge medical library here, no series of journals available to learn the things he had forgotten, the elementary, simple things to Copper, things that did not merit inclusion in the small library he had been forced to content himself with. Books are heavy, and every ounce of supplies had been freighted in by air.

McReady picked a barbiturate hopefully. Barclay and Van Wall went with him. One man never went anywhere alone in Big Magnet.

Ralsen had his sledge put away, and the physicists had moved off the table, the poker game broken up when they got back. Clark was putting out the food. The click of spoons and the muffled sounds of eating were the only sign of life in the room. There were no words spoken as the three returned; simply all eyes focused on them questioningly, while the jaws moved methodically.

McReady stiffened suddenly. Kinner was screeching out a hymn in a hoarse, cracked voice. He looked wearily at Van Wall with a twisted grin and shook his head. "Hu-uh."

Van Wall cursed bitterly, and sat down at the table. "We'll just plumb have to take that till his voice wears out. He can't yell like that forever."

"He's got a brass throat and a cast-iron larynx," Norris declared savagely. "Then we could be hopeful, and suggest he's one of our friends. In that case he could go on renewing his throat till doomsday."

Silence clamped down. For twenty minutes they ate without a word. Then Connant jumped up with an angry violence. "You sit as still as a bunch of graven images. You don't say a word, but oh, Lord, what expressive eyes you've got. They roll around like a bunch of glass marbles spilling down a table. They wink and blink and stare—and whisper things. Can you guys look somewhere else for a change, please?

"Listen, Mac, you're in charge here. Let's run movies for the rest of the night. We've been saving those reels to make 'em last. Last for what? Who is it's going to see those last reels, eh? Let's see 'em while we can, and look at something other than each other."

"Sound idea, Connant. I, for one, am quite willing to change this in any way I can."

"Turn the sound up loud, Dutton. Maybe you can drown out the hymns," Clark suggested.

"But don't," Norris said softly, "don't turn off the lights altogether."

"The lights will be out." McReady shook his head. "We'll show all the cartoon movies we have. You won't mind seeing the old cartoons, will you?"

"Goody, goody—a moom pitcher show. I'm just in the mood." McReady turned to look at the speaker, a lean, lanky New Englander, by the name of Caldwell. Caldwell was stuffing his pipe slowly, a sour eye cocked up to McReady.

The bronze giant was forced to laugh. "O.K., Bart, you win. Maybe we aren't quite in the mood for Popeye and trick ducks, but it's something."

"Let's play Classifications," Caldwell suggested slowly. "Or maybe you call it Guggenheim. You draw lines on a piece of paper, and put down classes of things—like animals, you know. One for 'H' and one for 'U' and so on. Like 'Human' and 'Unknown' for instance. I think that would be a hell of a lot better game. Classification, I sort of figure is what we need right now a lot more than movies. Maybe somebody's got a pencil that he can draw lines with, draw lines between the 'U' animals and the 'H' animals, for instance."

"McReady's trying to find that kind of a pencil," Van Wall

answered quietly, "but we've got three kinds of animals here, you know. One that begins with 'M'. We don't want any more."

"Mad ones, you mean. Uh-huh. Clark, I'll help you with those pots so we can get our little peep-show going." Caldwell got up slowly.

Dutton and Barclay and Benning, in charge of the projector and sound mechanism arrangements, went about their job silently, while the Ad Building was cleared and the dishes and pans disposed of. McReady drifted over toward Van Wall slowly, and leaned back in the bunk beside him. "I've been wondering, Van," he said with a wry grin, "whether or not to report my ideas in advance. I forgot the 'U animals' as Caldwell named it, could read minds. I've a vague idea of something that might work. It's too vague to bother with though. Go ahead with your show, while I try to figure out the logic of the thing. I'll take this bunk."

Van Wall glanced up, and nodded. The movie screen would be practically on a line with his bunk, hence making the pictures least distracting here, because least intelligible. "Perhaps you should tell us what you have in mind. As it is, only the unknowns know what you plan. You might be—unknown before you got it into operation."

"Won't take long, if I get it figured out right. But I don't want any more all-but-the-test-dog-monsters things. We better move Copper into this bunk directly above me. He won't be watching the screen either." McReady nodded toward Copper's gently snoring bulk. Garry helped them lift and move the doctor.

McReady leaned back against the bunk, and sank into a trance, almost, of concentration, trying to calculate chances, operations, methods. He was scarcely aware as the others distributed themselves silently, and the screen lit up. Vaguely Kinner's hectic, shouted prayers and his rasping hymn-singing annoyed him till the sound accompaniment started. The lights were turned out, but the large, light-colored areas of the screen reflected enough light for ready visibility. It made men's eyes sparkle as they moved restlessly. Kinner was still praying, shouting, his voice a raucous accompaniment to the mechanical sound. Dutton stepped up the amplification.

So long had the voice been going on, that only vaguely at first was McReady aware that something seemed missing. Lying as he was, just across the narrow room from the corridor leading to Cosmos House, Kinner's voice had reached him fairly clearly, despite the sound accompaniment of the pictures. It struck him abruptly that it had stopped.

"Dutton, cut that sound," McReady called as he sat up abruptly. The pictures flickered a moment, soundless and strangely futile in the sudden, deep silence. The rising wind on the surface above bubbled melancholy tears of sound down the stove pipes. "Kinner's stopped," McReady said softly.

"For God's sake, start that sound then, he may have stopped to listen," Norris snapped.

McReady rose and went down the corridor. Barclay and Van Wall left their places at the far end of the room to follow him. The flickers bulged and twisted on the back of Barclay's gray underwear as he crossed the still-functioning beam of the projector. Dutton snapped on the lights, and the pictures vanished.

Norris stood at the door as McReady had asked. Garry sat down quietly in the bunk nearest the door, forcing Clark to make room for him. Most of the others had stayed exactly where they were. Only Connant walked slowly up and down the room, in steady, unvarying rhythm.

"If you're going to do that, Connant," Clark spat, "we can get along without you altogether, whether you're human or not. Will you stop that damned rhythm?"

"Sorry." The physicist sat down in a bunk, and watched his toes thoughtfully. It was almost five minutes, five ages while the wind made the only sound, before McReady appeared at the door.

"We," he announced, "haven't got enough grief here already. Somebody's tried to help us out. Kinner has a knife in his throat, which was why he stopped singing, probably. We've got monsters, madmen and murderers. Any more 'M's' you can think of, Caldwell? If there are, we'll probably have 'em before long."

XI

"Is Blair loose?" someone asked.

"Blair is not loose. Or he flew in. If there's any doubt about where our gentle helper came from—this may clear it up." Van Wall held a foot-long, thin-bladed knife in a cloth. The wooden handle was half-burnt, charred with the peculiar pattern of the top of the galley stove.

Clark stared at it. "I did that this afternoon. I forgot the damn thing and left it on the stove."

Van Wall nodded. "I smelled it, if you remember. I knew the knife came from the galley."

"I wonder," said Benning, looking around at the party warily, "how many more monsters have we? If somebody could slip out of his place, go back of the screen to the galley and then down to the Cosmos House and back—he did come back, didn't he? Yes—everybody's here. Well, if one of the gang could do all that—"

"Maybe a monster did it," Garry suggested quietly. "There's that possibility."

"The monster, as you pointed out today, has only men left to imitate. Would he decrease his—supply, shall we say?" Van Wall pointed out. "No, we just have a plain, ordinary louse, a murderer to deal with. Ordinarily we'd call him an 'inhuman murderer' I suppose, but we have to distinguish now. We have inhuman murderers, and now we have human murderers. Or one at least."

"There's one less human," Norris said softly. "Maybe the monsters have the balance of power now."

"Never mind that," McReady sighed and turned to Barclay. "Bar, will you get your electric gadget? I'm going to make certain—"

Barclay turned down the corridor to get the pronged electrocuter, while McReady and Van Wall went back toward Cosmos House. Barclay followed them in some thirty seconds.

The corridor to Cosmos House twisted, as did nearly all corridors in Big Magnet, and Norris stood at the entrance again. But they heard, rather muffled, McReady's sudden shout. There was a savage scurry of blows, dull *ch-thunk*, *shluff* sounds. "Bar—bar—" And a curious, savage mewing scream, silenced before even quick-moving Norris had reached the bend.

Kinner—or what had been Kinner—lay on the floor, cut half in two by the great knife McReady had had. The meteorologist stood against the wall, the knife dripping red in his hand. Van Wall was stirring vaguely on the floor, moaning, his hand half-consciously rubbing at his jaw. Barclay, an unutterably savage gleam in his eyes, was methodically leaning on the pronged weapon in his hand, jabbing—jabbing, jabbing.

Kinner's arms had developed a queer, scaly fur, and the flesh had twisted. The fingers had shortened, the hand rounded, the fingernails become three-inch long things of dull red horn, keened to steel-hard razor-sharp talons.

McReady raised his head, looked at the knife in his hand and dropped it. "Well, whoever did it can speak up now. He was an inhuman murderer at that—in that he murdered an inhuman. I swear by all that's holy, Kinner was a lifeless corpse on the floor here when we arrived. But when It found we were going to jab it with the power—It changed."

Norris stared unsteadily. "Oh, Lord, those things can act. Ye gods—sitting in here for hours, mouthing prayers to a God it hated! Shouting hymns in a cracked voice—hymns about a Church it never knew. Driving us mad with its ceaseless howling—

"Well. Speak up, whoever did it. You didn't know it, but you did the camp a favor. And I want to know how in blazes you got out of that room without anyone seeing you. It might help in guarding ourselves."

"His screaming—his singing. Even the sound projector couldn't drown it." Clark shivered. "It was a monster."

"Oh," said Van Wall in sudden comprehension. "You were sitting right next to the door, weren't you! And almost behind the projection screen already."

Clark nodded dumbly. "He—it's quiet now. It's a dead—Mac, your test's no damn good. It was dead anyway, monster or man, it was dead."

McReady chuckled softly. "Boys, meet Clark, the only one we know is human! Meet Clark, the one who proves he's human by trying to commit murder—and failing. Will the rest of you please refrain from trying to prove you're human for a while? I think we may have another test."

"A test!" Connant snapped joyfully, then his face sagged in disappointment. "I suppose it's another either-way-you-want-it."

"No," said McReady steadily. "Look sharp and be careful. Come into the Ad Building. Barclay, bring your electrocuter. And somebody—Dutton—stand with Barclay to make sure he does it. Watch every neighbor, for by the Hell these monsters came from, I've got something, and they know it. They're going to get dangerous!"

The group tensed abruptly. An air of crushing menace entered into every man's body, sharply they looked at each other. More keenly than ever before—*is that man next to me an inhuman monster?*

"What is it?" Garry asked, as they stood again in the main room. "How long will it take?"

"I don't know, exactly," said McReady, his voice brittle with angry determination. "But I *know* it will work, and no two ways about it. It depends on a basic quality of the *monsters*, not on us. *'Kinner'* just convinced me." He stood heavy and solid in bronzed immobility, completely sure of himself again at last.

"This," said Barclay, hefting the wooden-handled weapon, tipped with its two sharp-pointed, charged conductors, "is going to be rather necessary, I take it. Is the power plant assured?"

Dutton nodded sharply. "The automatic stoker bin is full. The gas power plant is on stand-by. Van Wall and I set it for the movie operation and—we've checked it over rather carefully several times, you know. Anything those wires touch, dies," he assured them grimly. "*I* know that."

Dr. Copper stirred vaguely in his bunk, rubbed his eyes with fumbling hand. He sat up slowly, blinked his eyes blurred with sleep and drugs, widened with an unutterable horror of drug-ridden nightmares. "Garry," he mumbled, "Garry—listen. Selfish—from hell they came, and hellish shellfish—I mean self—— Do I? What do I mean?" he sank back in his bunk, and snored softly.

McReady looked at him thoughtfully. "We'll know presently," he nodded slowly. "But selfish is what you mean all right. You may have thought of that, half-sleeping, dreaming there. I didn't stop to think what dreams you might be having. But that's all right. Selfish is the word. They must be, you see." He turned to the men in the cabin, tense, silent men staring with wolfish eyes each at his neighbor. "Selfish, and as Dr. Copper said *every part is a whole*. Every piece is self-sufficient, an animal in itself.

"That, and one other thing, tell the story. There's nothing mysterious about blood; it's just as normal a body tissue as a piece of muscle, or a piece of liver. But it hasn't so much connective tissue, though it has millions, billions of life-cells."

McReady's great bronze beard ruffled in a grim smile. "This is satisfying, in a way. I'm pretty sure we humans still outnumber you—others. Others standing here. And we have what you, your other-world race, evidently doesn't. Not an imitated, but a bred-in-the-bone instinct, a driving, unquenchable fire that's genuine. We'll fight, fight with a ferocity you may attempt to imitate, but you'll never equal! We're human. We're real. You're imitations, false to the core of your every cell.

"All right. It's a showdown now. You know. You, with your mind reading. You've lifted the idea from my brain. You can't do a thing about it.

"Standing here—

"Let it pass. Blood is tissue. They have to bleed, if they don't bleed when cut, then, by Heaven, they're phony! Phony from hell! If they bleed—then that blood, separated from them, is an individual—*a newly formed individual in its own right, just as they, split, all of them, from one original, are individuals!*

"Get it, Van? See the answer, Bar?"

Van Wall laughed very softly. "The blood—the blood will not obey. It's a new individual, with all the desire to protect its own life that the original—the main mass from which it was split—has. The *blood* will live—and try to crawl away from a hot needle, say!"

McReady picked up the scalpel from the table. From the cabinet, he took a rack of test-tubes, a tiny alcohol lamp, and a length of platinum wire set in a little glass rod. A smile of grim satisfaction rode his lips. For a moment he glanced up at those around him. Barclay and Dutton moved toward him slowly, the wooden-handled electric instrument alert.

"Dutton," said McReady, "suppose you stand over by the splice there where you've connected that in. Just make sure no—thing pulls it loose."

Dutton moved away. "Now, Van, suppose you be first on this."

White-faced, Van Wall stepped forward. With a delicate precision, McReady cut a vein in the base of his thumb. Van Wall winced slightly, then held steady as a half inch of bright blood collected in the tube. McReady put the tube in the rack, gave Van Wall a bit of alum, and indicated the iodine bottle.

Van Wall stood motionlessly watching. McReady heated the platinum wire in the alcohol lamp flame, then dipped it into the tube. It hissed softly. Five times he repeated the test. "Human, I'd say." McReady sighed, and straightened. "As yet, my theory hasn't been actually proven—but I have hopes. I have hopes.

"Don't, by the way, get too interested in this. We have with us some unwelcome ones, no doubt. Van, will you relieve Barclay at the switch? Thanks. O.K., Barclay, and may I say I hope you stay with us? You're a damned good guy."

Barclay grinned uncertainly; winced under the keen edge of the scalpel. Presently, smiling widely, he retrieved his long-handled weapon.

"Mr. Samuel Dutt—*Bar!*"

The tensity was released in that second. Whatever of hell the monsters may have had within them, the men in that instant matched it. Barclay had no chance to move his weapon as a score of men poured down on that thing that had seemed Dutton. It mewed, and spat, and tried to grow fangs—and was a hundred broken, torn pieces. Without knives, or any weapon save the brute-given strength of a staff of picked men, the thing was crushed, rent.

Slowly they picked themselves up, their eyes smouldering, very quiet in their emotions. A curious wrinkling of their lips betrayed a species of nervousness.

Barclay went over with the electric weapon. Things smouldered and stank. The caustic acid Van Wall dropped on each spilled drop of blood gave off tickling, cough-provoking fumes.

McReady grinned, his deep-set eyes alight and dancing. "Maybe," he said softly, "I underrated man's abilities when I said nothing human could have the ferocity in the eyes of that thing we found. I wish we could have the opportunity to treat in a more befitting manner these things. Something with boiling oil, or melted lead in it, or maybe slow roasting in the power boiler. When I think what a man Dutton was—

"Never mind. My theory is confirmed by—by one who knew? Well, Van Wall and Barclay are proven. I think, then, that I'll try to show you what I already know. That I too am human." McReady swished the scalpel in absolute alcohol, burned it off the metal blade, and cut the base of his thumb expertly.

Twenty seconds later he looked up from the desk at the waiting men. There were more grins out there now, friendly grins, yet withal, something else in the eyes.

"Connant," McReady laughed softly, "was right. The huskies watching that thing in the corridor bend had nothing on you. Wonder why we think only the wolf blood had the right to ferocity? Maybe on spontaneous viciousness a wolf takes tops, but after these seven days—abandon all hope, ye wolves who enter here!

"Maybe we can save time. Connant, would you step for—"

Again Barclay was too slow. There were more grins, less tensity still, when Barclay and Van Wall finished their work.

Garry spoke in a low, bitter voice. "Connant was one of the finest men we had here—and five minutes ago I'd have sworn he was a man. Those damnable things are more than imitation." Garry shuddered and sat back in his bunk.

And thirty seconds later, Garry's blood shrank from the hot platinum wire, and struggled to escape the tube—struggled as frantically as a suddenly feral, red-eyed, dissolving imitation of Garry struggled to dodge the snake-tongue weapon. Barclay advanced at him, white-faced and sweating. The Thing in the test-tube screamed with a tiny, tinny voice as McReady dropped it into the glowing coal of the galley stove.

XII

"The last of it?" Dr. Copper looked down from his bunk with bloodshot, saddened eyes. "Fourteen of them—"

McReady nodded shortly. "In some ways—if only we could have permanently prevented their spreading—I'd like to have

even the imitations back. Commander Garry—Connant—Dutton
—Clark—"

"Where are they taking those things?" Copper nodded to the
stretcher Barclay and Norris were carrying out.

"Outside. Outside on the ice, where they've got fifteen smashed
crates, half a ton of coal, and presently will add ten gallons of
kerosene. We've dumped acid on every spilled drop, every torn
fragment. We're going to incinerate those."

"Sounds like a good plan." Copper nodded wearily. "I wonder,
you haven't said whether Blair—"

McReady started. "We forgot him! We had so much else! I
wonder—do you suppose we can cure him now?"

"If—" began Dr. Copper, and stopped meaningly.

McReady started a second time. "Even a madman. It imitated
Kinner and his praying hysteria—" McReady turned toward Van
Wall at the long table. "Van, we've got to make an expedition to
Blair's shack."

Van looked up sharply, the frown of worry faded for an instant
in surprised remembrance. Then he rose, nodded. "Barclay better
go along. He applied the lashings, and may figure how to get in
without frightening Blair too much."

Three quarters of an hour, through—37-degree cold, while the
Aurora curtain bellied overhead. The twilight was nearly twelve
hours long, flaming in the north on snow like white, crystalline
sand under their skis. A five-mile wind piled it in drift-lines
pointing off to the northwest. Three quarters of an hour to reach
the snow-buried shack. No smoke came from the little shack, and
the men hastened.

"Blair!" Barclay roared into the wind when he was still a
hundred yards away. "Blair!"

"Shut up," said McReady softly. "And hurry. He may be trying
a long hike. If we have to go after him—no planes, the tractors
disabled—"

"Would a monster have the stamina a man has?"

"A broken leg wouldn't stop it for more than a minute,"
McReady pointed out.

Barclay gasped suddenly and pointed aloft. Dim in the twilit
sky, a winged thing circled in curves of indescribable grace and

ease. Great white wings tipped gently, and the bird swept over them in silent curiosity. "Albatross—" Barclay said softly. "First of the season, and wandering way inland for some reason. If a monster's loose—"

Norris bent down on the ice, and tore hurriedly at his heavy, windproof clothing. He straightened, his coat flapping open, a grim blue-metaled weapon in his hand. It roared a challenge to the white silence of Antarctica.

The thing in the air screamed hoarsely. Its great wings worked frantically as a dozen feathers floated down from its tail. Norris fired again. The bird was moving swiftly now, but in an almost straight line of retreat. It screamed again, more feathers dropped and with beating wings it soared behind a ridge of pressure ice, to vanish.

Norris hurried after the others. "It won't come back," he panted.

Barclay cautioned him to silence, pointing. A curiously, fiercely blue light beat out from the cracks of the shack's door. A very low, soft humming sounded inside, a low, soft humming and a clink and clank of tools, the very sounds somehow bearing a message of frantic haste.

McReady's face paled. "Lord help us if that thing has—" He grabbed Barclay's shoulder, and made snipping motions with his fingers, pointing toward the lacing of control-cables that held the door.

Barclay drew the wire-cutters from his pocket, and kneeled soundlessly at the door. The snap and twang of cut wires made an unbearable racket in the utter quiet of the Antarctic hush. There was only that strange, sweetly soft hum from within the shack, and the queerly, hecticly clipped clicking and rattling of tools to drown their noises.

McReady peered through a crack in the door. His breath sucked in huskily and his great fingers clamped cruelly on Barclay's shoulder. The meteorologist backed down. "It isn't," he explained very softly, "Blair. It's kneeling on something on the bunk—something that keeps lifting. Whatever it's working on is a thing like a knapsack—and it lifts."

"All at once," Barclay said grimly. "No. Norris, hang back, and get that iron of yours out. It may have—weapons."

Together, Barclay's powerful body and McReady's giant strength struck the door. Inside, the bunk jammed against the door screeched madly and crackled into kindling. The door flung down from broken hinges, the patched lumber of the doorpost dropping inward.

Like a blue-rubber ball, a Thing bounced up. One of its four tentaclelike arms looped out like a striking snake. In a seven-tentacled hand a six-inch pencil of winking, shining metal glinted and swung upward to face them. Its line-thin lips twitched back from snake-fangs in a grin of hate, red eyes blazing.

Norris' revolver thundered in the confined space. The hate-washed face twitched in agony, the looping tentacle snatched back. The silvery thing in its hand a smashed ruin of metal, the seven-tentacled hand became a mass of mangled flesh oozing greenish-yellow ichor. The revolver thundered three times more. Dark holes drilled each of the three eyes before Norris hurled the empty weapon against its face.

The Thing screamed in feral hate, a lashing tentacle wiping at blinded eyes. For a moment it crawled on the floor, savage tentacles lashing out, the body twitching. Then it staggered up again, blinded eyes working, boiling hideously, the crushed flesh sloughing away in sodden gobbets.

Barclay lurched to his feet and dove forward with an ice-ax. The flat of the weighty thing crushed against the side of the head. Again the unkillable monster went down. The tentacles lashed out, and suddenly Barclay fell to his feet in the grip of a living, livid rope. The Thing dissolved as he held it, a white-hot band that ate into the flesh of his hands like living fire. Frantically he tore the stuff from him, held his hands where they could not be reached. The blind Thing felt and ripped at the tough, heavy, windproof cloth, seeking flesh—flesh it could convert—

The huge blow-torch McReady had brought coughed solemnly. Abruptly it rumbled disapproval throatily. Then it laughed gurglingly, and thrust out a blue-white, three-foot tongue. The Thing on the floor shrieked, flailed out blindly with tentacles that writhed and withered in the bubbling wrath of the blow-torch. It crawled and turned on the floor, it shrieked and hobbled madly, but always McReady held the blow-torch on the face, the dead eyes burning and bubbling uselessly. Frantically the Thing crawled and howled.

A tentacle sprouted a savage talon—and crisped in the flame. Steadily McReady moved with a planned, grim campaign. Helpless, maddened, the Thing retreated from the grunting torch, the caressing, licking tongue. For a moment it rebelled, squalling in inhuman hatred at the touch of icy snow. Then it fell back before the charring breath of the torch, the stench of its flesh bathing it. Hopelessly it retreated—on and on across the Antarctic snow. The bitter wind swept over it twisting the torch-tongue; vainly it flopped, a trail of oily, stinking smoke bubbling away from it—

McReady walked back toward the shack silently. Barclay met him at the door. "No more?" the giant meteorologist asked grimly.

Barclay shook his head. "No more. It didn't split?"

"It had other things to think about," McReady assured him. "When I left it, it was a glowing coal. What was it doing?"

Norris laughed shortly. "Wise boys, we are. Smash magnetos, so planes won't work. Rip the boiler tubing out of the tractors. And leave that Thing alone for a week in this shack. Alone and undisturbed."

McReady looked in at the shack more carefully. The air, despite the ripped door, was hot and humid. On a table at the far end of the room rested a thing of coiled wires and small magnets, glass tubing and radio tubes. At the center a block of rough stone rested. From the center of the block came the light that flooded the place, the fiercely blue light bluer than the glare of an electric arc, and from it came the sweetly soft hum. Off to one side was another mechanism of crystal glass, blown with an incredible neatness and delicacy, metal plates and a queer, shimmery sphere of insubstantiality.

"What is that?" McReady moved nearer.

Norris grunted. "Leave it for investigation. But I can guess pretty well. That's atomic power. That stuff to the left—that's a neat little thing for doing what men have been trying to do with 100-ton cyclotrons and so forth. It separates neutrons from heavy water, which he was getting from the surrounding ice."

"Where did he get all—oh. Of course. A monster couldn't be locked in—or out. He's been through the apparatus caches." McReady stared at the apparatus. "Lord, what minds that race must have—"

"The shimmery sphere—I think it's a sphere of pure force. Neutrons can pass through any matter, and he wanted a supply reservoir of neutrons. Just project neutrons against silica—calcium—beryllium—almost anything, and the atomic energy is released. That thing is the atomic generator."

McReady plucked a thermometer from his coat. "It's 120 degrees in here, despite the open door. Our clothes have kept the heat out to an extent, but I'm sweating now."

Norris nodded. "The light's cold. I found that. But it gives off heat to warm the place through that coil. He had all the power in the world. He could keep it warm and pleasant, as his race thought of warmth and pleasantness. Did you notice the light, the color of it?"

McReady nodded. "Beyond the stars is the answer. From beyond the stars. From a hotter planet that circled a brighter, bluer sun they came."

McReady glanced out the door toward the blasted, smoke-stained trail that flopped and wandered blindly off across the drift. "There won't be any more coming, I guess. Sheer accident it landed here, and that was twenty million years ago. What did it do all that for?" He nodded toward the apparatus.

Barclay laughed softly. "Did you notice what it was working on when we came? Look." He pointed toward the ceiling of the shack.

Like a knapsack made of flattened coffee-tins, with dangling cloth straps and leather belts, the mechanism clung to the ceiling. A tiny, glaring heart of supernal flame burned in it, yet burned through the ceiling's wood without scorching it. Barclay walked over to it, grasped two of the dangling straps in his hands, and pulled it down with an effort. He strapped it about his body. A slight jump carried him in a weirdly slow arc across the room.

"Anti-gravity," said McReady softly.

"Anti-gravity," Norris nodded. "Yes, we had 'em stopped, with no planes, and no birds. The birds hadn't come—but they had coffee-tins and radio parts, and glass and the machine shop at night. And a week—a whole week—all to itself. America in a single jump—with anti-gravity powered by the atomic energy of matter.

"We had 'em stopped. Another half hour—it was just tightening these straps on the device so it could wear it—and we'd have stayed in Antarctica, and shot down any moving thing that came from the rest of the world."

"The albatross—" McReady said softly. "Do you suppose—"

"With this thing almost finished? With that death weapon it held in its hand?

"No, by the grace of God, who evidently does hear very well, even down here, and the margin of half an hour, we keep our world, and the planets of the system too. Anti-gravity, you know, and atomic power. Because *They* came from another sun, a star beyond the stars. *They* came from a world with a bluer sun."

DOG STAR

Arthur C. Clarke

NEW YORK, 1956

Arthur Clarke's main interests lie under the sea and above the atmosphere, but he is no stranger to the interface between earth and air that most of us inhabit. Indeed, he has seen more of it than most humans; his services are always in demand, all over the civilized globe, and he is likely to be hobnobbing with astronauts in Houston on a Wednesday, lecturing in Acapulco on Friday, attending an international conference in London on Sunday and accepting an award in New York somewhere between flights. English by birth, Ceylonese by residency, Clarke is familiar with nearly all the continents and a majority of the countries on the globe. When he (and we) were guests at a symposium in Tokyo a few years ago, I was identified as a representative of the United States, Brian Aldiss as representing England, other writers as from other countries; but when Clarke's name came up, he was simply referred to as a citizen of the world.

Awards? He has them all. He is the only person ever to have accomplished the "hat trick" by winning Nebula, Hugo and International Fantasy Award, all three. Added to the Kalinga prize and several scores of others, he has enough trophies, plaques and statuettes to keep the servants busy dusting them. The science-fiction Worldcon paid him its well-deserved tribute in New York in 1956. Appropriately, it took place at what was then the biggest world convention ever held, since it went to a man who is surely one of the greatest science-fiction authors alive.

WHEN I heard Laika's frantic barking, my first reaction was one of annoyance. I turned over in my bunk and murmured sleepily, "Shut up, you silly bitch." That dreamy interlude lasted only a fraction of a second; then consciousness returned—and, with it, fear. Fear of loneliness, and fear of madness.

For a moment I dared not open my eyes; I was afraid of what I might see. Reason told me that no dog had ever set foot upon this world, that Laika was separated from me by a quarter of a million miles of space—and, far more irrevocably, five years of time.

"You've been dreaming," I told myself angrily. "Stop being a fool—open your eyes! You won't see anything except the glow of the wall paint."

That was right, of course. The tiny cabin was empty, the door tightly closed. I was alone with my memories, overwhelmed by the transcendental sadness that often comes when some bright dream fades into drab reality. The sense of loss was so desolating that I longed to return to sleep. It was well that I failed to do so, for at that moment sleep would have been death. But I did not know this for another five seconds, and during that eternity I was back on Earth, seeking what comfort I could from the past.

No one ever discovered Laika's origin, though the Observatory staff made a few enquiries and I inserted several advertisements in the Pasadena newspapers. I found her, a lost and lonely ball of fluff, huddled by the roadside one summer evening when I was driving up to Palomar. Though I have never liked dogs, or indeed any animals, it was impossible to leave this helpless little creature to the mercy of the passing cars. With some qualms, wishing that I had a pair of gloves, I picked her up and dumped her in the baggage compartment. I was not going to hazard the upholstery of my new '92 Vik, and felt that she could do little damage there. In this, I was not altogether correct.

When I had parked the car at the Monastery—the astronomers' residential quarters, where I'd be living for the next week—I inspected my find without much enthusiasm. At that stage, I had intended to hand the puppy over to the janitor; but then it whimpered and opened its eyes. There was such an expression of helpless trust in them that—well, I changed my mind.

Sometimes I regretted that decision, though never for long. I had no idea how much trouble a growing dog could cause, deliberately and otherwise. My cleaning and repair bills soared; I could never be sure of finding an unravaged pair of socks or an unchewed copy of the *Astrophysical Journal*. But eventually Laika was both house-trained and Observatory-trained: she must have been the only dog ever to be allowed inside the two-hundred-inch dome. She would lie there quietly in the shadows for hours, while I was up in the cage making adjustments, quite content if she could hear my voice from time to time. The other astronomers became equally fond of her (it was old Dr. Anderson who suggested her name), but from the beginning she was my dog, and would obey no one else. Not that she would always obey me.

She was a beautiful animal, about ninety-five per cent Alsatian. It was that missing five per cent, I imagine, that led to her being abandoned. (I still feel a surge of anger when I think of it, but since I shall never know the facts, I may be jumping to false conclusions.) Apart from two dark patches over the eyes, most of her body was a smoky gray, and her coat was soft as silk. When her ears were pricked up, she looked incredibly intelligent and alert; sometimes I would be discussing spectral types of stellar evolution with my colleagues, and it would be hard to believe that she was not following the conversation.

Even now, I cannot understand why she became so attached to

me, for I have made very few friends among human beings. Yet when I returned to the Observatory after an absence, she would go almost frantic with delight, bouncing around on her hind legs and putting her paws on my shoulders—which she could reach quite easily—all the while uttering small squeaks of joy which seemed highly inappropriate from so large a dog. I hated to leave her for more than a few days at a time, and though I could not take her with me on overseas trips, she accompanied me on most of my shorter journeys. She was with me when I drove north to attend that ill-fated seminar at Berkeley.

We were staying with university acquaintances; they had been polite about it, but obviously did not look forward to having a monster in the house. However, I assured them that Laika never gave the slightest trouble, and rather reluctantly they let her sleep in the living room. "You needn't worry about burglars tonight," I said. "We don't have any in Berkeley," they answered, rather coldly.

In the middle of the night, it seemed that they were wrong. I was awakened by a hysterical, high-pitched barking from Laika which I had heard only once before—when she had first seen a cow, and did not know what on earth to make of it. Cursing, I threw off the sheets and stumbled out into the darkness of the unfamiliar house. My main thought was to silence Laika before she roused my hosts—assuming that this was not already far too late. If there had been an intruder, he would certainly have taken flight by now. Indeed, I rather hoped that he had.

For a moment I stood beside the switch at the top of the stairs, wondering whether to throw it. Then I growled, "Shut up, Laika!" and flooded the place with light.

She was scratching frantically at the door, pausing from time to time to give that hysterical yelp. "If you want out," I said angrily, "there's no need for all that fuss." I went down, shot the bolt, and she took off into the night like a rocket.

It was very calm and still, with a waning Moon struggling to pierce the San Francisco fog. I stood in the luminous haze, looking out across the water to the lights of the city, waiting for Laika to come back so that I could chastise her suitably. I was still waiting when, for the second time in the twentieth century, the San Andreas Fault woke from its sleep.

Oddly enough, I was not frightened—at first. I can remember that two thoughts passed through my mind, in the moment before I realized the danger. Surely, I told myself, the geophysicists could have given us *some* warning. And then I found myself thinking, with great surprise, "I'd no idea that earthquakes make so much noise!"

It was about then that I knew that this was no ordinary quake; what happened afterward, I would prefer to forget. The Red Cross did not take me away until quite late the next morning, because I refused to leave Laika. As I looked at the shattered house containing the bodies of my friends, I knew that I owed my life to her; but the helicopter pilots could not be expected to understand that, and I cannot blame them for thinking that I was crazy, like so many of the others they had found wandering among the fires and the debris.

After that, I do not suppose we were ever apart for more than a few hours. I have been told—and I can well believe it—that I became less and less interested in human company, without being actively unsocial or misanthropic. Between them, the stars and Laika filled all my needs. We used to go for long walks together over the mountains; it was the happiest time I have ever known. There was only one flaw; I knew, though Laika could not, how soon it must end.

We had been planning the move for more than a decade. As far back as the nineteen-sixties it was realized that Earth was no place for an astronomical observatory. Even the small pilot instruments on the Moon had far outperformed all the telescopes peering through the murk and haze of the terrestrial atmosphere. The story of Mount Wilson, Palomar, Greenwich, and the other great names was coming to an end; they would still be used for training purposes, but the research frontier must move out into space.

I had to move with it; indeed, I had already been offered the post of Deputy Director, Farside Observatory. In a few months, I could hope to solve problems I had been working on for years.

Beyond the atmosphere, I would be like a blind man who had suddenly been given sight.

It was utterly impossible, of course, to take Laika with me. The only animals on the Moon were those needed for experimental purposes; it might be another generation before pets were allowed, and even then it would cost a fortune to carry them there—and to keep them alive. Providing Laika with her usual two pounds of meat a day would, I calculated, take several times my quite comfortable salary.

The choice was simple and straightforward. I could stay on Earth and abandon my career. Or I could go to the Moon—and abandon Laika.

After all, she was only a dog. In a dozen years, she would be dead, while I should be reaching the peak of my profession. No sane man would have hesitated over the matter; yet I did hesitate, and if by now you do not understand why, no further words of mine can help.

In the end, I let matters go by default. Up to the very week I was due to leave, I had still made no plans for Laika. When Dr. Anderson volunteered to look after her, I accepted numbly, with scarcely a word of thanks. The old physicist and his wife had always been fond of her, and I am afraid that they considered me indifferent and heartless—when the truth was just the opposite. We went for one more walk together over the hills; then I delivered her silently to the Andersons, and did not see her again.

Take-off was delayed almost twenty-four hours, until a major flare storm had cleared the Earth's orbit; even so, the Van Allen belts were still so active that we had to make our exit through the North Polar Gap. It was a miserable flight; apart from the usual trouble with weightlessness, we were all groggy with antiradiation drugs. The ship was already over Farside before I took much interest in the proceedings, so I missed the sight of Earth dropping below the horizon. Nor was I really sorry; I wanted no reminders, and intended to think only of the future. Yet I could not shake off that feeling of guilt; I had deserted someone who loved and trusted me, and was no better than those who had abandoned Laika when she was a puppy, beside the dusty road to Palomar.

The news that she was dead reached me a month later. There

was no reason that anyone knew; the Andersons had done their best, and were very upset. She had just lost interest in living, it seemed. For a while, I think I did the same; but work is a wonderful anodyne, and my program was just getting under way. Though I never forgot Laika, in a little while the memory ceased to hurt.

Then why had it come back to haunt me, five years later, on the far side of the Moon? I was searching my mind for the reason when the metal building around me quivered as if under the impact of a heavy blow. I reacted without thinking, and was already closing the helmet of my emergency suit when the foundations slipped and the wall tore open with a short-lived scream of escaping air. Because I had automatically pressed the General Alarm button, we lost only two men, despite the fact that the tremor—the worst ever recorded on Farside—cracked all three of the Observatory's pressure domes.

It is hardly necessary for me to say that I do not believe in the supernatural; everything that happened has a perfectly rational explanation, obvious to any man with the slightest knowledge of psychology. In the second San Francisco earthquake, Laika was not the only dog to sense approaching disaster; many such cases were reported. And on Farside, my own memories must have given me that heightened awareness, when my never-sleeping subconscious detected the first faint vibrations from within the Moon.

The human mind has strange and labyrinthine ways of going about its business; it knew the signal that would most swiftly rouse me to the knowledge of danger. There is nothing more to it than that; though in a sense one could say that Laika woke me on both occasions, there is no mystery about it, no miraculous warning across the gulf that neither man nor dog can ever bridge.

Of that I am sure, if I am sure of anything. Yet sometimes I wake now, in the silence of the Moon, and wish that the dream could have lasted a few seconds longer—so that I could have looked just once more into those luminous brown eyes, brimming with an unselfish, undemanding love I have found nowhere else on this or on any other world.

THE MONSTER

Lester del Rey

NEW YORK, 1967

Apart from being a famous writer, editor and anthologist, Lester del Rey is known to several million people for his hundreds of radio appearances on the Long John Nebel Show. Like most talk shows, this one invites people who are specialists in some area to discuss it on the air, and over the years Long John has had statesmen, scientists, billionaires, criminals, flying-saucer contactees and almost every other sort of person you can think of as guests. Each is chosen because of his specialized knowledge, but his Number One guest of all time is chosen regardless of the subject, no matter what the concerns of the day, because he can discuss anything. Not only discuss it, but often enough, confound and refute the so-called "experts" on their own ground.

Around the Long John Show, Lester del Rey is called "The Magnificent." Science-fiction readers would not disagree.

HIS feet were moving with an automatic monotony along the sound-deadening material of the flooring. He looked at them, seeing them in motion, and listened for the little taps they made. Then his eyes moved up along the rough tweed of his trousers to the shorter motion of his thighs. There was something good about the movement, almost a purpose.

He tried making his arms move, and found that they accepted the rhythm, the right arm moving forward with the left leg, giving a feeling of balance. It was nice to feel the movement, and nice to know that he could walk so smoothly.

His eyes tired of the motion quickly, however, and he glanced along the hall where he was moving. There were innumerable doors along it; it was a long hall, with a bend at the end. He reached the bend, and began to wonder how he could make the turn. But his feet seemed to know better than he, since one of them shortened its stride automatically, and his body swung right before picking up the smooth motion again.

The new hallway was like the old one, painted white, with the long row of doors. He began to wonder idly what might lie behind all the doors. A universe of hallways and doors that branched off into more hallways? It seemed purposeless to him. He slowed his steps, just as a series of sounds reached him from one of the doors. It was speech—and that meant there was someone else in this universe in which he had found himself. He stopped outside the door, turning his head to listen. The sounds were muffled, but he could make out most of the words.

Politics, his mind told him. The word had some meaning to him, but not much. Someone inside was talking to someone else about the best way to avoid the battle on the moon, now that both powers had bases there. There was a queer tone of fear to the comments on the new iron-chain reaction bombs and what they could do from the moon.

It meant nothing to him, except that he was not alone, and that it stirred up knowledge in his head of a world like a ball in space with a moon that circled it. He tried to catch more conversation, but it had stopped, and the other doors seemed silent. Then he found a door behind which a speaker was cursing at the idea of introducing robots into a world already a mess, calling another by name.

That hit the listener, sending shocks of awareness through his consciousness. He had no name! Who was he? Where was he? And what had come before he found himself here?

He found no answers, savagely though he groped through his reluctant mind. A single word emerged—amnesia, loss of memory. Did that mean he had once had memories? Then he tried to reason out whether an amnesiac would have a feeling of personality, but could not guess. He could not even be sure he had none.

He stared at the knob of the door, wondering if the men inside would know the answers. His hand moved to the knob slowly. Then, before he could act, there was the sudden, violent sound of running footsteps down the hall.

He swung about to see two men come plunging around the corner toward him. It hadn't occurred to him that legs could move so quickly. One man was thicker than he was, dressed in a dirty smock of some kind, and the other was neat and trim, in figure and dress, in a khaki outfit he wore like a badge. The one in khaki opened his mouth.

"There he is! Stop him! You—Expeto! Halt! George—"

Expeto—George Expeto! So he did have a name—unless the first name belonged to the other man. No matter, it was a name. George accepted it and gratitude ran through him sharply. Then he realized the senselessness of the order. How could he halt when he was already standing still? Besides, there were those rapid motions . . .

The two men let out a yell as George charged into motion, finding that his legs could easily hold the speed. He stared doubtfully at another corner, but somehow his responses were equal to it. He started to slow to a halt—just as something whined by his head and spattered against a white wall. His mind catalogued it as a bullet from a silent zep gun, and bullets were used in animosity. The two men were his enemies.

He considered it, and found he had no desire to kill them; besides, he had no gun. He doubled his speed, shot down another hall, ran into stairs and took them at a single leap. It was a mistake. They led to a narrower hallway, obviously recently blocked off, with a single door. And the man with the zep gun was charging after him as he hesitated.

He hit the door with his shoulder and was inside, in a strange room of machinery and tables and benches. Most of it was strange to his eyes, though he could recognize a small, portable boron-reactor and generator unit. It was obviously one of the new hundred-kilowatt jobs.

The place was a blind alley! Behind him the man in khaki leaped through the ruined door, his zep gun ready. But the panting older figure of the man in the smock was behind him, catching his arm.

"No! Man, you'd get a hundred years of Lunar Prison for shooting Expeto. He's worth his weight in general's stars! If he—"

"Yeah, if! George, we can't risk it. Security comes first. And if he isn't, we can't have another paranoiac running around. Remember the other?"

Expeto dropped his shoulders, staring at them and the queer fear that was in them. "I'm not George?" he asked slowly. "But I've got to be George. I've got to have a name."

The older man nodded. "Sure, George, you're George—George Expeto. Take it easy, Colonel Kallik! Sure you're George. And I'm George—George Enders Obanion. Take it easy, George, and you'll be all right. We're not going to hurt you. We want to help you."

It was a ruse, and Expeto knew it. They didn't want to help—he was somehow important, and they wanted him for something. His name wasn't George—just Expeto. The man was lying. But there was nothing else to do; he had no weapons.

He shrugged. "Then tell me something about myself."

Obanion nodded, catching at the other man's hand. "Sure, George. See that chart on the wall, there behind you— *Now!*"

Expeto had barely time to turn and notice there was no chart on the wall before he felt a violent motion at his back and a tiny catching reaction as the other's hand hit him. Then he blanked out.

He came back to consciousness abruptly, surprised to find that there was no pain in his head. A blow sufficient to knock him out should have left afterpains. He was alone with his thoughts.

They weren't good thoughts. His mind was seizing on the words the others had used, and trying to dig sense out of them. Amnesia was a rare thing—too rare. But paranoia was more common. A man might first feel others were persecuting him, then be sure of it, and finally lose all reality in his fantasies of persecution and his own importance. Then he was a paranoiac, making up fantastic lies to himself, but cunning enough and seemingly rational at times.

But they had been persecuting him! There'd been the man with the gun—and they'd said he was important! Or had he only imagined it? If someone important had paranoia, would they deliberately induce amnesia as a curative step?

And who was he and where? On the first, he didn't care— George Expeto would do. The second took more thought, but he had begun to decide it was a hospital—or asylum. The room here was whitewashed, and the bed was the only furniture. He stared down at his body. They'd strapped him down, and his arms were encased in thin metal chains!

He tried to recall all he could of hospitals, but nothing came. If he had ever been sick, there was no memory of it. Nor could he remember pain, or what it was like, though he knew the word.

The door opened then, cautiously, and a figure in white came in. Expeto stared at the figure, and a slow churning began in his head. The words were reluctant this time, but they came, mere surface whispers that he had to fight to retain. But the differences in the figure made them necessary. The longer hair, the softer face, the swelling at the breast, and something about the hips stirred his memories just enough.

"You're—woman!" He got the word out, not sure it would come.

She jumped at his voice, reaching for the door which she had closed slowly. Fear washed over her face, but she nodded, gulping. "I—of course. But I'm just a technician, and they'll be here, and— They've fastened you down!"

That seemed to bring her back to normal, and she came over, her eyes sweeping over him curiously, while one eyebrow lifted, and she whistled. "Um, not bad. Hi, Romeo. Too bad you're a monster! You don't look mean."

"So you came to satisfy your curiosity," he guessed, and his mind puzzled over it, trying to identify the urge that drove men to stare at beasts in cages. He was just a beast to them, a monster—but somehow important. And in the greater puzzle of it all, he couldn't even resent her remark. Instead, something that had been bothering him since he'd found the word came to the surface. "Why are there men and women—and who am I?"

She glanced at her watch, her ear to the door. Then she glided over to him. "I guess you're the most important man in the world—if you're a man, and not pure monster. Here."

She found his hand had limited freedom in the chains and moved it over her body, while he stared at her. Her eyes were intent on him. "Well. Now do you know why there are men and women?" Her stare intensified as he shook his head, and her lips firmed. "My God, it's true—you couldn't act that well! That's all I wanted to know! And now they'll take over the whole moon! Look, don't tell them I was here—they'll kill you if you do. Or do you know what death is? Yeah, that's it, *kaputt!* Don't talk, then. Not a word!"

She was at the door, listening. Finally she opened it, and moved out . . .

There was no sound from the zep gun, but the *splaatt* of the bullet reached Expeto's ears. He shuddered, writhing within himself as her exploding body jerked back out of sight. She'd been pleasant to look at. Maybe that was what women were for.

Obanion was over him then, while a crowd collected in the hall, all wearing khaki. "We're not going to kill you, Expeto. We knew she'd come—or hoped she would. Now, if I unfasten your chains, will you behave? We've only got four hours left. O.K., Colonel Kallik?"

The colonel nodded. Behind him, the others were gathering something up and leaving.

"She's the spy, all right. That must make the last of them. Clever. I'd have sworn she was O.K. But they tipped their hand in letting Expeto's door stay unbolted before. Well, the trap worked. Sorry about cutting down your time."

Obanion nodded, and now it was a group of men in white uniforms who came in, while the khaki-clad men left. They were wheeling in assorted machines, something that might have been an encephalograph, a unitary cerebrotrope, along with other instruments.

Expeto watched them, his mind freezing at the implications. But he wasn't insane. His thoughts were lucid. He opened his mouth to protest, just as Obanion swung around.

"Any feeling we're persecuting you, Expeto? Maybe you'd like to get in a few licks, to break my skull and run away where you'd be understood. You might get away with it; you're stronger than I am. Your reaction time is better too. See, I'm giving you the idea. And you've only got four hours in which to do it."

Expeto shook his head. That way lay madness. Let his mind feel he was persecuted and he'd surely be the paranoiac he'd heard mentioned. There had to be another answer. This was a hospital—and men were healed in hospitals. Even of madness. It could only be a test.

"No," he denied slowly, and was surprised to find it was true. "No, I don't want to kill you, Doctor. If I've been insane, it's gone. But I can't remember—I can't remember!"

He pulled his voice down from its shriek, shook his head again and tried to restrain himself. "I'll co-operate. Only tell me who I am. What have I done that makes people call me a monster? My God, give me an anchor to hold me steady, and then do what you want."

"You're better off not knowing, since you seem to be able to guess when I'm lying." Obanion motioned the other men up, and they waited while Expeto took the chair they pointed out. Then they began clamping devices on his head. "You're what the girl said—the spy. You're the most important man in the world right now—if you can stay sane. You're the one man who carries the secret of how we can live on the moon, protect Earth from aggressive powers, even get to the stars someday."

"But I can't remember—anything!"

"It doesn't matter. The secret's in you and we know how to use it. All right, now I'm going to give you some tests, and I want you to tell me exactly what comes into your mind. The instruments will check on it, so lying won't do any good. Ready?"

It went on and on, while new shifts came in. The clock on the wall indicated only an hour, but it might have been a century, when Obanion sighed and turned his work over to another.

Expeto's thoughts were reeling. He grabbed the breather gratefully, let his head thump back. There must be a way.

"What day is this?" he asked. At their silence he frowned. "Co-operate means both working together. I've been doing my part. Or is it too much to answer a simple question?"

The new man nodded slowly. "You're right. You deserve some answers, if I can give them without breaking security. It's June eighth, nineteen sixty-one—11 P.M."

It checked with figures that had appeared in the back of his mind, ruining the one theory he'd had. "The President is William Olsen?"

The doctor nodded, killing the last chance at a theory. For a time he'd thought that perhaps the aggressive countries had won, and that this was their dictatorship. If he'd been injured in a war— But it was nonsense, since no change had occurred in his time sense or in the Administration.

"How'd I get here?"

The doctor opened his mouth, then closed it firmly. "Forget that, Expeto. You're here. Get this nonsense of a past off your mind—you never had one, understand? And no more questions. We'll never finish in less than three hours, as it is."

Expeto stood up slowly, shaking himself. "You're quite right. You won't finish. I'm sick of this. Whatever I did, you've executed your justice in killing the me that was only a set of memories. And whatever I am, I'll find myself. To hell with the lot of you!"

He expected zep guns to appear, and he was right. The walls suddenly opened in panels, and six armed men were facing him, wearing the oppressive khaki. But something in him seemed to take over. He had the doctor in one arm and a zep gun from the hand of a major before anyone else could move. He faced them, waiting for the bullets that would come, but they drew back, awaiting orders. Expeto's foot found the door, kicked at it; the lock snapped.

Obanion's voice cut through it all. "Don't! No shooting! Expeto, I'm the one you want. Let Smith go, and I'll accompany you, until you're ready to let me go. Fair enough?"

Smith was protesting, but Obanion cut him short. "My fault, since I'm responsible. And the Government be damned. I'm not going to have a bunch of good men killed. His reaction's too fast. We can learn things this way, maybe better. All right, Expeto—or do you want to kill them?"

Expeto dropped the gun a trifle and nodded, while the emotions in his head threatened to make him blank out. He knew now that he could never kill even one of them. But they apparently weren't so sure. "Take me outside, and you can go back," he told Obanion.

The doctor wiped sweat from his forehead, managed a pasty smile and nodded. Surprisingly, he stepped through a different door, and down a short hall, where men with rifles stood irresolutely. Then they were outside.

Obanion turned to go back, and then hesitated. Surprisingly, he dropped an arm onto Expeto's shoulder. "Come on back inside. We can understand you. Or— All right, I guess you're going. Thanks for taking my offer."

The door closed, and Expeto was alone. Above him most of the building was dark, but he saw a few lighted windows, and some with men and women working over benches and with equipment. There was no sign of beds. All right, so it was some government laboratory.

The most important monster in the world, the useful paranoiac they'd saved by amnesia . . . The monster they intended to persecute back to paranoia, in hopes he'd recover his memory and the secret they wanted. Let them have the secret—but let him have peace and quiet, where his brain could recover by itself. Then he'd gladly give it to them. Or would he? Would he really be a monster again? Or might he learn the strange reason for there being men and women, the puzzle which seemed so simple that the woman had felt mere contact would solve it?

Funny that there were so many sciences, but no science of life—or was there? Maybe he'd been such a scientist—psychology, zoology, biology, whatever they'd call it from the Greek.

Maybe the secret lay there, and it had completely burned out that part of his mind.

Then he heard the sound of a motor and knew they weren't going to let him go. He wasn't to have a moment of freedom if they could prevent it. He swung about sharply, studying the horizon. There were lights and a town. There'd be people, and he could hide among them.

He whipped his legs into action, driving on at a full run. The light of the moon was barely enough for him to see the ground clearly, but he managed a good deal more speed than the hallways had permitted. He heard the car behind on the road he found, and doubled his speed, while the sound of the motor slowly weakened as the distance increased.

He breathed easier when he hit the outskirts of the town, and slowed to a casual walk, imitating the steps of a few people he saw about. This was better. In the myriad of streets and among countless others, he would be lost. The only trouble was that he was on a main street, and the lights would give him away to anyone who knew him.

He picked up a paper from a waste receptacle and moved off to the left, seeking a less brilliantly lighted street. Now and again he glanced at the print, looking for some trace. But aside from the news that his mind recognized as normal for the times, there was nothing on any mysterious, all-important person, nor on anyone who was either a monster or a savior.

Ahead of him a lone girl was tapping along on the sidewalk. He quickened his step, and she looked back, making the identity complete as her tiny bolero drifted back in the breeze to expose all but the tip of her breasts. She hesitated as he caught up with her, looking up uncertainly. "Yes?"

She couldn't know the answers. Obviously she had never seen him. How could she tell him what he wanted to know?

"Sorry. I thought you were someone else? No, wait. You can tell me something. Where can I find a place to stay?"

"Oh. Well, the Alhambra, I guess." She smiled a little. "Back there—see where the sign is?"

She brushed against his arm as she turned, and a faint gasp

sounded. Her hand suddenly contracted on his bare skin, then jerked back sharply. She began stepping slowly away.

"No!" It was a small wail as he caught her shoulder. Then she slumped against him, wilting as he pulled her toward his face. He released her, to see her fall down in a sagging heap.

For a moment the sickness in him rose in great waves, undulating and horrible as he dropped beside her. But when he felt the pulse in her hand still beating, it left. He hadn't killed her, only frightened her into unconsciousness.

He stood there, tasting that. *Only* frightened her that much!

And finally he turned about and headed for the Alhambra. There was nothing he could do for her; she'd recover, in time, and it would be better if she didn't see him there. Then maybe she'd decide it was all a fantasy.

Bitterly he watched a streak mount the horizon, remembering that the men had been discussing the two bases on the moon in the room where he'd first heard voices. They could face war and only fear it vaguely. But he could drive someone senseless by touching them!

He found the night clerk busy watching a television set with the screen badly adjusted to an overbalance of red, and signed the register with the full name he'd hoped once was his. George Expeto, from—make it from New York. It wouldn't matter.

"Five dollars," the clerk told him.

Dollars? He shook his head slowly, trying to think. Something about dollars and cents. But it made no sense.

The clerk's eyes were hard. "No dough, eh? O.K., try to fool someone else. No baggage, no dough, no room. Scram."

Expeto stood irresolutely, trying to make sense out of it still—something . . . The clerk had swung back to watching the set, and he reached out for the scrawny shoulder, drawing the man around.

"But look—" Then it was no use. The shoulder had crumpled in his hand like a rotten stick, and the man had lapsed into a faint with a single shriek.

Expeto stood outside, swinging while the sickness washed away slowly; he told himself the doctors would fix the man up—that

was what they were for. They'd fix him, and no real harm had
been done. He hadn't meant to hurt the man. He'd only meant to
ask him what dollars were and how to get them.

Then he moved on into a little park and dropped onto a seat.
But the sickness was still there, a sickness he hadn't noticed, but
which had been growing on him even before he'd hurt the clerk.
It was as if something were slowly eroding his mind. Even the
curious memory of ideas and words was going!

He was sitting there, his head in his hands, trying to catch
himself, when the car drove up. Obanion and Kallik got out, but
Obanion came over alone.

"Come on, Expeto. It won't work. You might as well come
back. And there's only an hour left!"

Expeto got up slowly, nodding wearily. The doctor was
right—there was no place in the world for such a monster as he.

"Left before what?" he asked dully, as he climbed into the rear
of the car and watched Obanion lock the door and the glass slide
between him and the front seat.

For a second Obanion hesitated, then he shrugged. "All right.
Maybe you should know. In another hour you'll be dead! And
nothing can prevent it."

Expeto took it slowly, letting the thought sink into the
muddying depths of his mind. But he was important—they'd told
him so. Or had they? They'd chased him about, bound him down,
refused to tell him what he needed, refused him even civil
decency and told him he was the hope of the world. Or had he
only imagined it?

"I never wanted anything but myself. Only myself. And they
wouldn't let me have that—not even for a few hours. They had to
hound me—" He realized he was muttering aloud and stopped it.

But from the front seat the voices came back, muffled by the
glass, Kallik speaking first. "See, paranoia all right. Thinks he's
being persecuted."

"He is." Obanion nodded slowly. "With the time limit the
Government insisted on, the ruin of our plans by the spies that got
through, and the need to get the facts, what else could we do? If
they'd let us animate him for a week—but six hours' limit on the
vital crystals! We've had to be brutal."

"You talk as if he were a human being. Remember the other —XP One? Crazy, killing people, or trying to. I tell you, the robots can't be made trustworthy yet, no matter what you cybernetics boys have found in the last ten years. This one only had six hours instead of ten for the other, and he's already threatened us and hurt two people."

"Maybe. We don't know all the story yet." Obanion wiped his forehead. "And damn it, he is human. That's what makes it tough, knowing we've got to treat him like a machine. Maybe we grew his brain out of silicones and trick metal crystals, and built his body in a laboratory, but the mechanical education he got made him a lot more human than some people, or should have made him so. If I can prove he isn't crazy—"

E x p e t o—Experiment Two—stared at the hand he held before his face. He bent the fingers, looking at the veins and muscles. Then, slowly, with his other hand, he twisted at them, stretching them out and out, until there could be no doubt that they were rubbery plastic.

A monster! A thing grown in a laboratory, made out of mechanical parts, and fed bits of human education from tapes in cybernetics machines! A thing that would walk on the moon without air and take over enemy bases, do men's work, but who could never be taken as a man by human beings, who grew from something or other but were never built. A thing to be animated for a few hours and deliberately set to die at the end of that time, as a precaution—because it had no real life, and it wasn't murder to kill a built thing!

A thing that somehow couldn't kill men, it seemed, judging by the sickness he'd felt when he'd hurt or threatened them. But a thing of which they couldn't be sure—until they'd tested him and found he was complete and sane.

He rocked back and forth on the seat, moaning a little. He didn't want to die; but already the eroded places in his brain were growing larger. It didn't matter; he had never been anyone; he never could be anyone. But he didn't want to die!

"Half an hour left," the cyberneticist, Obanion, said slowly. "And less than that unless we make sure he doesn't exert himself. He's about over."

Then the car was coming into the garage, and Obanion got out with Kallik. Expeto went with them quietly, knowing that Obanion was right. Already he was finding it hard to use his legs or control what passed for muscles. They went back to the room with the instruments and the waiting technicians.

For a moment he looked at the humans there. Obanion's eyes were veiled, but the others were open to his gaze. And there was no pity there. Men don't pity a car that is too old and must go to the scrap heap. He was only a machine, no matter how valuable. And after him other machines would see the faces of men turned away from them, generation after generation.

Slowly he kicked at the chair, tipping it over without splintering it, and his voice came out as high and shrill as his faltering control could force it. "No! No more! You've persecuted me enough. You've tried to kill me—me, the hope of your puny race! You've laughed at me and tortured me. But I'm smarter than you—greater than you! I can kill you—all of you—the whole world, with my bare hands."

He saw shock on Obanion's face, and sadness, and for that he was almost sorry. But the smug satisfaction of Kallik as the zep gun came up and the horror of the faces of the others counter-acted it. He yelled once, and charged at them.

For a moment he was afraid that he would not be stopped before he had to injure at least one of them. But then the zep gun in Kallik's hand spoke silently, and the bullet smashed against the mockery of Expeto's body.

He lay there, watching them slowly recover from their fright. It didn't matter when one of them came over and began kicking him senselessly. It didn't even matter when Obanion put a stop to it.

His senses were fading now, and he knew that the excitement had shortened his brief time, and that the crystals were about to break apart and put an end to his short existence. But in a curious way, while he still hated and feared death, he was resigned to it.

They'd be better off. Maybe the first experimental robot had known that. Expeto let the thought linger, finding it good. He couldn't believe the other had grown insane; it, too, must have found the bitter truth, and tried to do the only possible thing, even when that involved genuine injury to a few of the humans.

Now they'd have two such failures, and it would be perhaps years before they'd risk another when their checks failed to show the reason for the nonexistent flaws. They'd have to solve their own problems of war or peace without mechanical monsters to make them almost gods in power while teaching them the disregard of devils for life other than their own.

And there'd be no more of his kind to be used and despised and persecuted. Persecuted? The word stirred up thoughts—something about paranoia and insanity.

But it faded. Everything faded. And he sank through vague content into growing blackness. His thoughts were almost happy as death claimed him.

DUST

Lloyd Eshbach

CINCINNATI, 1949

Lloyd Arthur Eshbach was one of the big-name writers in science fiction in the thirties, but it is not for that that he was chosen Guest of Honor in Cincinnati. Eshbach did something far more significant than write stories; he started the first publishing company in the world to bring out a whole line of science-fiction books.

In those days the publication of a book of science fiction was an event that shook the fan world. Nearly all the sf published was in magazines, and although some publishers had brought out the novels of Wells and Huxley and Stapledon, and a few had even tried an anthology now and then, there was no such thing as a "category" of science fiction on any list in the world. Eshbach made it happen. He founded the firm called Fantasy Press, and started what has now become a multimillion-dollar industry.

ON THE *night of August 10th, at 9:38, astronomers on the west coast of the United States observed the sudden appearance of an amazingly brilliant meteor in the Constellation Virgo. It sped across the sky like a lance of silver radiance, until suddenly it vanished in the pallid light of the Moon* . . .

Jerry Blaine plodded wearily across the rugged face of a dead world. The weighted legs of his space suit stumbled over the jagged ribs of lava skeletons; he plowed and floundered through shadowed ravines, yard-deep with the accumulated cosmic dust of uncounted ages; he crawled with metal-clad fingers up precipitous walls of craters.

For thirty hours he had been struggling across the surface of the Moon. Hours of toil in a world of utter silence, of pitchy black shadows and harshly glaring light, of treacherous pitfalls and mountainous barriers. His heart thudded audibly; sweat streaked his face and body; his muscles groaned against the torture of prolonged, superhuman effort.

Yet behind the spherical glassite helmet of his space suit, the boyish face of Jerry Blaine bore an expression of triumph that no weariness could mar. His blue eyes twinkled joyously, and his wide mouth grew even wider with frequent grins of a somehow incredulous satisfaction. For he had succeeded where success had seemed impossible! He had made a discovery that had replaced the certainty of death with a promise of life.

Wait till Morkill heard the news! He'd throw off the cloak of gloom he'd been wearing since they had landed on the Moon. He was a skillful chemist—else he couldn't have formulated the radio-active compound that had made their Lunar flight possible —but he certainly couldn't be called a little ray of sunshine!

Thirty hours behind him lay the crater Tycho with its vast radiating streaks of light which had baffled astronomers of Earth for centuries. They need be baffled no longer! For he had seen what at one time must have been tremendous chasms in the Moon's surface, like—like cracks in a dried mudball—but now the cracks were filled. From the heart of Earth's satellite millenniums ago had spouted a crystalline lava to fill every crack and crevice with an indestructible mass of radiant matter. Lava that was pure quartz, somehow impregnated with an amazing store of—radium!

He might be mistaken, of course, but it must be some radio-active substance, or how could it continue glowing as it had for ages? At any rate, he'd know when he reached *The Apollo* for he had a fragment of the lava in the pack on his back for Morkill to test. And if it were radium, or any other radio-active material, they could return to Earth! They had headed for the Moon with what they thought was sufficient fuel for a two-way trip—but they had miscalculated the quantity needed. His discovery might mean release from their exile.

Jerry stumbled and fell headlong into a bed of finest dust. Awkwardly he crawled erect, his muscles rebelling against the added effort. Damn such a place! If only he could jump safely—but though the weaker Lunar gravity permitted his leaping through the emptiness like some amazing jumping jack, the procedure was anything but safe. He had tried it, and had taken some falls far worse than those that came with slower progress.

If it hadn't been so important that they conserve their little remaining fuel, both he and Morkill could have made the trip in *The Apollo* in a few minutes—or he could have made the trip alone in the little emergency sphere they kept in the vacuum chamber of the space ship—but . . . The thought ended abruptly as he saw the huge sphere before him. His heart leaped, and a shout burst from him to crash thunderously against his own ears.

He balanced himself for an instant on the tip of a ridge—and sprang mightily toward the gleaming, rivet-studded globe. Up— up he soared in a great arc that carried him across the broken ground to the level spot on which *The Apollo* rested. He landed awkwardly in a bank of cosmic dust, sinking deep into the downy mass; then he crawled out and made his way to the airlock.

It opened before him and closed behind him as he passed through the airlock into the main room of the sphere. He flung back his head-piece to greet Morkill coming from the control room.

"Well, Dave," he grinned at the other's dark, gloomy face. "I've brought home the bacon!"

"What?" David Morkill's black eyes burned intently into Jerry's. "You mean you've found—fuel?"

Jerry nodded. "Just that. Enough fuel to drive a thousand space ships from here to Antares and back again—and some to spare. Combined with the neo-hydrogen we have stored in the tanks, we have sufficient power to go home any time we want to. Help me out of this suit and I'll show you a sample."

Eagerly the big man peeled the space suit from his smaller companion, talking incessantly in a flood of relief. "You know, Jerry—this is a load off my mind. You probably didn't realize it, but I was worried. After all, there's still a lot for me to do in the world, and—and it's tough to pass out without any one knowing anything about it." Sudden anxiety shook his voice. "You're sure it's a radio-active mineral you've found?"

Stepping clear of his space suit, Jerry fumbled in the pack and drew out a lump of quartz. "Here it is. Suppose you decide what it will do—you're the chemist of the party."

Morkill grasped the glowing lava-fragment eagerly, examining it with experienced eyes. Nodding abruptly, he turned toward the little cubby hole beside the control room where he had outfitted a small chemical laboratory.

"While you're analyzing that," Jerry called after him, "I'm going to drink a gallon of water and eat two square meals. Then if that stuff pans out, we can hop over to Tycho."

In the control room of *The Apollo*, Jerry Blaine watched the pitted surface of the Moon drop away from the space ship, its bold highlights and night-black shadows standing out in sharp relief. Tycho, with its tremendous crystal-filled fissures, wide as rivers and straight as ruled lines, filled half the landscape. It was a sight of such splendor that it filled Jerry with awe. Seen from this vantage point, it looked like a queerly formed, uncut jewel of gigantic size, dropped on its somber setting by a careless denizen of space.

Abruptly Jerry turned from the controls to face David Morkill. There was a scowl on his face.

"Dave," he said earnestly, "this doesn't seem right to me. We had a chance to explore the Moon at our leisure—to see the dark side which no astronomer has ever seen—and as soon as you found we had sufficient fuel, you insisted on returning to Earth. A few days spent exploring wouldn't have made any difference to you and your plans, and it would have meant a lot to science."

Shrugging his broad shoulders, Morkill said curtly, "I think science can struggle along without knowing what's on the dark side of the Moon. And with something as big as this in my reach, I'm not taking chances of muffing it."

He waved a hand toward the central room of the space ship. Along one wall were roughly built bins filled with fragments of glowing quartz—quartz impregnated with radium. Morkill puffed out his big chest.

"There's enough radium there to make the stuff cheap—if I'd be foolish enough to let the price gc down. There's also enough there to make me the richest man in the world—enough to permit me to drive the biggest space ship money can build to any part of the Solar System. That radium means power—power to run space ships—and power to do anything I care to do. You don't think I'd let half of a dead satellite stop me, do you?"

Jerry Blaine ran one hand through his bristling brown hair, and surveyed Morkill in silent wonder for several moments.

"Tell me if I'm wrong," he began slowly, "but am I to get the idea that you're planning to use this stuff for the sole benefit of David Morkill? That cheap radium with its power to cure cancer—that cheap radium for the experimentation of scientists doesn't mean anything to you?"

Morkill smiled blandly. "I always had a lot of respect for your brilliance, Jerry," he said. "You've grasped the situation fully. And just in case you get any queer ideas," he added brusquely, "remember that this is *my* expedition—that *my* money financed it—and that you're only hired help, necessary because of your knowledge of astronomy—but not indispensable."

Jerry held his eyes fixed on those of the tall man for another moment, his face expressionless; then he turned to the vision screen with its image of the retreating world.

The Moon gleamed brilliantly against the black sky with its mosaic of stars. Lights and shadows were merging into one expanse of silvery radiance, out of which the mighty crater Tycho seemed to be glaring balefully.

Jerry heard Morkill's footsteps moving about the space ship, but he did not turn. His thoughts were busy with a heavy problem, weighing all the factors in a situation loaded with dynamite. If Morkill landed on Earth with this cargo of radium ore vastly richer than pitchblende, there was no telling what might happen. He'd have at his disposal wealth and power to do just about as he pleased. His could be a power for good—but since Morkill was Morkill, there'd be little good coming out of it. Jerry's jaw thrust out pugnaciously. One thing was certain. He'd find some way to wreck the other's plans.

He bent over the controls, carefully adjusting the course toward Earth. There'd be two full days in which to decide what had to be done . . .

"Jerry!" he heard an anxious voice from the other room. "Quick—what's this?"

He joined Morkill in an instant; saw him bending over something on the floor.

"I started eating a sandwich," the big man said jerkily. "Got it out of the food chest—and after the first bite, that—thing popped up before my eyes!"

Curiously, but with a feeling of repugnance, Jerry studied the queer growth at Morkill's feet. It was a plant, but it was unlike anything he had ever seen, a pallid, unhealthy, wax-like thing, growing out of the sandwich with visible speed. A long, slender stem terminated in a crest of colorless plumes folded together like a grotesque head of lettuce. As they watched, three branches shot out of its base to sink into the sandwich like a tripod, supporting the trunk and head. Slender rootlets spread through the food, absorbing it—and its speed of growth accelerated.

Morkill thrust a curious finger at the repulsive plant—and like a striking snake it lashed at him, the lettuce plumes flung back. Struck and clung, closing on his finger tip! Howling, Morkill sprang erect, dragging the growth with him—and threads of crimson spread through the plant, moving from its head, down through the stem, into the three limbs.

Cursing, Jerry seized the alien thing and wrenched, snapping it off below its head. The foot-long remnant, tough and leathery, whipped and coiled around Jerry's arms like a captured eel. With a shudder he tore it loose—hurled it to the floor—ground it underfoot to a pale pink pulp.

He faced Morkill in time to see him finish crushing the now crimson head of the thing against the smooth metal floor. The big man looked at Jerry, nursing a swollen, reddened forefinger. His face had become a sickly yellow, and beads of sweat stood out on his upper lip.

"I—maybe it's poisonous!" he exclaimed suddenly, his eyes bulging. In a panic he rushed into his laboratory. "Quick, Jerry—do something!"

"I don't think it's harmful," Jerry said with confidence he didn't feel. "A thing like that doesn't need poison to defend itself." Nevertheless, he applied a tourniquet while Morkill sucked blood from the gash; and after treating it with drugs, he bandaged it. While he worked, they tried to decide whence the growth had come, but every suggestion ended in blank uncertainty. They simply didn't know. Jerry thought that in some way a seed, long dormant on the Moon's surface, had found its way into *The Apollo*, and under the action of heat and light, had sprung to life. But how had it lodged upon that sandwich?

As they emerged from the laboratory, Jerry glanced sharply around, half expecting to see others of the repulsive plants; but none were visible.

"I haven't much appetite after that sandwich," Morkill remarked ruefully, "but I think we'd both better grab a bite, since we haven't eaten for eight or ten hours. Then I'll turn in, while you take the first watch at the controls."

Jerry Blaine nodded. "Good idea; but I'll take food with me and eat it at the panel. I don't like the way we're letting the course take care of itself, even if it's supposed to be automatic."

Seated in the control room, Jerry Blaine gulped down a hasty lunch, suspiciously inspecting each morsel before biting into it. He didn't think he'd find any man-eating plants sprouting before his eyes—but you never could tell.

With his lunch completed, he gave full attention to the controls, carefully adjusting their direction, and setting the atomic-drive at maximum speed, with a controlled neo-hydrogen flow and release of radium emanations.

He could hear Morkill moving around in the main room; then the lights clicked into darkness; and in a short while he could hear the big man's heavy breathing.

Time dragged for Jerry Blaine. There was nothing to disturb the monotony of his vigilance. *The Apollo* seemed to hang motionless in space; nothing marred the placid depths of star-studded velvet blackness through which he sped . . . He dozed.

A scream jarred him to his senses—a hideous scream of fear and pain! For a split second he stared into vacancy—then he sprang into the darkness of the other room. He heard heavy, panting breaths, heard the sound of scuffling feet—then a choking gasp and another terrified scream burst from Morkill.

Jerry's fingers found a light switch; and as white radiance flooded the chamber, his muscles froze in consternation. The spectacle before him burned its every detail into his brain—a vision only seconds in duration, yet which seemed to be a frozen eternity.

David Morkill struggled on the floor beside his bed in the grip of a monstrosity which looked like a gigantic, pale green leech. It had wrapped its noisome folds around his head and shoulders; and from it came a horrible, gurgling sound. Morkill's powerful fingers were buried deep in the flesh of the thing; and as the lights went on, he struggled erect, tore it free, and hurled it against the wall. A shower of blood spattered the floor; and blood oozed from gashes in Morkill's face and body . . . But that was not all . . .

From the food cabinet beyond the tall man gushed a squirming, nightmare mass of hideousness. Wriggling, crawling vegetable things; rending, ravenous animal things; things that were both animal and vegetable; things that were—neither! An incredible mound of teeming life, growing with insane speed as had that first plant thing! Growing and spreading like a liquid tide across the floor.

All this he saw in a breath—and now he heard a sound—a clash of metal against metal—and the door of the closet where their space suits were stored burst from its hinges! Out spewed a second nauseous mass of living things!

Paralyzed, Morkill mumbled through twisting lips, his arms and legs held rigid. Gripping his shoulder, Jerry dragged him back, his mind working swiftly. They couldn't fight this without weapons. They needed time. In the lab and control room they might find temporary safety; could decide what must be done. He thrust Morkill into his cubby hole.

"Inside!" he rasped. "Fix up your wounds—and keep your door closed!" Slamming it shut, he leaped into the control room. With a barrier between him and the madness outside, reaction set in and he dropped trembling into an air-cushioned chair. Cold perspiration oozed from every pore, and a fit of trembling seized him. He pressed his hands over his eyes to shut out the vision of living horrors spawned out of some impossible hell.

After a time he tried to give sane consideration to what he had seen. It wasn't a nightmare, that was certain—nor was he losing his mind. It had actually happened, hence it must have a natural explanation. The food—the growths couldn't have come from the food originally, for they had been drawing upon the same supply since they had left the Earth . . . The space suits! There must lie the answer! Something from the Moon had clung to their space suits, and in the warmth of the sphere had come to life.

The dust, of course! Dust—why, the Moon was covered with dust. There were places where chasms had accumulated dust several yards in thickness through the uncounted ages since the Moon had lost its atmosphere.

Jerry remembered something he had read—an idea of Svend Arrhenius, the scientist who had proposed the ionic theory. Life, so Arrhenius had reasoned, could exist under almost any condition—in absolute cold, in utter dryness, in a perfect vacuum. Bacteria, the minute spores of mosses and ferns, the almost microscopic seeds of fungi—all retained their fertility under amazing adversity. Breezes on living worlds blew them everywhere—always higher and higher—until at last they rose free of the atmosphere to drift through the vacuum of space. Light struck them and drove them farther and farther from their parent world—as light drove the tails of comets—until they found the warmth and air and moisture of another world, and again sprang to life.

So it must have been with the monstrosities beyond the door. For untold ages their seeds and spores had drifted through space.

Incalculable distances, some must have traversed, rising from life-supporting planets many light years away—planets utterly alien to Earth, where life obeyed other laws. And finally, as cosmic dust, life spores from worlds and ages separated by vast gulfs of time and space had come within the gravitational field of the Moon, and had settled there. And he and Morkill had carried them into *The Apollo* . . . Their rapid growth? Perhaps it was their nature to develop as they had—or perhaps the presence of all that radium had excited them to abnormally swift development.

Abruptly Jerry Blaine shrugged. The way things looked, all this conjecture probably wouldn't mean a thing. He and Morkill would be more than lucky if they got out of this alive. Anyway, thinking about the problem had brought back his self control.

"Dave," he called through the metal partition between the two small rooms, "are you all right?"

"All right?" Morkill quavered. "Hell, man, I'm practically cut to shreds! And—and what can we *do?* What—are these things?"

"I don't know what we can do—but I have a good idea of what they are, and what we're up against." Quickly Jerry sketched his theory of the origin of the monstrosities.

Morkill uttered a whining curse. "Then we're sunk! They'll keep on multiplying and growing and feeding on each other and everything else organic till they break in on us by sheer weight—just like they broke out of that closet! Do something— can't you? We—we can't pass out like this!"

Jerry could hear him panting through the wall; then he heard him gasp eagerly: "Quick, Jerry—drive for Earth with everything we've got! Maybe we can make it before they break in!"

"Don't be a fool, Dave," Jerry rasped disgustedly. "We can't land on Earth with this cargo! You'd let something like this loose on the human race just to save your own precious neck! Why not try to do something yourself? You're a chemist; you should be able to dope out a way to kill the things."

Frowning thoughtfully, Jerry looked at the image of Earth in the vision plate, a green and silver sphere glowing like a giant moon. That *was* a new idea that he had tossed at Morkill, one that hadn't occurred to him before. They *couldn't* land on Earth unless they wiped out every one of the monstrosities, and purged the space ship of every life spore. That brought him to his other problem. Jerry grinned mirthlessly. Maybe this was the answer! Morkill must not land on Earth, either, unless he could be parted from his radium—and with himself at the controls, *The Apollo* need never land—anywhere.

Jerry grimaced. A hell of a martyr he'd be! That was a way out—but he'd try to find another way if he could.

His glance fell on two unused space suits hanging against one wall, suits put there for an emergency. There were two other suits hanging in the laboratory, he remembered.

"Ho, Dave," he called, "put on a space suit. That'll be some protection if they do break in." He heard an eager grunt from the big man, and as he slipped into a suit of rubber-covered, metallized, spun-glass fabric, he heard sounds of activity beyond the partition.

A few moments later Morkill exclaimed: "Jerry—I've got something!" His voice shook with suppressed excitement and eagerness. "I'm sure it will work, but it'll take about ten minutes' time. Don't do anything till I call you."

"Good boy, Dave!"

Jerry crossed to the controls, holding the steady Earthward course. He was glad Morkill had snapped out of his whining spell—glad that he'd misjudged him. After all, there was no satisfaction in being teamed up with a coward who couldn't stand on his own feet. There had been times when he wondered how Morkill had found sufficient courage to attempt a space flight— but now that he considered it, enough had happened to him to make any one somewhat nervous.

Impatiently Jerry waited, wondering what means of attack Dave would use. It was a cinch that there wasn't a thing in the control room that could be used as a weapon. If salvation came, it had to come out of the laboratory. While he waited, he listened idly to the sounds outside his door. There wasn't much to hear—only an occasional thud as something fell to the floor, or an infrequent liquid gurgling that suggested loathsome, crawling things. Now he heard a loud, steady hissing, and to his nostrils came an acrid odor suggesting burning flesh. He frowned wonderingly, then shrugged as the sound broke off and the odor disappeared.

"How are you getting along, Dave?" he called finally. There was no answer. "Dave—" The words died in his throat, and Jerry gasped, his forehead furrowing into lines of consternation.

On the vision plate before him he saw the tiny emergency space boat they had kept in the vacuum chamber of *The Apollo!* He had forgotten it—but Morkill hadn't! And now Morkill had run out on him! He had the emergency rations that were kept in the little craft, as well as sufficient fuel to land on Earth! The dirty rat!

Jerry caught a glimpse of Morkill's grinning face at one of the glassite port holes—and he cursed savagely. The other had flung back his helmet—was laughing at him! Then suddenly the laugh broke off; and Jerry's eyes strained at the vision plate.

Something, a writhing mass of ropelike tentacles, had leaped from nowhere—had wrapped itself around David Morkill's head! Man and monster dropped from sight.

Rigidly Jerry watched. The little sphere drifted along beside *The Apollo* for endless minutes—then suddenly it fell behind the larger craft—back toward the Moon. Mechanically Jerry swung the space ship around; saw the life boat dropping plummetlike through emptiness. It vanished in moments in the brilliance of the dead world, falling free, flashing toward destruction.

With trembling fingers Jerry Blaine resumed the course toward Earth, then wiped cold perspiration from his forehead. That was—that! A horrible way to go out—yet Morkill deserved it. Yellow, clean through—and his cowardice had caught up with him. That hissing—it must have been a blow torch or the action of a chemical with which the big man had burned his way through the monster horde. He'd been sure his plan would work—and it had—but now he was gone. That solved one problem.

Jerry's eyes narrowed speculatively, and the muscles of his jaws knotted with sudden determination. There still remained the problem of the—things—and he'd soon settle it in one way or another. If he could reach the laboratory, he might have a chance. If he couldn't . . .

Jerry grinned with one side of his mouth as he snapped shut his glassite headpiece, and started the air purifier. Then he flung open the door and leaped out crouching. He heard a faint rush of air—and he stopped short.

Uncomprehending, he surveyed a spectacle that looked like a painting from the brush of an insane, alien artist. Everywhere incredible growths, splotches of jarring color, masses of disgusting forms coated floor and walls and ceiling. But in none was there sign of life! It seemed as though they had burst under internal pressure, and now drooped or lay flaccid in death!

Jerry's roving eyes saw the open airlock, saw the black of space beyond—and he knew the answer. Morkill in fleeing had failed to close the vacuum chamber! The air had rushed out; and with pressure removed, with atmosphere gone, the alien things had burst. Were dead!

There was justice in that, Jerry thought grimly, justice that David Morkill could never appreciate.

He started toward the airlock, then paused. If he closed it, and permitted the air supply to renew itself, there was every possibility that other growths might spring up. He had better destroy every vestige of the things first, perhaps even go over every inch of the walls and floor to be certain that no microscopic spore remained.

His glance fell on the bins with their heaps of radium ore, now hidden beneath a thick film of foulness. A fabulous fortune—and all his. But did he want it? Did he want to bring it to Earth? There was so much to consider. Was the human race ready for so vast an amount of radium? Could men be trusted with the power that this could create? He thought of the petty bickerings, the trivial wars, the selfishness and unrest, and he shook his head.

And what of its action upon these seeds of life he had brought from the Moon? Similar dust was settling to Earth every day, and nothing happened. Was the radium solely responsible for the spectacle before him?

With his mind a turmoil of uncertainty, Jerry Blaine returned to the control room and looked at the spreading disc of green and blue and silver beneath him. Suddenly his jaws clicked together. If there were some way in which he could land on Earth without the space ship, some way in which he could drift down through the miles of atmosphere alone, Man need never cope with this possible menace from the Moon.

Deep in thought Jerry watched the Earth draw closer. Hours passed while he weighed possible means of his landing safely. Then suddenly he rose, a broad grin on his face. He saw something out of childhood memories—a big balloon shaped like a bloated fat man, tugging at the end of a string . . . There was work for him to do . . .

A transformed Jerry Blaine tensely watched a sea of cloud rushing up toward him as he stood in the open airlock—a Jerry Blaine who looked like an inflated balloon. Over his own space suit he had put another, a suit designed for a much bigger man. And the space between the two suits he had filled with neo-hydrogen from the fuel tanks of *The Apollo*, a gas with vastly greater lifting power than ordinary hydrogen or helium. Tensely he watched for the moment when the space ship would enter Earth's stratosphere—the moment it would flash along a course almost parallel with the surface far below—the moment when he would leap free, would drift and float slowly downward to the world of men—and *The Apollo* with all its cargo, heated to incandescence by friction with the air, would drop like a flaming meteor to destruction . . .

On the night of August 10th at 9:38, astronomers on the west coast of the United States observed the sudden appearance of an amazingly brilliant meteor in the Constellation Virgo. It sped across the sky like a lance of silver radiance, until suddenly it vanished in the pallid light of the Moon—a visitant from space that drifted to Earth as impalpable, lifeless—dust . . .

THE PROPHETS OF DOOM

Hugo Gernsback

CHICAGO, 1952

What can one say to honor a man whose very name has been given to the awards with which science fiction honors its stars? Other people get *a Hugo; Hugo Gernsback was* Hugo. *European-born, Gernsback came to the United States early in this century and almost at once plunged into publishing—first magazines for electrical hobbyists which now and then ran imaginative stories about inventions and the future, then magazines which ran nothing else. Hugo Gernsback published the first science-fiction magazine in the world when in April, 1926, he brought out the first issue of* Amazing Stories. *A few years later, in a complicated stock problem, he lost control of* Amazing, *and instantly became his own competition by bringing out the rival magazines* Science Wonder Stories *and* Air Wonder Stories. *Later still, he published other science-fiction magazines, but it is for* Amazing Stories *that he is best remembered. He built well when he founded it. Not only has it produced scores of successors, but even now, pushing half a century later,* Amazing *itself still exists.*

The fame of Gernsback the editor drowns out the importance of Gernsback the writer; after his first few years as editor he did little science-fiction writing. But there, too, he showed the way. His most famous work is a novel called Ralph 124C41 + . *The title is meant to be read two ways: first, as the nomenclature of a future society in which everybody is identified by code numbers—with the "+" representing a truly superior person; second, as an allegorical title descriptive of the essence of Ralph: "One to Foresee for One." With a slight change, it becomes descriptive of Gernsback himself: One to Foresee for All.*

WHEN, in April, 1926, I launched the first issue of *Amazing Stories*, I called it "The Magazine of Scienti-fiction." Not a very elegant term, I admit, but I had the fixed idea, even in those early days of science fiction, that *Amazing Stories* henceforth was to be known as a scientific fiction monthly, to distinguish it from any other type of literature.

Not content with that slogan, after a good deal of thought I added a second, more explanatory one: "Extravagant Fiction Today—Cold Fact Tomorrow."

I carried both of these slogans on the editorial page between 1926 and 1929, as long as I published *Amazing Stories*.

Later, for Vol. I, No. 1, of *Science Wonder Stories* in June, 1929, I wrote another descriptive slogan: "Prophetic Fiction is the Mother of Scientific Fact." I think this still means what it says. Science fiction—under *any* term or name—must, in my opinion, deal first and foremost in futures.

It must, in story form, forecast *the wonders of man's progress to come.* That means distant exploits and exploration of space and time.

Contrary to the opinion of many latter-day so-called science-fiction authors, the genre of Jules Verne and H. G. Wells has now been prostituted to such an extent that it often is quite impossible to find any reference to science in what is popularly called science fiction today.

The classic science fiction of Jules Verne and H. G. Wells, with little exception, was serious and, yes, instructive and educational. *It was not primarily intended to entertain or to amuse.* These stories carried a message, and that is the great difference between technological science fiction and fantasy tales. I repeat: Either you have *science* fiction, with the emphasis on *science,* or you have fantasy. You cannot have both—the two genres bear no relation to each other.

In 1961 I expressed my displeasure with the decadence of modern science fiction in a talk which I gave before the "Eastern Science Fiction Association." I then stated: Once upon a time there was just the ordinary garden variety of *scientific* Science Fiction. Then, like atomic fission, science fiction began to proliferate into a chain reaction and we witnessed such mutations as (to name only a few): Pseudo Science Fiction, Fantasy Science Fiction, Sexy Science Fiction, Fairytale Science Fiction, and, lately—believe it or not—even Computer (i.e., *Analog*) Science Fiction, and then the so-called *psi* deviations, from psychic phenomena to spiritualism, including astrology.

Unfortunately, this state of affairs has degenerated lately with increasing momentum, chiefly because most authors know little about the incredibly vast future of science, nor have they the imagination to cope with coming events.

Also, let us admit that scientists as a rule are not good writers when it comes to inspiring literature and they are rarely *hommes de lettres.*

So the author, nine times out of ten, takes refuge in non-scientific fantasy. It is far easier to compose and probably reads better than a technical-science yarn that often is not easy to digest by the uneducated reader.

Often an author attempts to disguise his scientific poverty by using pseudo-scientific terminology. This point was made recently in the *New Scientist* of London, July 18, 1963, by science reviewer R. S. R. Fitter, in commenting on the book *The Web of Life* by

John H. Storer: "The book is written in extremely lucid and simple language, with none of the pseudo-scientific gobbledygook one associates with American scientific writing."

Hence the overwhelmingly large percentage of magazine and book editors can no longer buy true science-fiction stories as they did in the twenties. There are just not enough science-fiction authors today who can deliver adequate material with science-motivated content.

Let us state here without quibbling that I have never had, nor do I have now, the slightest quarrel with fantasy literature. In fact, I personally do like it, particularly if it is of the adult type, say the Edgar Allan Poe variety. What I detest is the parading of pure fantasy stories as science fiction and their sale as such to gullible readers. I consider this an out-and-out fraud.

It was particularly humiliating to me when I read the 1962 volume of the *Hugo Winners*, which the publisher, on the cover, lightheartedly labeled *"Nine prize-winning science-fiction stories."* Well, in my book it should have read "Eight fantasy tales, plus one science-fiction story."

I do not envy the editor who had to edit the book, because the selections had already been made by the World Science Fiction Convention. So he had no choice.

It is also an incontrovertible fact that true science fiction today is still avidly sought out and read by our country's industrial leaders, engineers and technicians because it still gives them invaluable ideas of events to come. Science fiction, believe it or not, is still a powerful force that stimulates thinking men whose destiny is tied up strongly in the future.

It also makes me sad when I see the constantly recurring scribbling of the many prophets of doom who have recently become fashionable in their endeavor to write off genuine science fiction as *passé*. Such bankruptcy of intellect can always be traced directly to the inability of such writers to comprehend the status and message of true prophetic science fiction. This fantastic lack of imagination often is as ludicrous as it is pathetic.

I quote only one recent writer—there are dozens of others everywhere—in the science-fiction fan magazine *Inside*, June, 1963. Curiously, too, although the writer of the 5,000-word opus quotes and lists the names of practically every "science-fiction" author, he forgets even to mention perhaps the most outstanding true science-fiction personality—with thirty-one books published in the United States—Arthur C. Clarke! Let us proceed with *Inside*'s forecast:

THE FUTURE OF SCIENCE FICTION

A question which naturally arises is, What of the future of science fiction? If it evolves through the discovery and working out of its congenital possibilities, what remains? What would be the next developments?

Personally, I do not see much of a future for science fiction. There are several reasons for hesitating to make such a statement—one of which is that the detective story seemed to be dead in the 1880's—but they are all general and negative. I see no specific and active reasons for supposing it has any very lively future.

In tracing out this general line of speculation, we quite naturally arrive at the thought that there will come a time when all possibilities are exhausted. Then science fiction will be completed. There will be nothing new, regardless of clever variations. It will have realized everything that is in it as a literary organism and will sink willingly, as it were, into extinction. Actually, it is difficult, perhaps impossible, to foresee a time in which there will not be published occasional stories of the marvelous, the fantastic, and of future science; but is not so difficult to believe that there will come a time, probably in our personal futures, in which there will no longer be a field—only a genre.

So much for one prophet of doom. The quoted statement brings to mind a long list of great unimaginative non-believers in the world's future. Nor are they unknown; some of them are quite famous in their own right—not as prophets, but as scientists and other highly placed celebrities.

Arthur C. Clarke, in his epoch-making book *Profiles of the*

Future, calls their deficiency "Failure of Imagination." Here are a few of those he mentions:

There was famed philosopher Auguste Comte, who in his *Cours de Philosophie* (1835) stated this about the heavenly bodies: "We see how we determine their forms, their distances, their bulk, their motions, but we can never know anything of their chemical or mineralogical structure . . . the stars serve us scientifically only as providing positions with which we may compare the interior movements of our system."

Let us not forget world-famed Lord Ernst Rutherford, who, perhaps more than any other mortal, was responsible for our insight into modern atomic science. Yet up to his death in 1937 he constantly ridiculed the idea that we would ever be able to harness the energy locked up in matter. Sad to relate, the first atomic chain reaction occurred only five years after his death!

Next listen to the great American astronomer Simon Newcomb (1835–1909), who wrote a celebrated essay that ended thus: "The demonstration that no possible combination of known substances, known forms of machinery and known forms of force, can be united in a practical machine, by which men shall fly long distances through the air, seems to the writer as complete as it is possible for the demonstration of any physical fact to be."

Not to be outdone by such a preposterous prophecy, the British professor A. W. Bickerton (1842–1929) wrote the following masterpiece, which I quote verbatim, in a paper published in 1926: "This foolish idea of shooting at the moon is an example of the absurd length to which vicious specialisation will carry scientists working in thought-tight compartments. Let us critically examine the proposal. For a projectile entirely to escape the gravitation of the earth, it needs a velocity of seven miles a second. The thermal energy of a gramme at this speed is 15,180 calories . . . The energy of our most violent explosive—nitroglycerine—is less than 1,500 calories per gramme. Consequently, even had the explosive nothing to carry, it has only one-tenth of the energy necessary to escape the earth . . . Hence the proposition appears to be basically impossible."

Lest you think that such recorded foolishness is rare and

isolated, rest assured that it is commonplace. All one has to do is to read our newspapers and magazines for the latest examples of total decay of imagination.

It is a measure of our times that just as the poor, misguided, unimaginative scientists whom we quoted failed to look into the future, so the present-day science-illiterate author cannot possibly comprehend the myriad of technical wonders still to come.

He cannot understand—nor extrapolate into future terms—that each new invention and discovery automatically opens the door to a host of new ideas that proliferate countless others.

And all of these are excellent springboards for novel, *true* science-fiction stories, never dreamt of before.

If these are often termed derisively "gadget stories" by the technologically illiterate, the more power to those far-seeing authors who have the imagination and the intellectual gifts to read the future aright so they can point out to their most modest and less fortunate brethren the direction in which the world is heading. Given enough such outstanding authors, true prophetic science fiction could very well stage a massive comeback—it could become the renaissance of the Jules Verne-H. G. Wells type of technological science fiction so badly needed in our present idea-improverished world.

Let me give a single example of what is coming in the next decade. You might call it educated-guess science fiction, because as yet it is not in existence, although we have practically all the scientific and technical elements now.

It is taken from an article I wrote a few weeks ago entitled "Microminiature Color Television." The idea deals with micro-miniaturized TV cameras so small that they can go through the hollow opening of a large-sized hypodermic needle. Before you scoff at that, electronic technicians will tell you that transistors have already shrunk into the microscopic, so minute that they cannot be seen by the naked eye. How small can a TV camera shrink? No one knows.

Next we combine the X-ray with the electron microscope and the TV color camera. This should give us enlargements of 300,000 diameters upwards.

The hardly visible microscopic TV camera can now be introduced through the hypodermic needle into practically every inaccessible part of the human anatomy.

Just imagine a 300,000-diameter enlargement of, say, an internal incipient cancer, or other disease! For all practical purposes, the entire human body will have become as transparent as if it were glass or plastic.

How many science-fiction plots can this single idea engender?

In technology, the probing microminiature TV color camera will literally have thousands of new uses. Coupled with the X-ray and the electron microscope, such future TV camera-probes will ferret out points of weaknesses and practically all potential failures, not apparent otherwise.

Take only one example: Our present-day rockets, missiles and our various satellites. Today's percentage of failure is intolerable. Its cost is well-nigh astronomical now. Often failures occur once the space vehicle has been placed in orbit. But most occur before they are off the ground.

Almost all these potential failures could be anticipated and overcome with miniature color TV probes *on the molecular level*. They would be cheap at *any* price. Does this give you any ideas?

THE LONG WATCH

Robert A. Heinlein

DENVER, 1941

*By the time of the third World Science Fiction Conven-
tion it was clear that conventions were here to stay, and
orderly-minded fans began devising a system to spread the joy
equitably—if not quite around the world, at least around the
United States. The first Worldcon had been in the Eastern Time
Zone, the second in the Central; clearly it made sense to move
majestically westward, one zone each year, returning to the East
Coast in the fifth year. And so it came to pass—at least as far as
Denver. Then things fell apart. First, the war began to bite—Pearl
Harbor occurred three months later, and for the next three years
there were no conventions at all. ("Is This Trip Necessary?"
demanded the posters in the railroad stations, and sf fans had to
admit that those trips did not seem necessary to anyone but*

themselves—anyway, the fans were rapidly going off into uniform.)

But Denver was a great convention, and its Guest of Honor was one of the greatest science-fiction writers of all time. There is not much point in saying anything about Robert A. Heinlein. It has all been said already; the author of Stranger in a Strange Land *is no stranger to anyone who reads.*

"NINE ships blasted off from Moon Base. Once in space, eight of them formed a globe around the smallest. They held this formation all the way to Earth.

"The small ship displayed the insignia of an admiral—yet there was no living thing of any sort in her. She was not even a passenger ship, but a drone, a robot ship intended for radioactive cargo. This trip she carried nothing but a lead coffin—and a Geiger counter that was never quiet."

—from the editorial *After Ten Years*, film 38, 17 June 2009, Archives of the *N. Y. Times*

I

Johnny Dahlquist blew smoke at the Geiger counter. He grinned wryly and tried it again. His whole body was radioactive by now. Even his breath, the smoke from his cigarette, could make the Geiger counter scream.

How long had he been here? Time doesn't mean much on the Moon. Two days? Three? A week? He let his mind run back: the last clearly marked time in his mind was when the Executive Officer had sent for him, right after breakfast—

"Lieutenant Dahlquist, reporting to the Executive Officer."

Colonel Towers looked up. "Ah, John Ezra. Sit down, Johnny. Cigarette?"

Johnny sat down, mystified but flattered. He admired Colonel Towers, for his brilliance, his ability to dominate, and for his battle record. Johnny had no battle record; he had been commissioned on completing his doctor's degree in nuclear physics and was now junior bomb officer of Moon Base.

The Colonel wanted to talk politics; Johnny was puzzled. Finally Towers had come to the point; it was not safe (so he said) to leave control of the world in political hands; power must be held by a scientifically selected group. In short—the Patrol.

Johnny was startled rather than shocked. As an abstract idea, Towers' notion sounded plausible. The League of Nations had folded up; what would keep the United Nations from breaking up, too, and thus lead to another World War. "And you know how bad such a war would be, Johnny."

Johnny agreed. Towers said he was glad that Johnny got the point. The senior bomb officer could handle the work, but it was better to have both specialists.

Johnny sat up with a jerk. "You are going to *do* something about it?" He had thought the Exec was just talking.

Towers smiled. "We're not politicians; we don't just talk. We act."

Johnny whistled. "When does this start?"

Towers flipped a switch. Johnny was startled to hear his own voice, then identified the recorded conversation as having taken place in the junior officers' messroom. A political argument, he remembered, which he had walked out on . . . a good thing, too! But being spied on annoyed him.

Towers switched it off. "We *have* acted," he said. "We know who is safe and who isn't. Take Kelly—" He waved at the loudspeaker. "Kelly is politically unreliable. You noticed he wasn't at breakfast?"

"Huh? I thought he was on watch."

"Kelly's watch-standing days are over. Oh, relax; he isn't hurt."

Johnny thought this over. "Which list am I on?" he asked. "Safe or unsafe?"

"Your name has a question mark after it. But I have said all along that you could be depended on." He grinned engagingly. "You won't make a liar of me, Johnny?"

Dahlquist didn't answer; Towers said sharply, "Come now—what do you think of it? Speak up."

"Well, if you ask me, you've bitten off more than you can chew. While it's true that Moon Base controls the Earth, Moon Base itself is a sitting duck for a ship. One bomb—*blooie!*"

Towers picked up a message form and handed it over; it read: I HAVE YOUR CLEAN LAUNDRY—ZACK. "That means every bomb in the *Trygve Lie* has been put out of commission. I have reports from every ship we need worry about." He stood up. "Think it over and see me after lunch. Major Morgan needs your help right away to change control frequencies on the bombs."

"The control frequencies?"

"Naturally. We don't want the bombs jammed before they reach their targets."

"What? You said the idea was to *prevent* war."

Towers brushed it aside. "There won't be a war—just a psychological demonstration, an unimportant town or two. A little bloodletting to save an all-out war. Simple arithmetic."

He put a hand on Johnny's shoulder. "You aren't squeamish, or you wouldn't be a bomb officer. Think of it as a surgical operation. And think of your family."

Johnny Dahlquist had been thinking of his family. "Please, sir, I want to see the Commanding Officer."

Towers frowned. "The Commodore is not available. As you know, I speak for him. See me again—after lunch."

The Commodore was decidedly not available; the Commodore was dead. But Johnny did not know that.

Dahlquist walked back to the messroom, bought cigarettes, sat down and had a smoke. He got up, crushed out the butt, and headed for the Base's west airlock. There he got into his space suit and went to the lockmaster. "Open her up, Smitty."

The marine looked surprised. "Can't let anyone out on the surface without word from Colonel Towers, sir. Hadn't you heard?"

"Oh, yes! Give me your order book." Dahlquist took it, wrote a pass for himself, and signed it "by direction of Colonel Towers." He added, "Better call the Executive Officer and check it."

The lockmaster read it and stuck the book in his pocket. "Oh, no, Lieutenant. Your word's good."

"Hate to disturb the Executive Officer, eh? Don't blame you." He stepped in, closed the inner door, and waited for the air to be sucked out.

Out on the Moon's surface he blinked at the light and hurried to the track-rocket terminus; a car was waiting. He squeezed in, pulled down the hood, and punched the starting button. The rocket car flung itself at the hills, dived through and came out on a plain studded with projectile rockets, like candles on a cake. Quickly it dived into a second tunnel through more hills. There was a stomach-wrenching deceleration and the car stopped at the underground atom-bomb armory.

As Dahlquist climbed out he switched on his walkie-talkie. The space suited guard at the entrance came to port-arms. Dahlquist said, "Morning, Lopez," and walked by him to the airlock. He pulled it open.

The guard motioned him back. "Hey! Nobody goes in without the Executive Officer's say-so." He shifted his gun, fumbled in his pouch and got out a paper. "Read it, Lieutenant."

Dahlquist waved it away. "I drafted that order myself. *You* read it; you've misinterpreted it."

"I don't see how, Lieutenant."

Dahlquist snatched the paper, glanced at it, then pointed to a line. "See? '—except persons specifically designated by the Executive Officer.' That's the bomb officers, Major Morgan and me."

The guard looked worried. Dahlquist said, "Damn it, look up 'specifically designated'—it's under *'Bomb Room, Security, Procedure for,'* in your standing orders. Don't tell me you left them in the barracks!"

"Oh, no, sir! I've got 'em." The guard reached into his pouch. Dahlquist gave him back the sheet; the guard took it, hesitated, then leaned his weapon against his hip, shifted the paper to his left hand, and dug into his pouch with his right.

Dahlquist grabbed the gun, shoved it between the guard's legs, and jerked. He threw the weapon away and ducked into the airlock. As he slammed the door he saw the guard struggling to his feet and reaching for his side arm. He dogged the outer door shut and felt a tingle in his fingers as a slug struck the door.

He flung himself at the inner door, jerked the spill lever, rushed back to the outer door and hung his weight on the handle. At once he could feel it stir. The guard was lifting up; the lieutenant was pulling down, with only his low Moon weight to anchor him. Slowly the handle raised before his eyes.

Air from the bomb room rushed into the lock through the spill valve. Dahlquist felt his space suit settle on his body as the pressure in the lock began to equal the pressure in the suit. He quit straining and let the guard raise the handle. It did not matter; thirteen tons of air pressure now held the door closed.

He latched open the inner door to the bomb room, so that it could not swing shut. As long as it was open, the airlock could not operate; no one could enter.

Before him in the room, one for each projectile rocket, were the atom bombs, spaced in rows far enough apart to defeat any faint possibility of spontaneous chain reaction. They were the deadliest things in the known universe, but they were his babies. He had placed himself between them and anyone who would misuse them.

But, now that he was here, he had no plan to use his temporary advantage.

The speaker on the wall sputtered into life. "Hey! Lieutenant! What goes on here? You gone crazy?" Dahlquist did not answer. Let Lopez stay confused—it would take him that much longer to make up his mind what to do. And Johnny Dahlquist needed as many minutes as he could squeeze. Lopez went on protesting. Finally he shut up.

Johnny had followed a blind urge not to let the bombs—*his* bombs!—be used for "demonstrations on unimportant towns." But what to do next? Well, Towers couldn't get through the lock. Johnny would sit tight until hell froze over.

Don't kid yourself, John Ezra! Towers could get in. Some high explosive against the outer door—then the air would whoosh out, our boy Johnny would drown in blood from his burst lungs—and the bombs would be sitting there, unhurt. They were built to stand the jump from Moon to Earth; vacuum would not hurt them at all.

He decided to stay in his space suit; explosive decompression didn't appeal to him. Come to think about it, death from old age was his choice.

Or they could drill a hole, let out the air, and open the door without wrecking the lock. Or Towers might even have a new airlock built outside the old. Not likely, Johnny thought; a *coup d'etat* depended on speed. Towers was almost sure to take the quickest way—blasting. And Lopez was probably calling the Base right now. Fifteen minutes for Towers to suit up and get here, maybe a short dicker—then *whoosh!* the party is over.

Fifteen minutes—

In fifteen minutes the bombs might fall back into the hands of the conspirators; in fifteen minutes he must make the bombs unusable.

An atom bomb is just two or more pieces of fissionable metal, such as plutonium. Separated, they are no more explosive than a pound of butter; slapped together, they explode. The complications lie in the gadgets and circuits and gun used to slap them together in the exact way and at the exact time and place required.

These circuits, the bomb's "brain," are easily destroyed—but the bomb itself is hard to destroy because of its very simplicity. Johnny decided to smash the "brains"—and quickly!

The only tools at hand were simple ones used in handling the bombs. Aside from a Geiger counter, the speaker on the walkie-talkie circuit, a television rig to the base, and the bombs themselves, the room was bare. A bomb to be worked on was taken elsewhere—not through fear of explosion, but to reduce radiation exposure for personnel. The radioactive material in a bomb is buried in a "tamper"—in these bombs, gold. Gold stops alpha, beta, and much of the deadly gamma radiation—but not neutrons.

The slippery, poisonous neutrons which plutonium gives off had to escape, or a chain reaction—explosion!—would result. The room was bathed in an invisible, almost undetectable rain of neutrons. The place was unhealthy; regulations called for staying in it as short a time as possible.

The Geiger counter clicked off the "background" radiation, cosmic rays, the trace of radioactivity in the Moon's crust, and secondary radioactivity set up all through the room by neutrons. Free neutrons have the nasty trait of infecting what they strike, making it radioactive, whether it be concrete wall or human body. In time the room would have to be abandoned.

Dahlquist twisted a knob on the Geiger counter; the instrument stopped clicking. He had used a suppressor circuit to cut out noise of "background" radiation at the level then present. It reminded him uncomfortably of the danger of staying here. He took out the radiation exposure film all radiation personnel carry; it was a direct-response type and had been fresh when he arrived. The most sensitive end was faintly darkened already. Half way down the film a red line crossed it. Theoretically, if the wearer was exposed to enough radioactivity in a week to darken the film to that line, he was, as Johnny reminded himself, a "dead duck."

Off came the cumbersome space suit; what he needed was speed. Do the job and surrender—better to be a prisoner than to linger in a place as "hot" as this.

He grabbed a ball hammer from the tool rack and got busy, pausing only to switch off the television pick-up. The first bomb bothered him. He started to smash the cover plate of the "brain," then stopped, filled with reluctance. All his life he had prized fine apparatus.

He nerved himself and swung; glass tinkled, metal creaked. His mood changed; he began to feel a shameful pleasure in destruction. He pushed on with enthusiasm, swinging, smashing, destroying!

So intent was he that he did not at first hear his name called. "Dahlquist! Answer me! Are you there?"

He wiped sweat and looked at the TV screen. Towers' perturbed features stared out.

Johnny was shocked to find that he had wrecked only six bombs. Was he going to be caught before he could finish? Oh, no! He *had* to finish. Stall, son, stall! "Yes, Colonel? You called me?"

"I certainly did! What's the meaning of this?"

"I'm sorry, Colonel."

Towers' expression relaxed a little. "Turn on your pick-up, Johnny, I can't see you. What was that noise?"

"The pick-up is on," Johnny lied. "It must be out of order. That noise—uh, to tell the truth, Colonel, I was fixing things so that nobody could get in here."

Towers hesitated, then said firmly, "I'm going to assume that you are sick and send you to the Medical Officer. But I want you to come out of there, right away. That's an order, Johnny."

Johnny answered slowly. "I can't just yet, Colonel. I came here to make up my mind and I haven't quite made it up. You said to see you after lunch."

"I meant you to stay in your quarters."

"Yes, sir. But I thought I ought to stand watch on the bombs, in case I decided you were wrong."

"It's not for you to decide, Johnny. I'm your superior officer. You are sworn to obey me."

"Yes, sir." This was wasting time; the old fox might have a squad on the way now. "But I swore to keep the peace, too. Could you come out here and talk it over with me? I don't want to do the wrong thing."

Towers smiled. "A good idea, Johnny. You wait there. I'm sure you'll see the light." He switched off.

"There," said Johnny. "I hope you're convinced that I'm a half-wit—you slimy mistake!" He picked up the hammer, ready to use the minutes gained.

He stopped almost at once; it dawned on him that wrecking the "brains" was not enough. There were no spare "brains," but there was a well-stocked electronics shop. Morgan could jury-rig control circuits for bombs. Why, he could himself—not a neat job, but one that would work. Damnation! He would have to wreck the bombs themselves—and in the next ten minutes.

But a bomb was solid chunks of metal, encased in a heavy tamper, all tied in with a big steel gun. It couldn't be done—not in ten minutes.

Damn!

Of course, there was one way. He knew the control circuits; he also knew how to beat them. Take this bomb: if he took out the safety bar, unhooked the proximity circuit, shorted the delay circuit, and cut in the arming circuit by hand—then unscrewed *that* and reached in *there*, he could, with just a long, stiff wire, set the bomb off.

Blowing the other bombs and the valley itself to Kingdom Come.

Also Johnny Dahlquist. That was the rub.

All this time he was doing what he had thought out, up to the step of actually setting off the bomb. Ready to go, the bomb seemed to threaten, as if crouching to spring. He stood up, sweating.

He wondered if he had the courage. He did not want to funk—and hoped that he would. He dug into his jacket and took out a picture of Edith and the baby. "Honeychile," he said, "if I get out of this, I'll never even try to beat a red light." He kissed the picture and put it back. There was nothing to do but wait.

What was keeping Towers? Johnny wanted to make sure that Towers was in blast range. What a joke on the jerk! Me—sitting here, ready to throw the switch on him. The idea tickled him; it led to a better: why blow himself up—alive?

There was another way to rig it—a "dead man" control. Jigger up some way so that the last step, the one that set off the bomb, would not happen as long as he kept his hand on a switch or a lever or something. Then, if they blew open the door, or shot him, or anything—up goes the balloon!

Better still, if he could hold them off with the threat of it, sooner or later help would come—Johnny was sure that most of the Patrol was not in this stinking conspiracy—and then: Johnny comes marching home! What a reunion! He'd resign and get a teaching job; he'd stood his watch.

All the while, he was working. Electrical? No, too little time. Make it a simple mechanical linkage. He had it doped out but had hardly begun to build it when the loudspeaker called him. "Johnny?"

"That you, Colonel?" His hands kept busy.

"Let me in."

"Well, now, Colonel, that wasn't in the agreement." Where in blue blazes was something to use as a long lever?

"I'll come in alone, Johnny, I give you my word. We'll talk face to face."

His word! "We can talk over the speaker, Colonel." Hey, that was it—a yardstick, hanging on the tool rack.

"Johnny, I'm warning you. Let me in, or I'll blow the door off."

A wire—he needed a wire, fairly long and stiff. He tore the antenna from his suit. "You wouldn't do that, Colonel. It would ruin the bombs."

"Vacuum won't hurt the bombs. Quit stalling."

"Better check with Major Morgan. Vacuum won't hurt them; explosive decompression would wreck every circuit." The Colonel was not a bomb specialist; he shut up for several minutes. Johnny went on working.

"Dahlquist," Towers resumed, "that was a clumsy lie. I checked with Morgan. You have sixty seconds to get into your suit, if you aren't already. I'm going to blast the door."

"No, you won't," said Johnny. "Ever hear of a 'dead man' switch?" Now for a counterweight—and a sling.

"Eh? What do you mean?"

"I've rigged number seventeen to set off by hand. But I put in a gimmick. It won't blow while I hang on to a strap I've got in my hand. But if anything happens to me—*up she goes!* You are about fifty feet from the blast center. Think it over."

There was a short silence. "I don't believe you."

"No? Ask Morgan. He'll believe me. He can inspect it, over the TV pick-up." Johnny lashed the belt of his space suit to the end of the yardstick.

"You said the pick-up was out of order."

"So I lied. This time I'll prove it. Have Morgan call me."

Presently Major Morgan's face appeared. "Lieutenant Dahlquist?"

"Hi, Stinky. Wait a sec." With great care Dahlquist made one last connection while holding down the end of the yardstick. Still careful, he shifted his grip to the belt, sat down on the floor, stretched an arm and switched on the TV pick-up. "Can you see me, Stinky?"

"I can see you," Morgan answered stiffly. "What is this nonsense?"

"A little surprise I whipped up." He explained it—what circuits he had cut out, what ones had been shorted, just how the jury-rigged mechanical sequence fitted in.

Morgan nodded. "But you're bluffing, Dahlquist. I feel sure that you haven't disconnected the 'K' circuit. You don't have the guts to blow yourself up."

Johnny chuckled. "I sure haven't. But that's the beauty of it. It can't go off, *so long as I am alive.* If your greasy boss, ex-Colonel Towers, blasts the door, then I'm dead and the bomb goes off. It won't matter to me, but it will to him. Better tell him." He switched off.

Towers came on over the speaker shortly. "Dahlquist?"

"I hear you."

"There's no need to throw away your life. Come out and you will be retired on full pay. You can go home to your family. That's a promise."

Johnny got mad. "You keep my family out of this!"

"Think of them, man."

"Shut up. Get back to your hole. I feel a need to scratch and this whole shebang might just explode in your lap."

II

Johnny sat up with a start. He had dozed, his hand hadn't let go the sling, but he had the shakes when he thought about it.

Maybe he should disarm the bomb and depend on their not daring to dig him out? But Towers' neck was already in hock for treason; Towers might risk it. If he did and the bomb were disarmed, Johnny would be dead and Towers would have the bombs. No, he had gone this far; he wouldn't let his baby girl grow up in a dictatorship just to catch some sleep.

He heard the Geiger counter clicking and remembered having used the suppressor circuit. The radioactivity in the room must be increasing, perhaps from scattering the "brain" circuits—the circuits were sure to be infected; they had lived too long too close to plutonium. He dug out his film.

The dark area was spreading toward the red line.

He put it back and said, "Pal, better break this deadlock or you are going to shine like a watch dial." It was a figure of speech; infected animal tissue does not glow—it simply dies, slowly.

The TV screen lit up; Towers' face appeared. "Dahlquist? I want to talk to you."

"Go fly a kite."

"Let's admit you have us inconvenienced."

"Inconvenienced, hell—I've got you stopped."

"For the moment. I'm arranging to get more bombs—"

"Liar."

"—but you are slowing us up. I have a proposition."

"Not interested."

"Wait. When this is over I will be chief of the world government. If you cooperate, even now, I will make you my administrative head."

Johnny told him what to do with it. Towers said, "Don't be stupid. What do you gain by dying?"

Johnny grunted. "Towers, what a prime stinker you are. You spoke of my family. I'd rather see them dead than living under a two-bit Napoleon like you. Now go away—I've got some thinking to do."

Towers switched off.

Johnny got out his film again. It seemed no darker but it reminded him forcibly that time was running out. He was hungry and thirsty—and he could not stay awake forever. It took four days to get a ship up from Earth; he could not expect rescue any sooner. And he couldn't last four days—once the darkening spread past the red line he was a goner.

His only chance was to wreck the bombs beyond repair, and get out—before that film got much darker.

He thought about ways, then got busy. He hung a weight on the sling, tied a line to it. If Towers blasted the door, he hoped to jerk the rig loose before he died.

There was a simple, though arduous, way to wreck the bombs beyond any capacity of Moon Base to repair them. The heart of each was two hemispheres of plutonium, their flat surface polished smooth to permit perfect contact when slapped together.

Anything less would prevent the chain reaction on which atomic explosion depended.

Johnny started taking apart one of the bombs.

He had to bash off four lugs, then break the glass envelope around the inner assembly. Aside from that the bomb came apart easily. At last he had in front of him two gleaming, mirror-perfect half globes.

A blow with the hammer—and one was no longer perfect. Another blow and the second cracked like glass; he had trapped its crystalline structure just right.

Hours later, dead tired, he went back to the armed bomb. Forcing himself to steady down, with extreme care he disarmed it. Shortly its silvery hemispheres too were useless. There was no longer a usable bomb in the room—but huge fortunes in the most valuable, most poisonous, and most deadly metal in the known world were spread around the floor.

Johnny looked at the deadly stuff. "Into your suit and out of here, son," he said aloud. "I wonder what Towers will say?"

He walked toward the rack, intending to hang up the hammer. As he passed, the Geiger counter chattered wildly.

Plutonium hardly affects a Geiger counter; secondary infection from plutonium does. Johnny looked at the hammer, then held it closer to the Geiger counter. The counter screamed.

Johnny tossed it hastily away and started back toward his suit.

As he passed the counter it chattered again. He stopped short.

He pushed one hand close to the counter. Its clicking picked up to a steady roar. Without moving he reached into his pocket and took out his exposure film.

It was dead black from end to end.

III

Plutonium taken into the body moves quickly to bone marrow. Nothing can be done; the victim is finished. Neutrons from it smash through the body, ionizing tissue, transmuting atoms into radioactive isotopes, destroying and killing. The fatal dose is unbelievably small; a mass a tenth the size of a grain of table salt is more than enough—a dose small enough to enter through the tiniest scratch. During the historic "Manhattan Project" immediate high amputation was considered the only possible first-aid measure.

Johnny knew all this but it no longer disturbed him. He sat on the floor, smoking a hoarded cigarette, and thinking. The events of his long watch were running through his mind.

He blew a puff of smoke at the Geiger counter and smiled without humor to hear it chatter more loudly. By now even his breath was "hot"—carbon-14, he supposed, exhaled from his blood stream as carbon dioxide. It did not matter.

There was no longer any point in surrendering, nor would he give Towers the satisfaction—he would finish out this watch right here. Besides, by keeping up the bluff that one bomb was ready to blow, he could stop them from capturing the raw material from which bombs were made. That might be important in the long run.

He accepted, without surprise, the fact that he was not unhappy. There was a sweetness about having no further worries of any sort. He did not hurt, he was not uncomfortable, he was no longer even hungry. Physically he still felt fine and his mind was at peace. He was dead—he knew that he was dead; yet for a time he was able to walk and breathe and see and feel.

He was not even lonesome. He was not alone; there were comrades with him—the boy with his finger in the dike, Colonel Bowie, too ill to move but insisting that he be carried across the line, the dying Captain of the *Chesapeake* still with deathless challenge on his lips, Rodger Young peering into the gloom. They gathered about him in the dusky bomb room.

And of course there was Edith. She was the only one he was aware of. Johnny wished that he could see her face more clearly. Was she angry? Or proud and happy?

Proud though unhappy—he could see her better now and even feel her hand. He held very still.

Presently his cigarette burned down to his fingers. He took a final puff, blew it at the Geiger counter, and put it out. It was his last. He gathered several butts and fashioned a roll-your-own with a bit of paper found in a pocket. He lit it carefully and settled back to wait for Edith to show up again. He was very happy.

.   .   .

He was still propped against the bomb case, the last of his salvaged cigarettes cold at his side, when the speaker called out again. "Johnny? Hey, Johnny! Can you hear me? This is Kelly. It's all over. The *Lafayette* landed and Towers blew his brains out. Johnny? *Answer me.*"

When they opened the outer door, the first man in carried a Geiger counter in front of him on the end of a long pole. He stopped at the threshold and backed out hastily. "Hey, chief!" he called. "Better get some handling equipment—uh, and a lead coffin, too."

"*Four days it took the little ship and her escort to reach Earth. Four days while all of Earth's people awaited her arrival. For ninety-eight hours all commercial programs were off television; instead there was an endless dirge—the* Dead March *from* Saul, *the* Valhalla *theme,* Going Home, *the Patrol's own* Landing Orbit.

"*The nine ships landed at Chicago Port. A drone tractor removed the casket from the small ship; the ship was then refueled and blasted off in an escape trajectory, thrown away into outer space, never again to be used for a lesser purpose.*

"*The tractor progressed to the Illinois town where Lieutenant Dahlquist had been born, while the dirge continued. There it placed the casket on a pedestal, inside a barrier marking the distance of safe approach. Space marines, arms reversed and heads bowed, stood guard around it; the crowds stayed outside this circle. And still the dirge continued.*

"*When enough time had passed, long, long after the heaped flowers had withered, the lead casket was enclosed in marble, just as you see it today.*"

SANITY

Fritz Leiber

NEW ORLEANS, 1951

When Fritz Leiber first began writing wonderful science-fiction stories he signed himself Fritz Leiber, Jr. His father was still alive and still active and well known as a famous Shakespearean actor on the stage (and still is to be seen now and then on the Late, Late Show, playing a cardinal or a duke in a costume drama). Fritz the Younger was an actor himself, and an impressive figure of a man—tall, handsome, with the voice of a baritone Barrymore. He still is, and though he gave up acting long since, he still continues to do the thing he does best of all: write science-fiction stories as no one else writes them ever.

For many years Leiber doubled as editor of Science Digest, *bringing to it, and enriching in it, a background of understanding of science. In his youth he studied for the ministry. One can recognize in his work the knowledge and concerns of science and religion, but what makes them unique is his marvelously individual insight into the follies and perversities of mankind.*

"COME in, Phy, and make yourself comfortable."

The mellow voice—and the suddenly dilating doorway—caught the general secretary of the World playing with a blob of greenish gasoid, squeezing it in his fist and watching it ooze between his fingers in spatulate tendrils that did not dissipate. Slowly, crookedly, he turned his head. World Manager Carrsbury became aware of a gaze that was at once oafish, sly, vacuous. Abruptly the expression was replaced by a nervous smile. The thin man straightened himself, as much as his habitually drooping shoulders would permit, hastily entered, and sat down on the extreme edge of a pneumatically form-fitting chair.

He embarrassedly fumbled the blob of gasoid, looking around for a convenient disposal vent or a crevice in the upholstery. Finding none, he stuffed it hurriedly into his pocket. Then he repressed his fidgetings by clasping his hands resolutely together, and sat with downcast eyes.

"How are you feeling, old man?" Carrsbury asked in a voice that was warm with a benign friendliness.

The general secretary did not look up.

"Anything bothering you, Phy?" Carrsbury continued solicitously. "Do you feel a bit unhappy, or dissatisfied, about your . . . er . . . transfer, now that the moment has arrived?"

Still the general secretary did not respond. Carrsbury leaned forward across the dully silver, semicircular desk and, in his most winning tones, urged, "Come on, old fellow, tell me all about it."

The general secretary did not lift his head, but he rolled up his strange, distant eyes until they were fixed directly on Carrsbury. He shivered a little, his body seemed to contract, and his bloodless hands tightened their interlocking grip.

"I know," he said in a low, effortful voice. "You think I'm insane."

Carrsbury sat back, forcing his brows to assume a baffled frown under the mane of silvery hair.

"Oh, you needn't pretend to be puzzled," Phy continued, swiftly now that he had broken the ice. "You know what that word means as well as I do. Better—even though we both had to do historical research to find out.

"Insane," he repeated dreamily, his gaze wavering. "Significant departure from the norm. Inability to conform to basic conventions underlying all human conduct."

"Nonsense!" said Carrsbury, rallying and putting on his warmest and most compelling smile. "I haven't the slightest idea of what you're talking about. That you're a little tired, a little strained, a little distraught—that's quite understandable, considering the burden you've been carrying, and a little rest will be just the thing to fix you up, a nice long vacation away from all this. But as for your being . . . why, ridiculous!"

"No," said Phy, his gaze pinning Carrsbury. "You think I'm insane. You think all my colleagues in the World Management Service are insane. That's why you're having us replaced with those men you've been training for ten years in your Institute of Political Leadership—ever since, with my help and connivance, you became World Manager."

Carrsbury retreated before the finality of the statement. For the first time his smile became a bit uncertain. He started to say something, then hesitated and looked at Phy, as if half hoping he would go on.

But that individual was once again staring rigidly at the floor.

Carrsbury leaned back, thinking. When he spoke it was in a more natural voice, much less consciously soothing and fatherly.

"Well, all right, Phy. But look here, tell me something, honestly. Won't you—and the others—be a lot happier when you've been relieved of all your responsibilities?"

Phy nodded somberly. "Yes," he said, "we will . . . but"—his face became strained—"you see—"

"But—?" Carrsbury prompted.

Phy swallowed hard. He seemed unable to go on. He had gradually slumped toward one side of the chair, and the pressure had caused the green gasoid to ooze from his pocket. His long fingers crept over and kneaded it fretfully.

Carrsbury stood up and came around the desk. His sympathetic frown, from which perplexity had ebbed, was now quite genuine.

"I don't see why I shouldn't tell you all about it now, Phy," he said simply. "In a queer sort of way I owe it all to you. And there isn't any point now in keeping it a secret . . . there isn't any danger—"

"Yes," Phy agreed with a quick bitter smile, "you haven't been in any danger of a *coup d'état* for some years now. If ever we should have revolted, there'd have been"—his gaze shifted to a point in the opposite wall where a faint vertical crease indicated the presence of a doorway—"your secret police."

Carrsbury started. He hadn't thought Phy had known. Disturbingly, there loomed in his mind a phrase: *the cunning of the insane.* But only for a moment. Friendly complacency flooded back. He went behind Phy's chair and rested his hands on the sloping shoulders.

"You know, I've always had a special feeling toward you, Phy," he said, "and not only because your whims made it a lot easier for me to become World Manager. I've always felt that you were different from the others, that there were times when—" He hesitated.

Phy squirmed a little under the friendly hands. "When I had my moments of sanity?" he finished flatly.

"Like now," said Carrsbury softly, after a nod the other could not see. "I've always felt that sometimes, in a kind of twisted, unrealistic way, you *understood.* And that has meant a lot to me. I've been alone, Phy, dreadfully alone, for ten whole years. No companionship anywhere, not even among the men I've been training in the Institute of Political Leadership—for I've had to play a part with them too, keep them in ignorance of certain facts, for fear they would try to seize power over my head before they were sufficiently prepared. No companionship anywhere, except for my hopes—and for occasional moments with you. Now that it's over and a new regime is beginning for us both, I can tell you that. And I'm glad."

There was silence. Then—Phy did not look around, but one lean hand crept up and touched Carrsbury's. Carrsbury cleared his throat. Strange, he thought, that there could be even a momentary rapport like this between the sane and the insane. But it was so.

He disengaged his hands, strode rapidly back to his desk, turned.

"I'm a throwback, Phy," he began in a new, unused, eager voice. "A throwback to a time when human mentality was far sounder. Whether my case was due chiefly to heredity, or to certain unusual accidents of environment, or to both, is unimportant. The point is that a person had been born who was in a position to criticize the present state of mankind in the light of the past, to diagnose its condition, and to begin its cure. For a long time I refused to face the facts, but finally my researches—especially those in the literature of the twentieth century—left me no alternative. The mentality of mankind had become—aberrant. Only certain technological advances, which had resulted in making the business of living infinitely easier and simpler, and the fact that war had been ended with the creation of the present world state, were staving off the inevitable breakdown of civilization. But only staving it off—delaying it. The great masses of mankind had become what would once have been called hopelessly neurotic. Their leaders had become . . . you said it first, Phy . . . insane. Incidentally, this latter phenomenon—the drift of psychological aberrants toward leadership—has been noted in all ages."

He paused. Was he mistaken, or was Phy following his words with indications of a greater mental clarity than he had ever noted before, even in the relatively nonviolent World Secretary? Perhaps—he had often dreamed wistfully of the possibility—there was still a chance of saving Phy. Perhaps, if he just explained to him clearly and calmly—

"In my historical studies," he continued, "I soon came to the conclusion that the crucial period was that of the Final Amnesty, concurrent with the founding of the present world state. We are taught that at that time there were released from confinement millions of political prisoners—and millions of others. Just who were those others? To this question, our present histories gave only vague and platitudinous answers. The semantic difficulties I encountered were exceedingly obstinate. But I kept hammering away. Why, I asked myself, have such words as insanity, lunacy, madness, psychosis, disappeared from our vocabulary—and the concepts behind them from our thought? Why has the subject 'abnormal psychology' disappeared from the curricula of our schools? Of greater significance, why is our modern psychology strikingly similar to the field of abnormal psychology as taught in the twentieth century, and to that field alone? Why are there no longer, as there were in the twentieth century, any institutions for the confinement and care of the psychologically aberrant?"

Phy's head jerked up. He smiled twistedly. "Because," he whispered slyly, "everyone's insane now."

The cunning of the insane. Again that phrase loomed warningly in Carrsbury's mind. But only for a moment. He nodded.

"At first I refused to make that deduction. But gradually I reasoned out the why and wherefore of what had happened. It wasn't only that a highly technological civilization had subjected mankind to a wider and more swiftly tempoed range of stimulations, conflicting suggestions, mental strains, emotional wrenchings. In the literature of twentieth-century psychiatry there are observations on a kind of psychosis that results from success. An unbalanced individual keeps going so long as he is fighting something, struggling toward a goal. He reaches his goal—and goes to pieces. His repressed confusions come to the surface, he realizes that he doesn't know what he wants at all, his energies hitherto engaged in combatting something outside himself are turned against himself, he is destroyed. Well, when war was finally outlawed, when the whole world became one unified state, when social inequality was abolished . . . you see what I'm driving at?"

Phy nodded slowly. "That," he said in a curious, distant voice, "is a very interesting deduction."

"Having reluctantly accepted my main premise," Carrsbury went on, "everything became clear. The cyclic six-months' fluctuations in world credit—I realized at once that Morgenstern of Finance must be a manic-depressive with a six-months' phase, or else a dual personality with one aspect a spendthrift, the other a miser. It turned out to be the former. Why was the Department of Cultural Advancement stagnating? Because Manager Hobart was markedly catatonic. Why the boom in Extraterrestrial Research? Because McElvy was a euphoric."

Phy looked at him wonderingly. "But naturally," he said, spreading his lean hands, from one of which the gasoid dropped like a curl of green smoke.

Carrsbury glanced at him sharply. He replied, "Yes, I know that you and several of the others have a certain warped awareness of the differences between your . . . personalities, though none whatsoever of the basic aberration involved in them all. But to get on. As soon as I realized the situation, my course was marked out. As a sane man, capable of entertaining fixed realistic purposes, and surrounded by individuals of whose inconsistencies and delusions it was easy to make use, I was in a position to attain, with time and tact, any goal at which I might aim. I was already in the Managerial Service. In three years I became World Manager. Once there, my range of influence was vastly enhanced. Like the man in Archimedes' epigram, I had a place to stand from which I could move the world. I was able, in various guises and on various pretexts, to promulgate regulations the actual purpose of which was to soothe the great neurotic masses by curtailing upsetting stimulations and introducing a more regimented and orderly program of living. I was able, by humoring my fellow executives and making the fullest use of my greater capacity for work, to keep world affairs staggering along fairly safely—at least stave off the worst. At the same time I was able to begin my Ten Years' Plan—the training, in comparative isolation, first in small numbers, then in larger, as those instructed could in turn become instructors, of a group of prospective leaders carefully selected on the basis of their relative freedom from neurotic tendencies."

"But that—" Phy began rather excitedly, starting up.

"But what?" Carrsbury inquired quickly.

"Nothing," muttered Phy dejectedly, sinking back.

"That about covers it," Carrsbury concluded, his voice suddenly grown a little duller. "Except for one secondary matter. I couldn't afford to let myself go ahead without any protection. Too much depended on me. There was always the risk of being wiped out by some ill-coordinated but none the less effective spasm of violence, momentarily uncontrollable by tact, on the part of my fellow executives. So, only because I could see no alternative, I took a dangerous step. I created"—his glance strayed toward the faint crease in the side wall—"my secret police. There is a type of insanity known as paranoia, an exaggerated suspiciousness involving delusions of persecution. By means of the late-twentieth-century Rand technique of hypnotism, I inculcated a number of these unfortunate individuals with the fixed idea that their lives depended on me and that I was threatened from all sides and must be protected at all costs. A distasteful expedient, even though it served its purpose. I shall be glad, very glad, to see it discontinued. You can understand, can't you, why I had to take that step?"

He looked questioningly at Phy—and became aware with a shock that that individual was grinning at him vacuously and holding up the gasoid between two fingers.

"I cut a hole in my couch and a lot of this stuff came out," Phy explained in a thick naïve voice. "Ropes of it got all over my office. I kept tripping." His fingers patted at it deftly, sculpturing it into the form of a hideous transparent green head, which he proceeded to squeeze out of existence. "Queer stuff," he rambled on, "rarefied liquid. Gas of fixed volume. And all over my office floor, tangled up with the furniture."

Carrsbury leaned back and shut his eyes. His shoulders slumped. He felt suddenly a little weary, a little eager for his day of triumph to be done. He knew he shouldn't be despondent because he had failed with Phy. After all, the main victory was won. Phy was the merest of side issues. He had always known that, except for flashes, Phy was hopeless as the rest. Still—

"You don't need to worry about your office floor, Phy," he said with a listless kindliness. "Never any more. Your successor will have to see about cleaning it up. Already, you know, to all intents and purposes, you have been replaced."

"That's just it!" Carrsbury started at Phy's explosive loudness. The World Secretary jumped up and strode toward him, pointing an excited hand. "That's what I came to see you about! That's what I've been trying to tell you! I can't be replaced like that!

None of the others can, either! It won't work! You can't do it!"

With a swiftness born of long practice, Carrsbury slipped behind his desk. He forced his features into that expression of calm, smiling benevolence of which he had grown unutterably weary.

"Now, now, Phy," he said brightly, soothingly, "if I can't do it, of course I can't do it. But don't you think you ought to tell me why? Don't you think it would be very nice to sit down and talk it all over and you tell me why?"

Phy halted and hung his head, abashed.

"Yes, I guess it would," he said slowly, abruptly falling back into the low, effortful tones. "I guess I'll have to. I guess there just isn't any other way. I had hoped, though, not to have to tell you everything." The last sentence was half question. He looked up wheedlingly at Carrsbury. The latter shook his head, continuing to smile. Phy went back and sat down.

"Well," he finally began, gloomily kneading the gasoid, "it all began when you first wanted to be World Manager. You weren't the usual type, but I thought it would be kind of fun—yes, and kind of helpful." He looked up at Carrsbury. "You've really done the World a lot of good in quite a lot of ways, always remember that," he assured him. "Of course," he added, again focusing on the tortured gasoid, "they weren't exactly the ways you thought."

"No?" Carrsbury prompted automatically. *Humor him. Humor him.* The wornout refrain droned in his mind.

Phy sadly shook his head. "Take those regulations you promulgated to soothe people—"

"Yes?"

"—they kind of got changed on the way. For instance, your prohibition, regarding reading tapes, of all exciting literature . . . oh, we tried a little of the soothing stuff you suggested at first. Everyone got a great kick out of it. They laughed and laughed. But afterward, well, as I said, it kind of got changed—in this case to a prohibition of all *unexciting* literature."

Carrsbury's smile broadened. For a moment the edge of his mind had toyed with a fear, but Phy's last remark had banished it.

"Every day I coast past several reading stands," Carrsbury said gently. "The fiction tapes offered for sale are always in the most chastely and simply colored containers. None of those wild and lurid pictures that one used to see everywhere."

"But did you ever buy one and listen to it? Or project the visual text?" Phy questioned apologetically.

"For ten years I've been a very busy man," Carrsbury answered. "Of course I've read the official reports regarding such matters, and at times glanced through sample résumés of taped fiction."

"Oh, sure, that sort of official stuff," agreed Phy, glancing up at the wall of tape files beyond the desk. "What we did, you see, was to keep the monochrome containers but go back to the old kind of contents. The contrast kind of tickled people. Remember, as I said before, a lot of your regulations have done good. Cut out a lot of unnecessary noise and inefficient foolishness, for one thing."

That sort of official stuff. The phrase lingered unpleasantly in Carrsbury's ears. There was a trace of irrepressible suspicion in his quick over-the-shoulder glance at the tiered tape files.

"Oh, yes," Phy went on, "and that prohibition against yielding to unusual or indecent impulses, with a long listing of specific categories. It went into effect all right, but with a little rider attached: 'unless you really want to.' That seemed absolutely necessary, you know." His fingers worked furiously with the gasoid. "As for the prohibition of various stimulating beverages— well, in this locality they're still served under other names, and an interesting custom has grown up of behaving very soberly while imbibing them. Now when we come to that matter of the eight-hour working day—"

Almost involuntarily, Carrsbury had got up and walked over to the outer wall. With a flip of his hand through an invisible U-shaped beam, he switched on the window. It was as if the outer wall had disappeared. Through its near-perfect transparency, he peered down with fierce curiosity past the sleekly gleaming façades to the terraces and parkways below.

The modest throngs seemed quiet and orderly enough. But then there was a scurry of confusion—a band of people, at this angle all tiny heads with arms and legs, came out from a shop far below and began to pelt another group with what looked like foodstuffs.

While, on a side parkway, two small ovoid vehicles, seamless drops of silver because their vision panels were invisible from the outside, butted each other playfully. Someone started to run.

Carrsbury hurriedly switched off the window and turned around. Those were just off-chance occurrences, he told himself angrily. Of no real statistical significance whatever. For ten years mankind had steadily been trending toward sanity despite occasional relapses. He'd seen it with his own eyes, seen the day-by-day progress—at least enough to know. He'd been a fool to let Phy's ramblings affect him—only tired nerves had made that possible.

He glanced at his timepiece.

"Excuse me," he said curtly, striding past Phy's chair, "I'd like to continue this conversation, but I have to get along to the first meeting of the new Central Managerial Staff."

"Oh but you can't!" Instantly Phy was up and dragging at his arm. "You just can't do it, you know! It's impossible!"

The pleading voice rose toward a scream. Impatiently Carrsbury tried to shake loose. The seam in the side wall widened, became a doorway. Instantly both of them stopped struggling.

In the doorway stood a cadaverous giant of a man with a stubby dark weapon in his hand. Straggly black beard shaded into gaunt cheeks. His face was a cruel blend of suspicion and fanatical devotion, the first directed along with the weapon at Phy, the second—and the somnambulistic eyes—at Carrsbury.

"He was threatening you?" the bearded man asked in a harsh voice, moving the weapon suggestively.

For a moment an angry, vindictive light glinted in Carrsbury's eyes. Then it flicked out. What could he have been thinking, he asked himself. This poor lunatic World Secretary was no one to hate.

"Not at all, Hartman," he remarked calmly. "We were discussing something and we became excited and allowed our voices to rise. Everything is quite all right."

"Very well," said the bearded man doubtfully, after a pause. Reluctantly he returned his weapon to its holster, but he kept his hand on it and remained standing in the doorway.

"And now," said Carrsbury, disengaging himself, "I must go."

He had stepped onto the corridor slidewalk and had coasted halfway to the elevator before he realized that Phy had followed him and was plucking timidly at his sleeve.

"You can't go off like this," Phy pleaded urgently, with an apprehensive backward glance. Carrsbury noted that Hartman had also followed—an ominous pylon two paces to the rear. "You must give me a chance to explain, to tell you why, just like you asked me."

Humor him. Carrsbury's mind was deadly tired of the drone, but mere weariness prompted him to dance to it a little longer. "You can talk to me in the elevator," he conceded, stepping off the slidewalk. His finger flipped through a U-beam and a serpentine movement of light across the wall traced the elevator's obedient rise.

"You see, it wasn't just that matter of prohibitory regulations," Phy launched out hurriedly. "There were lots of other things that never did work out like your official reports indicated. Departmental budgets for instance. The reports showed, I know, that appropriations for Extraterrestrial Research were being regularly slashed. Actually, in your ten years of office, they increased tenfold. Of course, there was no way for you to know that. You couldn't be all over the world at once and see each separate launching of suprastratospheric rockets."

The moving light became stationary. A seam dilated. Carrsbury stepped into the elevator. He debated sending Hartman back. Poor babbling Phy was no menace. Still—*the cunning of the insane.* He decided against it, reached out and flipped the control beam at the sector which would bring them to the hundredth and top floor. The door snipped softly shut. The cage became a surging darkness in which floor numerals winked softly. Twenty-one. Twenty-two. Twenty-three.

"And then there was the Military Service. You had it sharply curtailed."

"Of course I did." Sheer weariness stung Carrsbury into talk. "There's only one country in the world. Obviously, the only military requirement is an adequate police force. To say nothing of the risks involved in putting weapons into the hands of the present world population."

"I know," Phy's answer came guiltily from the darkness. "Still, what's happened is that, unknown to you, the Military Service has been increased in size, and recently four rocket squadrons have been added."

Fifty-seven. Fifty-eight. *Humor him.* "Why?"

"Well, you see we've found out that Earth is being reconnoitered. Maybe from Andromeda. Maybe hostile. Have to be prepared. We didn't tell you . . . well, because we were afraid it might excite you."

The voice trailed off. Carrsbury shut his eyes. How long, he asked himself, how long? He realized with dull surprise that in the last hour people like Phy, endured for ten years, had become unutterably wearisome to him. For the moment even the thought of the conference over which he would soon be presiding, the conference that was to usher in a sane world, failed to stir him. Reaction to success? To the end of a ten years' tension?

"Do you know how many floors there are in this building?"

Carrsbury was not immediately conscious of the new note in Phy's voice, but he reacted to it.

"One hundred," he replied promptly.

"Then," asked Phy, "just where are we?"

Carrsbury opened his eyes to the darkness. One hundred twenty-seven, blinked the floor numeral. One hundred twenty-eight. One hundred twenty-nine.

Something cold dragged at Carrsbury's stomach, pulled at his brain. He felt as if his mind were being slowly and irresistibly twisted. He thought of hidden dimensions, of unsuspected holes in space. Something remembered from elementary physics danced through his thoughts: If it were possible for an elevator to keep moving upward with uniform acceleration, no one inside an elevator could determine whether the effects they were experiencing were due to acceleration or to gravity—whether the elevator were standing motionless on some planet or shooting up at ever-increasing velocity through free space.

One hundred forty-one. One hundred forty-two.

"Or as if you were rising through consciousness into an unsuspected realm of mentality lying above," suggested Phy in his new voice, with its hint of gentle laughter.

One hundred forty-six. One hundred forty-seven. It was slowing now. One hundred forty-nine. One hundred fifty. It had stopped.

This was some trick. The thought was like cold water in Carrsbury's face. Some cunning childish trick of Phy's. An easy thing to hocus the numerals. Carrsbury groped irascibly about in the darkness, encountered the slick surface of a holster, Hartman's gaunt frame.

"Get ready for a surprise," Phy warned from close at his elbow.

As Carrsbury turned and grabbed, bright sunlight drenched him, followed by a gripping, heart-stopping spasm of vertigo.

He, Hartman, and Phy, along with a few insubstantial bits of furnishings and controls, were standing in the air fifty stories above the hundred-story summit of World Managerial Center.

For a moment he grabbed frantically at nothing. Then he realized they were not falling and his eyes began to trace the hint of walls and ceiling and floor and, immediately below them, the ghost of a shaft.

Phy nodded. "That's all there is to it," he assured Carrsbury casually. "Just another of those charmingly odd modern notions against which you have legislated so persistently—like our incomplete staircases and roads to nowhere and those charming garden paths which ended in drops, not stairs, and the British called 'ha-has.' The Buildings and Grounds Committee decided to extend the range of the elevator for sightseeing purposes. The shaft was made air-transparent to avoid spoiling the form of the original building and to improve the view. This was achieved so satisfactorily that an electronic warning system had to be installed for the safety of passing airjets and other craft. Treating the surfaces of the cage like windows was an obvious detail."

He paused and looked quizzically at Carrsbury. "All very simple," he observed, "but don't you find a kind of symbolism in it? For ten years now you've been spending most of your life in that building below. Every day you've used this elevator. But not once have you dreamed of these fifty extra stories. Don't you think that something of the same sort may be true of your observations of other aspects of contemporary social life?"

Carrsbury gaped at him stupidly.

Phy turned to watch the growing speck of an approaching

aircraft. "You might look at it too," he remarked to Carrsbury, "for it's going to transport you to a far happier, more restful life."

Carrsbury parted his lips, wet them. "But—" he said, unsteadily. "But—"

Phy smiled. "That's right, I didn't finish my explanation. Well, you might have gone on being World Manager all your life, in the isolation of your office and your miles of taped official reports and your occasional confabs with me and the others. Except for your Institute of Political Leadership and your Ten-Years' Plan. That upset things. Of course, we were as much interested in it as we were in you. It had definite possibilities. We hoped it would work out. We would have been glad to retire from office if it had. But, most fortunately, it didn't. And that sort of ended the whole experiment."

He caught the downward direction of Carrsbury's gaze.

"No," he said, "I'm afraid your pupils aren't waiting for you in the conference chamber on the hundredth story. I'm afraid they're still in the Institute." His voice became gently sympathetic. "And I'm afraid that it's become . . . well . . . a somewhat different sort of institute."

Carrsbury stood very still, swaying a little. Gradually his thoughts and his will power were emerging from the waking nightmare that had paralyzed them. *The cunning of the insane*— he had neglected that trenchant warning. In the very moment of victory—

No! He had forgotten Hartman! This was the very emergency for which that counterstroke had been prepared.

He glanced sideways at the chief member of his secret police. The black giant, unconcerned by their strange position, was glaring fixedly at Phy as if at some evil magician from whom any malign impossibility could be expected.

Now Hartman became aware of Carrsbury's gaze. He divined his thought.

He drew his dark weapon from its holster, pointed it unwaveringly at Phy.

His black-bearded lips curled. From them came a hissing sound.

Then, in a loud voice, he cried, "You're dead, Phy! I disintegrated you."

Phy reached over and took the weapon from his hand.

"That's another respect in which you completely miscalculated the modern temperament," he remarked to Carrsbury, a shade argumentatively. "All of us have certain subjects on which we're a trifle unrealistic. That's only human nature. Hartman's was his suspiciousness—a weakness for ideas involving plots and persecutions. You gave him the worst sort of job—one that catered to and encouraged his weaknesses. In a very short time he became hopelessly unrealistic. Why, for years he's never realized that he's been carrying a dummy pistol.

"But," he added, "give him the proper job and he'd function well enough—say, something in creation or exploration or social service. Fitting the man to the job is an art with infinite possibilities. That's why we had Morgenstern in Finance—to keep credit fluctuating in a safe, predictable rhythm. That's why a euphoric is made manager of Extraterrestrial Research—to keep it booming. Why a catatonic is given Cultural Advancement—to keep it from tripping on its face in its haste to get ahead."

He turned away. Dully, Carrsbury observed that the aircraft was hovering close to the cage and sidling slowly in.

"But in that case why—" he began stupidly.

"Why were you made World Manager?" Phy finished easily. "Isn't that fairly obvious? Haven't I told you several times that you did a lot of good, indirectly? You interested us, don't you see? In fact, you were practically unique. As you know, it's our cardinal principle to let every individual express himself as he wants to. In your case, that involved letting you become World Manager. Taken all in all it worked out very well. Everyone had a good time, a number of constructive regulations were promulgated, we learned a lot—oh, we didn't get everything we hoped for, but one never does. Unfortunately, in the end, we were forced to discontinue the experiment."

The aircraft had made contact.

"You understand, of course, why that was necessary?" Phy continued hurriedly, as he urged Carrsbury toward the opening port. "I'm sure you must. It all comes down to a question of sanity. What is sanity—now, in the twentieth century, any time? Adherence to a norm. Conformity to certain basic conventions underlying all human conduct. In our age, departure from the norm has become the norm. Inability to conform has become the standard of conformity. That's quite clear, isn't it? And it enables you to understand, doesn't it, your own case and that of your protégés? Over a long period of years you persisted in adhering to a norm, in conforming to certain basic conventions. You were completely unable to adapt yourself to the society around you. You could only pretend—and your protégés wouldn't have been able to do even that. Despite your many engaging personal characteristics, there was obviously only one course of action open to us."

In the port Carrsbury turned. He had found his voice at last. It was hoarse, ragged. "You mean that all these years you've just been *humoring* me?"

The port was closing. Phy called, "There was an Oglala Sioux Indian named Crazy Horse. He licked Crook and he licked Custer. Don't think I'm underestimating your strength, Carrsbury."

As the aircraft edged out, he waved farewell with the blob of green gasoid.

"It'll be very pleasant where you're going," he shouted encouragingly. "Comfortable quarters, adequate facilities for exercise, and a complete library of twentieth-century literature to while away your time."

He watched Carrsbury's rigid face, staring whitely from the vision port, until the aircraft had diminished to a speck.

Then he turned away, looked at his hands, noticed the gasoid, tossed it out the open door of the cage, studied its flight for a few moments, then flicked the downbeam.

"I'm glad to see the last of that fellow," he muttered, more to himself than to Hartman, as they plummeted toward the roof. "He was beginning to have a very disturbing influence on me. In fact, I was beginning to fear for my"—his expression became suddenly vacuous—"insanity."

THE MEANING
OF THE WORD "IMPOSSIBLE"

Willy Ley

PHILADELPHIA, 1953

Willy Ley was one of that early band of rocket enthusiasts in Germany who dreamed of space travel when even the airplane was fantastic enough for most people. (A very junior member of that group was young Werner von Braun.) Unfortunately, for German rocketry and German science fiction, Ley had a distaste for dictators, and when it became clear that Hitler was no passing madness, Ley emigrated to the United States—very fortunately for Americans. Like most of the German rocketeers, Ley had been a long-time fan of science fiction. (During the war von Braun managed to keep up his subscription to Astounding *by having it forwarded from neutral Sweden.) As soon as Ley hit American shores, he borrowed a typewriter and began writing scientific articles, and now and then a story, for the sf magazines. His column* For Your Information *was the most popular single feature in* Galaxy, *and continued from its first issues until his death. He did not confine himself exclusively to science fiction. He was Walt Disney's technical advisor on Tomorrowland, author of any number of books and, for some years, science editor for the New York newspaper* PM. *(Which ran a regular picture feature by "Olga, PM's Exercise Girl," a ballerina who soon became Mrs. Willy Ley.)*

The 1953 Philadelphia convention made him its Guest of Honor in recognition of his services to science fiction. In recognition of his services to space travel he achieved a rather special honor: the International Astronomical Association named one of the craters of the moon "Ley."

THE story goes that the first steamship that crossed the Atlantic Ocean had a book on board in which it was proved that such a transatlantic crossing was impossible—on the ground that the ship could not carry the necessary amount of fuel.

I cannot be sure about this story—and I have not read the book in question; I don't even know its title—but I do have a book in my library (published in 1929) that shows that it is impossible for a rocket to attain the velocity of seven miles per second required to escape from the earth's gravitational field. The author of the book had carefully checked the energy content of all known fuels and high explosives and could show that none of them contained enough energy even to accelerate itself to escape velocity. Since the fuel could not even carry itself to that speed, how could anyone expect it to accelerate a rocket body and a payload too?

And then there was the French philosopher Auguste Comte, who wrote, "Astronomers can determine the shapes, distances, sizes and motions of planets and stars . . . but never, by any means, will we be able to study their chemical compositions . . ." For good measure, he added that "Every notion of the true mean temperature of the stars will necessarily always be concealed from us."

Of course steamships did cross the Atlantic, rockets impart

escape velocity to their payloads as a matter of course, and spectrum analysis—which does just what Comte declared to be impossible—was invented only a quarter of a century after his resounding declaration saw print.

On the other hand, let us consider the case of a loan between two friends whom we'll call Orlin and Mark. It is around the time of the year when the income tax falls due, and Orlin says to Mark: "I happen to be two hundred dollars short, but as you know I have a good job. Lend me the two hundred now so that I can clean up the tax bill. I'll return one hundred next payday to prove my goodwill; but then I'll be nearly broke, so on the following payday I'll only be able to give you fifty dollars. On the payday after that you'll get twenty-five dollars, and so forth, until the whole two hundred dollars has been paid off."

Mathematician Root has been a witness to the transaction and keeps quiet with some misgivings because he does not want to disturb their friendship. But he later repeats the story to his wife, saying that Mark will never get all of his two hundred dollars back, even if the agreement is kept to the letter. Mrs. Root, making a very rapid mental calculation, cannot see why not and says so. Doctor Root, in his very best classroom manner, explains that the agreement amounts to an infinite series—there will have to be another payment on every one of Orlin's paydays, even if both Orlin and Mark live forever. And Mrs. Root, who was willing to concede that Mark may not get all of his money back (for any number of reasons, including sickness, bankruptcy of Orlin's employer, or plain automobile accident), immediately turns around and says that she does not know what an infinite series is, but that it is clear that an infinite number of payments will add up to an infinite amount of money.

Of course if you have an infinite series in which the single "links," or "members," remain the same or even increase, the final result is bound to be infinite. But as this example shows, the final result is, in fact, less than two hundred dollars. It is quite likely that Mark, after the tenth payment, will consider the loan repaid, but the mathematician will still be correct in his declaration that it is impossible for Mark to get his entire two hundred dollars back in this manner. It does not matter that after, say, 15 payments, there is no coinage small enough to be used. Even if there were it would not work.

The rather finite result of an infinite series:

Amount of Loan	$200.00	
First payment		$100.00
Second payment		50.00
Third payment		25.00
Fourth payment		12.50
Fifth payment		6.25
Interim addition	$200.00	$193.75
	− 193.75	
Amount still to be paid:	$ 6.25	
Sixth payment		3.12\frac{1}{2}$
Seventh payment		1.56$\frac{1}{4}$
Eighth payment		0.78$\frac{1}{8}$
Ninth payment		0.39$\frac{1}{16}$
Tenth payment		0.19$\frac{17}{32}$
Interim addition	$6.25	6.05\frac{15}{32}$
Amount still to be paid	0.19\frac{17}{32}$	
Eleventh payment will be (Continue *ad libitum* and *ad infinitum!*)[1]		0.09\frac{49}{64}$

Obviously we are dealing with two kinds of "impossibles" here, but the solution happens to be quite simple. The "impossibilities" of the 4,000-mile voyage under steam, of the rocket that cannot reach escape velocity, and of Auguste Comte's statement are merely the result of careless assumptions coupled with sloppy

[1] That an infinite series can produce a finite result is most simply shown by the decimal equivalent of $\frac{1}{3}$, namely, 0.3 + 0.03 + 0.003 + 0.0003 + 0.00003 . . . , etc.

language. The man who "proved" that the steamship could not make the trip assumed, if I am correctly informed, that the steam engine would be fed with cordwood. Coal is different, and if one thinks of atomic fuel one man could carry enough to drive a passenger liner across the Atlantic, both ways. The man who calculated that the rocket could not reach escape velocity forgot that the fuel is *not* carried along but is left behind during the ascent. As for Auguste Comte, he made the "impossible" assumptions that no new inventions would come along and that no new discoveries would be made.

Of course it is impossible to travel from New York to Paris in seven hours by steamship. It is just like the objection of a Baltimore gentleman upon being told that the recently introduced telephone would enable him to speak with a friend in Washington from his own home. Having a speaking tube in mind, he declared that it is impossible to shout loud enough to be heard over this distance. True.

His remark sounds so silly to us now because he made the assumption that the telephone, like a speaking tube, carried the sound of his voice instead of a modulated electric current.[2]

Now, was the mathematician who said that Mark would never get all his money back just lucky with his "impossible"? No, and that is the difference to be explained. Those other impossibles were either based on plain mistakes (like the rocket calculation) or else on the assumption that the means and methods available at the moment were the only means and methods possible. But when a mathematician says "impossible," he does not speak about what

[2] That it is only too easy to make a ridiculous statement is illustrated by a story that was told to me by a retired German army officer in 1925. During World War I he had been the commander of a battery of heavy howitzers that had a maximum range of nine miles. One day he received a phone call from a staff officer who said that a cluster of French batteries had proved to be a major nuisance and that he, the staff officer, hereby authorized the expenditure of sixty heavy shells to end the existence of that French emplacement. The battery commander did not even have to look at a map; he knew all about the French position. He also knew that it was eleven miles from his own position and explained that it was impossible for his battery to carry out that order. The reply: "Well, if you say so, but one should think that with a little more dedication . . ." *Click.*

can be done at the moment, he is speaking about a *theoretical* impossibility. It is impossible that $15 + 16 = 43$ if you use our system of decimal numbers. There might be a number system where that equation makes sense—though I doubt it—in our own it is impossible.

The mathematician (discounting possible individual mistakes) says "impossible" only where the impossibility has been proved. Just as a chemist can say that it is impossible to oxidize carbon dioxide (CO_2) because in that compound the carbon atom is already holding all the oxygen atoms that it can hold, or as an electrical engineer will declare that it is impossible for the same electric current to have two different voltages at the same instant, so the mathematician has quite a number of cases where he can safely speak about a "mathematical impossibility."

SF, THE SPIRIT OF YOUTH

Frank R. Paul

NEW YORK, 1939

*1939 was the first Worldcon ever. I have a personal pique
about that convention, because with Donald A. Wollheim, Robert
W. Lowndes and a few others I helped to conceive and plan it.
Those were stormy days in science-fiction fandom, given to
vendettas and power struggles, and somehow or other, in the
course of a fan feud, our side lost out; the convention was held,
but none of us were allowed to attend it. It was a gala affair—so I
am told.*

    *And the Guest of Honor was the most uniquely famous artist
science fiction has ever produced. Frank R. Paul loved machines,
and loved to draw them. Hugo Gernsback discovered this about
him early on, and as exciting drawings of strange machinery were
what Hugo liked to publish in his magazines, Paul was Gernsback's principal artist for a couple of decades. He was probably the*

first human being ever to make a living drawing pictures of spaceships, and he did it so well and so persuasively that when in the last few years the human race came to build real spaceships, quite a few of them looked a lot like Frank R. Paul's illustrations.

To represent him in this collection, we have selected the speech he gave at that very first of all Worldcons.

FELLOW science-fiction fans: I am mighty glad to be here among as fine a crowd of live wires and go-getters that has ever assembled under one roof. I always pictured you science fans just as you are. Always ready for any adventure and to argue any question at the drop of a hat.

In every age there have been people whose natural inclination and curiosity urged them on to decipher and analyze the riddles of the universe, notwithstanding the sneers and jeers of the less active-minded. You see, in a well-ordered society you are suppose to think only the thoughts approved by contemporary authorities.

When the earth was considered flat, it was folly to think it otherwise, and to suggest that by some chance it might be round, was nothing less than blasphemy. And since the majority was of the "flat" opinion, inspired by the leading minds of the time, it was much easier, and less dangerous, to be on the jeering side than to profess rebellious ideas.

However, there were devil-may-care free-thinkers who had the audacity to question accepted "facts."

After many of these nebulous "facts" had been proven humbugs, people began to feel more and more tolerant of the rebels, and thanks to that tolerance, the world has seen more progress in research of all branches of science, and utilization of findings for the good of all mankind in the last fifty years than during the preceding five thousand years.

Two thousand years ago a meeting such as this, with all these rebellious, adventurous minds, would have been looked upon as a very serious psychological phenomenon, and the leaders would have been put in chains or at least burned at the stake. But today it may well be considered the healthiest sign of youthful, wide-awake minds—to discuss subjects far beyond the range of the average provincial mind.

The science-fiction fan may well be called the advance guard of progress. We are the fellows who are willing to give every new idea a chance for a tryout, without ridicule. We did not mind in the least to be called nuts and hams in the early days of radio, when we were literally relegated to the doghouse with our homemade squealing and yowling sets—but, oh boy, what a thrill when we got a few dots and dashes! We are the ones who popularized the new radio vocabulary.

To my mind, a science-fiction fan is intensely interested in everything going on around him, differing radically from his critic. His critic is hemmed in by a small provincial horizon of accepted orthodox and humdrum realities, and either does not dare or is too lazy to reach beyond that horizon. The science-fiction fan, on the other hand, has a horizon as big as the universe itself, and has been known to peek even beyond that—a fascinating hobby sharpening the imagination and incidentally absorbing a lot of knowledge—and familiarize himself with the scientific terms which so mystify his critics.

You have often heard them proudly proclaim: "Don't expect *me* to know any of that stuff" or "I don't want to know anything like that." Of course we have no quarrel with that kind of an individual, but it would be rather interesting to find out by what mental process he arrives at the conclusion that it's smart to be stupid.

The science-fiction fan is alive to every new development in every branch of science by hungrily reading everything printed about it. You cannot easily fool him on any subject. I am sure no fan was fooled when they pulled the Martian Invasion stunt over the radio.

To say that by reading science-fiction you become a believer in all sorts of supernatural things is like saying that by frequenting the movies you are bound to become a criminal.

Once in a while we also find eminent scientists throwing cold water on our enthusiasm, for instance, Dr. Robert A. Millikan the other day said we should stop dreaming about atomic power and solar power. Well, we love the doctor as one of our foremost scientists of the day, but that is no reason for us to give up hope that some scientist of the future might not attack the problem and ride it. What seems utterly impossible today may be commonplace tomorrow. I need not cite just such examples, as you know them possibly better than I do.

But I do want to illustrate what I mean. Just suppose for a moment that any of you could by some machine method return, say, only about two hundred years and visit one of the great miniature portrait painters and watch them work. You would naturally ask him how many of these exquisite portraits he can turn out in a day. You would be told that four or five is the absolute limit, providing the light is right, and so forth.

Now, if you should tell one of these speed masters that you, without being an artist, could produce a portrait, guaranteed likeness in every way, and not only of one person, but two, three, or a whole group of people in one-twenty-fifth part of a second, you would no doubt not only be laughed at, but very likely be hustled off to the eighteenth-century insane asylum.

The master would tell you that to pick up his brush would take longer than that, and he is quite right—the only way he could imagine of producing a portrait was the way he knew how. You can readily imagine his amazement if you showed him a photograph, and he would tell you, "Yes, but that is not painted." Of course not, but it's a portrait and more accurate than any portrait painter could paint. And so it is with most discoveries and inventions: it's the results that count.

The science-fiction fan's ideal is Dr. Arthur H. Campton, who sees all kind of forces in nature with exciting and thrilling possibilities which are waiting for discovery and exploration.

Science fiction is the spirit of youth, ever ready to plunge into the unknown for new adventures.

Science fiction is growing up. More and more people are becoming science-conscious by seeing scientific marvels in their daily life, and they can no longer ignore or scoff.

It gives me a lot of satisfaction and pride to be identified with the development of this thrilling and informative kind of reading.

During the past twenty years, which mark the beginning of science fiction in America, my work has been familiar to a great many of you, and I want to thank all of you for taking the lively interest in it which you have shown. I also want to thank you for the kind letters you have sent me and the editors. There have been bouquets and brickbats a-plenty.

Of course, to please everybody is one of the few things that even a science-fiction fan will admit is quite impossible. I have always tried to interpret what the author had in mind, but you'll admit I have never tried to scare you with the purely grotesque. I conclude with the conviction that in the future we will have bigger and better science fiction, with the accent on the science.

From *THE SKYLARK OF SPACE*

Edward Elmer Smith, Ph.D.

CHICAGO, 1940

The first writer ever made Guest of Honor at a World Science Fiction Convention was, by nearly unanimous consensus, the one who most deserved it. Doc Smith—no one, neither his wife and children nor the most casual acquaintance, ever called him anything but "Doc"—was the man who, single-handed, had created the whole interstellar-adventure field of science fiction, with the Skylark stories and the Lensman stories in all their dozen volumes.

Like most of the major science-fiction writers whose first story appeared in the decades after 1926 (when Amazing Stories *came out and introduced science fiction as a category of publishing), Doc Smith's growth as a writer was identified with the sf magazines. Unlike most of them, however, Smith didn't come across a science-fiction magazine and then decide to try to write something for it; he wrote* The Skylark of Space *in 1919, and let it gather dust in a desk drawer for nearly a decade until a magazine appeared that would publish it. Nearly everything he wrote was full book length; and so he is represented here not by a short story—which would have been thoroughly untypical of his work—but by an extract from his Skylark stories. They were the first things he wrote—and the last. We were in London at the 1965 convention when we got the cable announcing his death in California. The final installment of his last novel,* Skylark Du-Quesne, *was just appearing on the newsstands that month.*

THE MASTERY OF MIND OVER MATTER

THEY descended rapidly, directly over a large and imposing city in the middle of a vast, level, beautifully planted plain. While they were watching it the city vanished and the plain was transformed into a heavily timbered mountain summit, the valleys falling away upon all sides as far as the eye could reach.

"Well, I'll say that's *some* mirage!" exclaimed Seaton, rubbing his eyes in astonishment. "I've seen mirages before, but never anything like that. Wonder what this air's made of? But we'll land, anyway, if we finally have to swim!"

The ship landed gently upon the summit, the occupants half expecting to see the ground disappear before their eyes. Nothing happened, however, and they disembarked, finding walking somewhat difficult because of the great mass of the planet. Looking around, they could see no sign of life, but they *felt* a presence near them—a vast, invisible something.

Suddenly, out of the air in front of Seaton, a man materialized; a man identical with him in every detail, even to the smudge of grease under one eye, the small wrinkles in his heavy blue serge suit, and the emblem of the American Chemical Society which formed the pendant of his watch-fob.

"Hello, folks," the stranger began in Seaton's characteristic careless speech. "I see you're surprised at my knowing your language. You're a very inferior race of animals—don't even understand telepathy, don't understand the luminiferous ether, or the relation between time and space. Your greatest things, such as the Skylark and your object-compass, are merely toys."

Changing instantly from Seaton's form to that of Dorothy, likewise a perfect imitation, the stranger continued, without a break: "Atoms and electrons and things, spinning and whirling in their dizzy little orbits . . ." It broke off abruptly, continuing in the form of DuQuesne: "Couldn't make myself clear as Miss Vaneman—not a scientific convolution in her foolish little brain. You are a freer type, DuQuesne; unhampered by foolish, soft fancies. But you are very clumsy, although working fairly well with your poor tools—Brookings and his organization, the Perkins Cafe and its clumsy communications system. All of you are very low in the scale. You have millions of years to go before you will amount to anything; before you will even rise above death and its attendant necessity, sex."

The strange being then assumed form after form with bewildering rapidity, while the spectators stared in dumb astonishment. In rapid succession it took on the likeness of each member of the party, of the vessel itself, of a watch in Seaton's pocket; reappearing as Seaton.

"Well, bunch," it said in a matter-of-fact voice, "there's no mental exercise in you and you're such a low form of life that you're of no use on this planet; so I'll dematerialize you."

A peculiar light came into its eyes as they stared intently into Seaton's, and he felt his senses reel under the impact of an awful force, but he fought back with all his power and remained standing.

"What's this?" the stranger demanded in surprise. "This is the first time in thousands of millions of cycles that mere matter—which is only a manifestation of mind—has refused to obey mind. There's a screw loose somewhere.

"I must reason this out," it continued analytically, changing instantaneously into Crane's likeness. "Ah! I am not a perfect reproduction; there is some subtle difference. The external form is the same, the organic structure likewise. The molecules of substance are arranged as they should be, as are also the atoms in the molecule. The electrons in the atom—ah! There is the difficulty. The arrangement and number of electrons, as well as positive charges, are entirely different from what I had supposed. I must derive the formula."

"Let's go, folks!" said Seaton hastily, drawing Dorothy back toward the Skylark. "This dematerialization stunt may be play for him, but I don't want any of it in mine."

"No, you really *must* stay," remonstrated the stranger. "Much as it is against my principles to employ brute force, you must stay and be properly dematerialized, alive or dead. Science demands it."

As he spoke he started to draw his automatic pistol. Being in Crane's form he drew slowly, as Crane did; and Seaton, with the dexterity of much sleight-of-hand practice and of years of familiarity with his weapon, drew and fired simultaneously, before the other had withdrawn the pistol from his pocket. The X-plosive shell completely volatized the stranger and hurled the party backward toward the Skylark, into which they fled hastily. As Crane, the last one to enter the vessel, fired his pistol and closed the massive door, Seaton leaped to the levers. As he did so, he saw a creature materialize in the air of the vessel and fall to the floor with a crash as he threw on the power. It was a frightful thing, like nothing ever before seen upon any world; with great teeth, long, sharp claws, and an automatic pistol clutched firmly in a human hand. Forced flat by the acceleration of the vessel, it was unable to lift either itself or the weapon, and lay helpless.

"We take one trick, anyway," blazed Seaton, as he threw on the power of the attractor and diffused its force into a screen over the party, so that the enemy could not materialize in the air above them and crush them by mere weight. "As pure mental force you're entirely out of my class, but when you come down to matter which I can understand, I'll give you a run for your money until your ankles catch fire."

"That is a childish defiance. It speaks well for your courage, but ill for your intelligence," the animal said, and vanished.

A moment later Seaton's hair almost stood on end as he saw an automatic pistol appear upon the board directly in front of him, clamped to it by bands of steel. Paralyzed by this unlooked-for demonstration of the mastery of mind over matter, unable to move a muscle, he lay helpless, staring at the engine of death in front of him. Although the whole proceeding occupied only a fraction of a second, it seemed to Seaton as though he watched the weapon for hours as the sleeve drew back, cocking the pistol and throwing a cartridge into the chamber; the trigger moved; and the hammer descended to speed on its way the bullet which was to blot out his life. There was a sharp click as the hammer fell—Seaton was surprised to find himself still alive until a voice spoke, apparently from the muzzle of the pistol, with the harsh sound of a metallic diaphragm.

"I was almost sure that it wouldn't explode," the stranger said chattily. "You see, I haven't derived the formula yet, so couldn't make a real explosive. I could, of course, materialize beside you, under your protective screen, and crush you; or I could, by sufficient expenditure of energy, materialize a planet around your ship and crush it: but you have given me a great deal of mental exercise already, and in return I am going to give you one chance for your lives. I can't dematerialize either you or your vessel until I work out the formula for your peculiar atomic structure. If I can't derive the formula before you reach the boundaries of my home-space, beyond which I cannot go, I shall let you go free, without using brute force to stop you. Deriving the formula will be a nice little problem. It should be fairly easy, as it involves only a simple integration in ninety-seven dimensions."

Silence ensued, and Seaton advanced his lever to the limit of his ability to retain consciousness. Almost overcome by the horror of their position, in an agony of suspense, expecting every instant to be hurled into nothingness, he battled on, with no thought of yielding, even in the face of those overwhelming mental odds.

"You can't do it, old top," he thought savagely, concentrating all the power of his highly trained mind against the intellectual monster. "You can't dematerialize us, and you can't integrate above ninety dimensions to save your neck. You can't do it—you're all balled up right now."

For more than an hour the silent battle raged, during which time the Skylark flew millions and billions of miles toward Earth. Finally the stranger spoke again.

"You three win," it said abruptly. In answer to the unspoken surprise of all three men, it continued: "Yes, all three of you got the same idea and Crane even forced his body to retain consciousness to fight me. Your efforts were very feeble, but enough to interrupt my calculations at a delicate stage, every time. You are a low form of life, undoubtedly, but with more mentality than I supposed at first. I could get that formula, of course, in spite of you, if I had time, but we are rapidly approaching the limits of my territory, outside of which even I could not think my way back. That is one thing in which your mechanical devices are superior to anything my own race developed before we became pure intellectuals. They point the way back to your Earth, which is so far away that even my mentality cannot grasp the meaning of the distance. I can understand the Earth, can visualize it, from your minds, but I cannot project myself any nearer to it than we are at present. Before I leave you, I will say that you have conferred a real favor upon me—you have given me something to think about for thousands of cycles to come. Goodbye."

THE HURKLE IS A HAPPY BEAST

Theodore Sturgeon

CHICAGO, 1962

Theodore Sturgeon's first story appeared in the same year as the first Worldcon. He was one of that galaxy of great new writers John Campbell found and encouraged to fill the pages of Astounding *in that golden age long gone, and one of the greatest of them. I still remember the impact of* Killdozer *(recently made into a full-length film) and* Microcosmic God *and a dozen others in those early years, and any number of fine stories since.*

Sturgeon's convention was Chicon III. He had a suite, inhabited round the clock by himself, his guitar, his family—and at one time or another by nearly all of the thousand or so other people at the convention. About the only time it was empty was during the banquet, when Sturgeon made his Guest of Honor speech. There have been good GoH speeches and bad ones, funny ones, inspiring ones, scholarly ones, angry ones . . . but Ted Sturgeon's was

*surely the most warmly moving and touching speech ever made.
As befitted a writer who has—so he says—always written on a
single subject: love.*

*His story in this volume is, of course, also about love, although
an undirected and perhaps somewhat undesirable kind of love.
When it first appeared I read it while on vacation in Cape Cod,
and was moved to write Ted a comment in verse on the back of a
view of Provincetown:*

> *The hurkle is a happy beast.*
> *Its rays itch felon, foe and priest.*
> *How lucky for the happy hurkles*
> *They do not feel each other's spurkles.*

THIS all happened quite a long time ago . . .

Lirht is either in a different universal plane or in another island
galaxy. Perhaps these terms mean the same thing. The fact
remains that Lirht is a planet with three moons, one of which is
unknown, and a sun, which is as important in its universe as is
ours.

Lirht is inhabited by gwik, its dominant race, and by several
less highly developed species which, for purposes of this narrative,
can be ignored. Except, of course, for the hurkle. The hurkle are
highly regarded by the gwik as pets, in spite of the fact that a
hurkle is so affectionate that it can have no loyalty.

The prettiest of the hurkle are blue.

Now, on Lirht, in its greatest city, there was trouble, the nature
of which does not matter to us, and a gwik named Hvov, whom
you may immediately forget, blew up a building which was
important for reasons we cannot understand. This event caused
great excitement, and gwik left their homes and factories and
strubles and streamed toward the center of town, which is how a
certain laboratory door was left open.

In times of such huge confusion, the little things go on. During
the "Ten Days That Shook the World" the cafés and theaters of
Moscow and Petrograd remained open, people fell in love, sued

each other, died, shed sweat and tears; and some of these were tears of laughter. So on Lirht, while the decisions on the fate of the miserable Hvov were being formulated, gwik still fardled, funted, and fupped. The great central hewton still beat out its mighty pulse, and in the anams the corsons grew . . .

Into the above-mentioned laboratory, which had been left open through the circumstances described, wandered a hurkle kitten. It was very happy to find itself there; but then, the hurkle is a happy beast. It prowled about fearlessly—it could become invisible if frightened—and it glowed at the legs of the tables and at the glittering, racked walls. It moved sinuously, humping its back and arching along on the floor. Its front and rear legs were as stiff and straight as the legs of a chair; the middle pair had two sets of knees, one bending forward, one back. It was engineered as ingeniously as a scorpion, and it was exceedingly blue.

Occupying almost a quarter of the laboratory was a huge and intricate machine, unhoused, showing the signs of development projects the galaxies over—temporary hook-ups from one component to another, cables terminating in spring clips, measuring devices standing about on small tables near the main work. The kitten regarded the machine with curiosity and friendly intent, sending a wave of radiations outward which were its glow, or purr. It arched daintily around to the other side, stepping delicately but firmly on a floor switch.

Immediately there was a rushing, humming sound, like small birds chasing large mosquitoes, and parts of the machine began to get warm. The kitten watched curiously, and saw, high up inside the clutter of coils and wires, the most entrancing muzziness it had ever seen. It was like heat flicker over a fallow field; it was like a smoke vortex; it was like red neon lights on a wet pavement. To the hurkle kitten's senses, that red-orange flicker was also like the smell of catnip to a cat, or anise to a terrestrial terrier.

It reared up toward the glow, hooked its forelegs over a bus bar—fortunately there was no ground potential—and drew itself upward. It climbed from transformer to power pack, skittered up a variable condenser—the setting of which was changed thereby —disappeared momentarily as it felt the bite of a hot tube, and finally teetered on the edge of the glow.

The glow hovered in mid-air in a sort of cabinet, which was surrounded by heavy coils embodying tens of thousands of turns of small wire and great loops of bus. One side, the front, of the cabinet was open, and the kitten hung there fascinated, rocking back and forth to the rhythm of some unheard music it made to contrast this sourceless flame. Back and forth, back and forth it rocked and wove, riding a wave of delicious, compelling sensation. And once, just once it moved its center of gravity too far from its point of support. Too far—far enough. It tumbled into the cabinet, into the flame.

One muggy mid-June day a teacher, whose name was Stott and whose duties were to teach seven subjects to forty moppets in a very small town, was writing on a blackboard. He was writing the word Madagascar, and the air was so sticky and warm that he could feel his undershirt pasting and unpasting itself on his shoulderblade with each round "a" he wrote.

Behind him there was a sudden rustle from the moist seventh-graders. His schooled reflexes kept him from turning from the board until he had finished what he was doing, by which time the room was in a young uproar. Stott about-faced, opened his mouth, closed it again. A thing like this would require more than a routine reprimand.

His forty-odd charges were writhing and squirming in an extraordinary fashion, and the sound they made, a sort of whimpering giggle, was unique. He looked at one pupil after another. Here a hand was busily scratching a nape; there a boy was digging guiltily under his shirt; yonder a scrubbed and shining damsel violently worried her scalp.

Knowing the value of individual attack, Stott intoned, "Hubert, what seems to be the trouble?"

The room immediately quieted, though diminished scrabblings continued. "Nothin', Mister Stott," quavered Hubert.

Stott flicked his gaze from side to side. Wherever it rested, the scratching stopped and was replaced by agonized control. In its wake was rubbing and twitching. Stott glared, and idly thumbed a lower left rib. Someone snickered. Before he could identify the source, Stott was suddenly aware of an intense itching. He checked the impulse to go after it, knotted his jaw, and swore to himself that he wouldn't scratch as long as he was out there, front and center. "The class will—" he began tautly, and then stopped.

There was a—a *something* on the sill of an open window. He blinked and looked again. It was a translucent, bluish cloud which was almost nothing at all. It was less than a something should be, but it was indeed more than a nothing. If he stretched his imagination just a little, he might make out the outlines of an arched creature with too many legs; but of course that was ridiculous.

He looked away from it and scowled at his class. He had had two unfortunate experiences with stink bombs, and in the back of his mind was the thought of having seen once, in a trick-store window, a product called "itching powder." Could this be it, this terrible itch? He knew better, however, than to accuse anyone yet; if he was wrong, there was no point in giving the little geniuses any extracurricular notions.

He tried again. "The cl—" He swallowed. This itch was . . . "The class will—" He noticed that one head, then another and another, was turning toward the window. He realized that if the class got too interested in what he thought he saw on the window sill, he'd have a panic on his hands. He fumbled for his ruler and rapped twice on the desk. His control was not what it should have been at the moment; he struck far too hard, and the reports were like gunshots. The class turned to him as one, and behind them the thing on the window sill appeared with great distinctness.

It was blue—a truly beautiful blue. It had a small spherical head and an almost identical knob at the other end. There were four stiff, straight legs, a long, sinuous body, and two central limbs with a boneless look about them. On the side of the head were four pairs of eyes, of graduated sizes. It teetered there for perhaps ten seconds, and then, without a sound, leaped through the window and was gone.

Mr. Stott, pale and shaking, closed his eyes. His knees trembled and weakened, and a delicate, dewy mustache of perspiration appeared on his upper lip. He clutched at the desk and forced his eyes open; and then, flooding him with relief, pealing into his terror, swinging his control back to him, the bell rang to end the class and the school day.

"Dismissed," he mumbled, and sat down. The class picked up and left, changing itself from a twittering pattern of rows to a rowdy kaleidoscope around the bottleneck doorway. Mr. Stott slumped down in his chair, noticing that the dreadful itch was gone, had been gone since he had made that thunderclap with the ruler.

Now, Mr. Stott was a man of method. Mr. Stott prided himself on his ability to teach his charges to use their powers of observation and all the machinery of logic at their command. Perhaps, then, he had more of both at his command—after he recovered himself—than could be expected of an ordinary man.

He sat and stared at the open window, not seeing the sunswept lawns outside. And after going over these events a half-dozen times, he fixed on two important facts:

First, that the animal he had seen, or thought he had seen, had six legs.

Second, that the animal was of such a nature as to make anyone who had not seen it believe he was out of his mind.

These two thoughts had their corollaries:

First, that every animal he had ever seen which had six legs was an insect.

Second, that if anything was to be done about this fantastic creature, he had better do it by himself. And whatever action he took must be taken immediately. He imagined the windows being kept shut to keep the thing out—in this heat—and he cowered away from the thought. He imagined the effect of such a monstrosity if it bounded into the midst of a classroom full of children in their early teens, and he recoiled. No, there could be no delay in this matter.

He went to the window and examined the sill. Nothing. There was nothing to be seen outside, either. He stood thoughtfully for a moment, pulling on his lower lip and thinking hard. Then he went downstairs to borrow five pounds of DDT powder from the janitor for an "experiment." He got a wide, flat wooden box and an electric fan, and set them up on a table he pushed close to the window. Then he sat down to wait, in case, just in case the blue beast returned.

When the hurkle kitten fell into the flame, it braced itself for a fall at least as far as the floor of the cabinet. Its shock was tremendous, then, when it found itself so braced and already resting on a surface. It looked around, panting with fright, its invisibility reflex in full operation.

The cabinet was gone. The flame was gone. The laboratory with its windows, lit by the orange Lirhtian sky, its ranks of shining equipment, its hulking, complex machine—all were gone.

The hurkle kitten sprawled in an open area, a sort of lawn. No colors were right; everything seemed half-lit, filmy, out of focus. There were trees, but they were not low and flat and bushy like honest Lirhtian trees; these had straight naked trunks and leaves like a portle's tooth. The different atmospheric gases had colors; clouds of fading, changing faint colors obscured and revealed everything. The kitten twitched its cafmors and ruddled its kump, right there where it stood, for no amount of early training could overcome a shock like this.

It gathered itself together and tried to move, and then it got its second shock. Instead of arching over inchworm-wise, it floated into the air and came down three times as far as it had ever jumped in its life.

It cowered on the dreamlike grass, darting glances all about, under, and up. It was lonely and terrified and felt very much put upon. It saw its shadow through the shifting haze, and the sight terrified it even more, for it had no shadow when it was frightened on Lirht. Everything here was all backwards and wrong way up; it got more visible, instead of less, when it was frightened; its legs didn't work right, it couldn't see properly, and there wasn't a single, solitary malapek to be throdded anywhere. It thought some music; happily, that sounded all right inside its round head, though somehow it didn't resonate as well as it had.

It tried, with extreme caution, to move again. This time its trajectory was shorter and more controlled. It tried a small, grounded pace, and was quite successful. Then it bobbed for a moment, seesawing on its flexing middle pair of legs, and, with utter abandon, flung itself skyward. It went up perhaps fifteen feet, turning end over end, and landed with its stiff forefeet in the turf.

It was completely delighted with this sensation. It gathered itself together, gryting with joy, and leaped up again. This time it made more distance than altitude, and bounced two long, happy bounces as it landed.

Its fears were gone in the exploration of this delicious new freedom of motion. The hurkle, as has been said before, is a happy beast. It curveted and sailed, soared and somersaulted, and at last brought up against a brick wall with stunning and unpleasant results. It was learning, the hard way, a distinction between weight and mass. The effect was slight but painful. It drew back and stared forlornly at the bricks. Just when it was beginning to feel friendly again . . .

It looked upward, and saw what appeared to be an opening in the wall some eight feet above the ground. Overcome by a spirit of high adventure, it sprang upward and came to rest on a window sill—a feat of which it was very proud. It crouched there, preening itself, and looked inside.

It saw a most pleasing vista. More than forty amusingly ugly animals, apparently imprisoned by their lower extremities in individual stalls, bowed and nodded and mumbled. At the far end of the room stood a taller, more slender monster with a naked head—naked compared with those of the trapped ones, which were covered with hair like a mawson's egg. A few moments' study showed the kitten that in reality only one side of the heads was hairy; the tall one turned around and began making tracks in the end wall, and its head proved to be hairy on the other side too.

The hurkle kitten found this vastly entertaining. It began to radiate what was, on Lirht, a purr, or glow. In this fantastic place it was not visible; instead, the trapped animals began to respond with most curious writhings and squirmings and susurrant rubbings of their hides with their claws. This pleased the kitten even more, for it loved to be noticed, and it redoubled the glow. The receptive motions of the animals became almost frantic.

Then the tall one turned around again. It made a curious sound or two. Then it picked up a stick from the platform before it and brought it down with a horrible crash.

The sudden noise frightened the hurkle kitten half out of its wits. It went invisible; but its visibility system was reversed here, and it was suddenly outstandingly evident. It turned and leaped outside, and before it reached the ground, a loud metallic shrilling pursued it. There were gabblings and shufflings from the room which added force to the kitten's consuming terror. It scrambled to a low growth of shrubbery and concealed itself among the leaves.

Very soon, however, its irrepressible good nature returned. It lay relaxed, watching the slight movement of the stems and leaves—some of them may have been flowers—in a slight breeze. A winged creature came humming and dancing about one of the blossoms. The kitten rested on one of its middle legs, shot the other out, and caught the creature in flight. The thing promptly jabbed the kitten's foot with a sharp black probe. This the kitten ignored. It ate the thing, and belched. It lay still for a few minutes, savoring the sensation of the bee in its clarfel. The experiment was suddenly not a success. It ate the bee twice more and then gave it up as a bad job.

It turned its attention again to the window, wondering what those racks of animals might be up to now. It seemed very quiet up there . . . Boldly the kitten came from hiding and launched itself at the window again. It was pleased with itself; it was getting quite proficient at precision leaps in this mad place. Preening itself, it balanced on the window sill and looked inside.

Surprisingly, all the smaller animals were gone. The larger one was huddled behind the shelf at the end of the room. The kitten and the animal watched each other for a long moment. The animal leaned down and stuck something into the wall.

Immediately there was a mechanical humming sound and something on a platform near the window began to revolve. The next thing the kitten knew it was enveloped in a cloud of pungent dust.

It choked and became as visible as it was frightened, which was very. For a long moment it was incapable of motion; gradually, however, it became conscious of a poignant, painfully penetrating sensation which thrilled it to the core. It gave itself up to the feeling. Wave after wave of agonized ecstasy rolled over it, and it began to dance to the waves. It glowed brilliantly, though the emanation served only to make the animal in the room scratch hysterically.

The hurkle felt strange, transported. It turned and leaped high into the air, out from the building.

Mr. Stott stopped scratching. Disheveled indeed, he went to the window and watched the odd sight of the blue beast, quite invisible now, but coated with dust, so that it was like a bubble in a fog. It bounced across the lawn in huge floating leaps, leaving behind it diminishing patches of white powder in the grass. He smacked his hands one on the other and, smirking, withdrew to straighten up. He had saved the earth from battle, murder, and bloodshed forever, but he did not know that. No one ever found out what he had done. So he lived a long and happy life.

And the hurkle kitten?

It bounded off through the long shadows, and vanished in a copse of bushes. There it dug itself a shallow pit, working drowsily, more and more slowly. And at last it sank down and lay motionless, thinking strange thoughts, making strange music, and racked by strange sensations. Soon even its slightest movements ceased, and it stretched out stiffly, motionless . . .

For about two weeks. At the end of that time, the hurkle, no longer a kitten, was possessed of a fine, healthy litter of just under two hundred young. Perhaps it was the DDT, and perhaps it was the new variety of radiation that the hurkle received from the terrestrial sky, but they were all parthenogenetic females, even as you and I.

And the humans? Oh, we *bred* so! And how happy we were!

But the humans had the slidy itch, and the scratchy itch, and the prickly or tingly or titillative paresthetic formication. And there wasn't a thing they could do about it.

So they left.

Isn't this a lovely place?

ABDICATION

A. E. Van Vogt and E. Mayne Hull

LOS ANGELES, 1946

Los Angeles in 1946 was the first world convention after the layoff of World War II; and it was also the first to have not one, but two, Guests of Honor. It was not merely that E. Mayne Hull was less formally known as Mrs. A. E. Van Vogt; they were not just husband and wife, they were collaborators on the startlingly original kind of science-fiction stories that the two of them, and nobody else, produced in such huge and pleasant volume in almost every issue of Astounding.

Sometimes they wrote together, sometimes separately. When they collaborated, the results might appear under either name, or both. Their collaboration endured until Mayne's tragic death, while this book was in preparation.

THE big man came aboard the space liner from one of the obscure planets in that group of stars known as the Ridge.

The Ridge is not visible as such from Earth. It lies well to the "upper" edge of the Milky Way; and the long, jerky line of stars that compose it point *at* Earth, thus showing as a little, bright cluster in an Earth telescope. Seen from Kidgeon's Blackness, far to the right, the Ridge stands out beautifully clear, one of the more easily distinguishable guidemarks in our Galaxy.

The area is not well serviced. Once a week an interstellar liner flashes down the row of stars, stopping off according to advance notices received from its agents on the several score little-known planets. On reaching the edge of the Ridge, the ship heads for the central communication center, Dilbau III, where transfer is made to the great ships that traffic to distant Earth.

The entire trip requires about three weeks; and anyone who moved around as much as I did soon learned that the most interesting part of the journey is watching the passengers who get on and off at the way ports.

That's how I came to see the big man as soon as I did.

Even before he came aboard from the surface craft that had flashed up to where we lay about a hundred thousand miles above the planet, I could see that the new passenger was *somebody*.

It was his luggage, case after case of it being hoisted by the cranes, which gave that information. Beside me, a ship's officer gasped to a fellow officer: "Good heavens, that's ninety tons of the stuff so far!"

That made me straighten up with interest. They don't allow freight on these liners; and ninety tons makes up a lot of personal belongings. The officer spoke again: "It's the permanent move, looks like to me. Somebody's made his pile, and he's going home to Earth. Look! It's Jim Rand."

It was.

I have a little theory of my own about legendary men of space like Jim Rand. It's their reputations that enable them to accomplish their greatest and most widely publicized coups.

Initial momentum is necessary, naturally, and boundless energy and courage, but that only makes millions. It's reputation that pushes such men into the billion stellar class.

Jim Rand's deep, familiar voice broke my reverie: "Hello, there," he said. "I believe I know you, but I can't place you."

He had stopped a few feet from where I stood, and was staring at me.

He was a man of about fifty, with a small mustache, and a nose that looked as if it had been broken, and then repaired under emergency conditions. That slight twist in it didn't hurt his looks any, rather it added a curious strength to the muscular lines of his face. His eyes were blue-green, bright now with puzzlement.

I knew exactly how he was feeling. People whom I've met, and meet again later, always wonder whether or not they know me; and sometimes they become very exasperated with their memories. It's up to me, then, to recall the occasion. Sometimes, I do that; sometimes I don't.

I said now: "Yes, Mr. Rand, I was introduced to you by a mutual friend when you were organizing the Wild Mines of Guurdu. Your mind was probably on more weighty matters at the time. My name is Delton—Chris Delton."

His gaze was curiously steady. "Maybe," he said finally. "But I don't think I'd forget a man of your appearance."

I shrugged. They always say that. I saw that his face was clearing.

"Will you meet me in the lounge in about an hour?" he said. "Perhaps we can talk."

I nodded. "Happy to."

I watched him walk off along the brilliantly lighted corridor, redcaps wheeling several trunks and bags after his tall, powerful form.

He did not look back.

Beneath my feet I could feel the shudder of engines. The great ship was getting under way.

"Yes," said Jim Rand an hour and a half later, "I'm through, I'm retiring, quitting for good. No more wildcat stuff. I've bought an estate; I'm going to get married, have some children and settle down."

We were sitting in the lounge, and we had become more

friendly than I had thought possible. The great, glittering room was practically deserted, nearly everybody having answered the first call for dinner.

I said: "I don't wish to seem a cynic, but you know the old story: All this out here, these untamed planets, the measureless wealth, the dark vastness of space itself—it's supposed to get into a man's blood."

I finished as coolly as I could: "Actually, the most important thing in your life at the moment is that at least two, possibly four, men have been watching you for the past three minutes."

"Yes," said Jim Rand. "I know. They've been there since we came in."

"Do you know them?"

"Never saw them before in my life." He shrugged. "And I don't give a damn either. Five years ago, even last year, I might have got myself excited about the possibilities. Not now. I'm through. My mind is made up. I've laid my plans."

He settled back in the lounge chair, a big, alert man, smiling at me with a faint, amused expression in his eyes.

"I'm glad you were aboard," he said, "though I still can't remember our last meeting. It would have been boring alone with all these little minds."

He waved a great hand with a generous gesture that took in half the ship. I couldn't suppress a smile. I said: "Boredom—there'll be plenty of that on Earth for a man of action. The place is closed in by the damnedest laws—all kinds of queer regulations about not carrying energy guns—and if anybody bothers you, or starts trouble, you've got to settle it in court. Why, do you know, they sentence you to jail simply for owning an invisibility suit?"

Rand smiled lazily. "That won't bother me. I gave all mine away."

I stared at him, frowning. "You know," I said finally, "I've found that trouble never asks whether it's welcome or not. Don't look now, but somebody's just got out of the elevator, and is coming toward you."

I finished: "If you need any help, just call on me."

"Thank you," said Jim Rand. He smiled his lazy smile, but I

could see the gathering alertness in him. "I usually handle my own trouble."

It was I who had the vantage point. I was facing the elevator. Rand was sitting sidewise to it; and, superb actor that he was, he did not deign to glance around, or so much as flick an eyelash.

I studied the stranger who was approaching without looking at him directly. His eyes, I saw, were dark in color, rather close-set behind a long, thin nose. It was a wolfish face thus set off, with thin, cruel lips and a receding chin that yet gave no suggestion of weakness. The man eased his lank body into the lounge beside Rand.

Ignoring me, he said: "We might as well understand each other."

If Rand was startled by that, there was no indication on his face. He smiled, then pursed his lips.

"By all means," he said. "Misunderstandings are bad, bad."

He clicked his tongue sadly, as if the memory of past misunderstandings and resultant tragedies was passing through his mind. It was magnificently done, and I could not restrain a thrill of admiration.

"You are meddling in something which is no business of yours."

Rand nodded thoughtfully to that, and I could see that the movement was more than an actor's gesture. It must be occurring to him by now that he had better put some thought to such an open threat.

His voice was light, however, as he said: "Now, there, you have touched on one of my pet subjects—business ethics."

The man's dark-brown eyes flamed. He spat his words: "We have already been compelled to kill three men. I am sure, *Mr. Blord*, you would not want to be the fourth."

That startled Rand. His eyes widened; and there was no doubt that he was shocked at the discovery that he was being mistaken for someone else, particularly *that* someone.

I don't know whether I'm qualified to speak about Artur Blord.

He's simply one of several dozen similar types of men who made the Ridge their stamping ground. Cities spring up where the heavy hand of their money points. And that brings more money, which they concentrate elsewhere.

Blord differed from the others only in that he was a mystery, and few people had ever seen him. For some reason, this added to his reputation, so much so that I have heard people speak about him in hushed whispers.

The shock faded from Rand's face. His eyes narrowed. He said coldly: "If there must be a fourth dead man, I assure you it won't be me."

The wolf-faced man actually changed color. That's what reputation can do. He said hastily, his tone conciliatory: "There's no reason for us to be fighting. There're nine of us now, all good men that even you, Blord, cannot afford to antagonize. I should have known I couldn't scare you. Here's our real proposition: We'll give you ten million stellors, payable in cash, *within an hour,* provided you sign an agreement stating that you will NOT get off this ship tomorrow at Zand."

He leaned back. "Now, isn't that a fair and square offer?"

"Perfectly," said Rand, emphatically, "perfectly fair."

"Then you'll do it!"

"No!" said Jim Rand. And moved his right arm about a foot. It was a long distance for that powerful arm to gather momentum; and its effect was comparatively devastating.

"I don't like," said Jim Rand, "people who threaten me."

The man was moaning, clutching at his broken nose. He stumbled blindly to his feet and headed for the elevator. His four companions gathered around him, and they all vanished into the glistening interior.

As soon as the elevator door closed, Rand whirled on me. "Did you get that?" he said. "Blord! Artur Blord is mixed up in this. Do you realize what it could mean? He's the biggest operator on this side of Dilbau III. He's got a technique for using other men that's absolutely the last word. I've always wanted to stack up against him but—"

He stopped, then hissed: "Wait here!"

He walked swiftly toward the elevator, stood for a moment staring at the floor indicator of the machine the others had taken, then climbed into the adjoining lift. Ten minutes later, he settled softly in the seat he had left. "Have you ever seen a wounded nid?" he said exultantly. "It heads straight for home without regard to the trail it may leave."

There was bright fire in his gaze, as he went on briskly: "The chap whom I hit is called Tansey; and he and his gang have taken Apartments 300–308. The outfit must be new to the Ridge stars. Proof is they mistook a person as well known as I am for Blord. They—"

Rand stopped short there. He looked at me sharply. "What's the matter?"

"I'm thinking," said I, "of a man who's retiring; his plans are all made, estate, wife, children—"

"Oh!" said Jim Rand.

The glow faded from his eyes. Some of the life went out of him. He sat very still frowning; and I didn't have to be a mind reader to see the struggle that was taking place in his mind.

At last, he laughed ruefully, "I *am* through," he said. "It's true I forgot myself for a moment, but I must expect occasional lapses. My will remains unalterable."

He paused; then: "Will you have dinner with me?"

I said: "I had dinner served in my apartment before I came to meet you."

"Well, then," he persisted, "how about coming up to my rooms a couple of hours from now?" He smiled. "I can see you're skeptical about me, and so you may be interested in proof that I'm really in earnest. I've got the presidential suite, by the way. Will you come?"

"Why, sure," I said. I sat watching him walk off toward the dining room.

It was half-past eight—all these stellar ships are operated on Earth time—when Rand opened the door for me, and led me into his living room. The whole room was littered with three-dimensional maps, each in its long case; and I was familiar enough with the topography that was visible to recognize the planet Zand II.

Rand looked at me quickly, laughed and said: "Don't get any wrong ideas. I'm not planning anything. I'm merely curious about the situation on Zand."

I looked at him carefully. He had seated himself; and he seemed at ease, casual, without a real worry in him. I said, finally: "I wouldn't dismiss the matter as readily as that. Remember, you didn't invite their attention in the first place; they're not liable to wait for future invitations, either."

Rand waved an impatient arm. "To hell with them. They'll be off the ship in fifteen hours."

I said slowly: "You may not realize it, but your position in relation to such men is different than it's ever been. For the first time in your existence, you're thinking in terms of your personal future.

"In the past, death was an incident, and, if necessary you were ready to accept it. Wasn't that the general philosophy?"

Rand was scowling: "What are you getting at?"

"You can't afford to take any chances. I'm going to suggest that I go to Apartment 300, and tell them who you are."

Rand's gaze was suspicious. "Are you kidding?" he said. "Do you think I'm going to eat dirt for a bunch of cheap crooks? If I have to handle them, I'll do it my way."

He shrugged. "But never mind. I can see you mean well. Take a look at this, will you?"

He indicated one of the long map plates, on which showed a section of the third continent of the planet Zand II. His finger touched a curling tongue of land that jutted into the Sea of Iss. I nodded questioningly, and he went on: "Last time I was on Zand, they were building a city there. It was mostly tents, with a population of about a hundred thousand, about three hundred murders a week, and atomic engineering was just coming in. That was six years ago."

"I was there last year," I said. "The population then was a million. There are twenty-seven skyscrapers of fifty to a hundred stories, and everything was built of the indestructible plastics. The city is called Grenville after—"

Rand cut me off grimly. "I know him. He used to work for me, and I had a run-in with him when I was on Zand. Had to leave fast at the time because I was busy elsewhere, and because he had the power."

A thoughtful frown creased his face. "I always intended to go back."

I nodded. "I know. Unfinished business."

He started to nod to that. And then he sat up and stared at me. I was absolutely amazed at the passion that flared in his voice, as he raged: "If I went around fishing up all the business I've started, and paying off all the ingrates, I'd still be here a thousand years from now."

His anger faded. He looked at me sheepishly. "I beg your pardon."

There was silence. Finally, Rand mused: "So there're a million people there now. Where the devil do they all come from?"

"Not on these liners," I said. "It's too expensive. They come packed into small freighters, men and women crowded together in the same rooms."

Rand nodded. "I'd almost forgotten. That's the way I came. You'd think it was romantic to hear some people talk. It's not. I've had my skinful of frontier stuff. I'm settling in one of the garden cities of Earth in a fifteen-million-stellor palace with a wife that will—"

He broke off. His eyes lighted. "That's what I want to show you," he said. "My future home, my future wife."

Rand led the way into the second sitting room—the lady's sitting room, it's called in the circulars—and I saw with surprise that he had had a screen fitted up against a wall and there was a compact projector standing on the table.

Rand switched off the lights and turned on the projector. A picture flashed on the screen, the picture of a palatial house.

The first look made me whistle. I couldn't help it. They say that men don't dream of homes, but if ever anything looked like a dream come alive, this was it. There was a flow in the design, and a sense of space. I can't just describe that. The mansion actually looked smaller than it was; it seemed like a jewel in its garden setting, a white jewel glittering in the sun.

There was a click; the picture faded from the screen, and Rand said slowly: "That's the house, built, paid for, fully staffed. Am I committed, or am I not?"

In the half darkness, I said: "It can't possibly cost more than a million stellors a year to maintain. Say, another million to operate a space yacht and to cover the overhead of watching your holdings. Your share of the Guurdu Mines alone will pay for it all ten times over."

A light blinked on; and I saw that Rand was glaring at me. "You're hard to convince," he said.

"I know the hold," I said, "that the Ridge stars get on a man."

He leaned back, relaxing. "All right, I'll admit everything you say. But I'm going to show you something now that you can't set up against a money value."

He reached toward a table on which lay some X-ray plates. I had noticed them before. Now, Rand picked up the top one and handed it to me. It was one of a woman's spine. Beside it, on the plate was written in some species of white ink:

> Dear Jim:
>   The most perfect spine I have ever seen in a woman. When you consider that her I.Q. is 140, the answer is: don't let her get away. With the right father, her children will all be super.
>
>   Karn Grayson, M.D.

"Is that the woman?" I asked.

"That's she." I could see that he was looking at me sharply, studying my face. "I've got more plates here, but I'm not going to show them to you. They simply prove that she's physically perfect. I've never met her personally, of course. My agents advertised discreetly, and among all the trashy women who answered was this marvel."

In my life, in conversation with strong men, I've never been anything but frank. "I'm wondering," I said steadily, "about the kind of woman who sends her specification like a prize animal."

"I wondered about that, too," said Jim Rand. "But I'll show you."

He did.

There will always be women like Gady Mellerton, I suppose, but not many. They're scattered here and there through time and space; and each time the mold is destroyed, and must be painstakingly re-created. Invariably, they know their worth, and have no intention of wasting themselves on little men.

On the screen, she seemed tall, about five feet six, I judged. She had dark hair and—distinction. That was the essence of her appearance. She looked the way a queen ought to look and never does.

Her voice, when she spoke, was a golden, vibrant music: "All I've seen of you, Jim Rand, is a picture your agent gave me. I like your face. It's strong, determined; where you are you're a man among men. And you don't look dissipated. I like that, too.

"I don't like being up here, parading myself like a show horse. I don't like those X rays that I had to have taken, but even in that I can appreciate that, far away as you are, you must set up standards and judge by them. I'm supposed to describe my life, and I like that least of all."

Click! Rand cut off the voice, leaving the picture. "I'll tell you the rest," he said.

He told me about her, as I sat there unable to unloose my gaze from the screen.

"She's a multi-operator. That's one of those damn jobs out of which you can't save any money. I don't mean that the salary isn't good. But they grab a piece out of it for old age insurance, for sickness, for compulsory holidays, and so much for clothes a year, so much for housing, entertainment. You've got to live up to your income. You know the kind of stuff.

"For the people as a whole, it's paradise, a dream come true, but the only way a woman can break out of it is to marry somebody. Actually, when a first-rater gets caught in one of those perfect jobs, she's sunk. It's the purest form of slavery. It's hell with a capital H. Can't you just picture it?"

I said nothing. I sat there looking at the woman on the screen. She was about twenty-five; and I could picture her going to and from work, on her holidays, swimming. I could picture the beautiful children she would have.

I grew aware that Rand was pacing the floor. He seemed to realize my unqualified approval, for he was like a little boy who has shown off a new, remarkable toy. He glowed. He grinned at me. He rubbed his hands together.

"Isn't she wonderful?" he said. *"Isn't she?"*

I said at last, slowly: "So wonderful that you can't afford to take any chances with her future. So wonderful that I'm going to loan you an invisibility suit, and you're going to sleep on the floor tonight."

Rand paused in his pacing, confronted me. "There you go again," he scoffed. "What do you think I am, a little sissy? I'm not hiding from anybody."

His arrogance silenced me. If I had been asked at that moment whether Jim Rand was heading straight for Earth, my answer would have been an unqualified "yes."

It was an hour later when we separated, and nearly two hours after that when my doorbell sounded. I answered at once. Jim Rand stood there.

He looked startled when he saw that I was fully dressed. "I thought you'd be in bed," he said, as I shut the door after him.

"What's the matter?" I asked. "Anything happen?"

"Not exactly." He spoke slowly, and he did not look straight at me. "But after I went to bed I realized that I'd been very foolish."

My mind leaped instantly to the girl, Gady Mellerton. "You mean," I said sharply, "you're not going to Earth?"

"Don't be silly." His tone was irritable. He sank into a chair. "Damn you, Delton, you've been a bad influence on me. Your crass assumption that I'm lost if I deviate in the slightest degree from my purpose actually had me leaning over backward, suppressing all my normal impulses, my natural curiosity, even my mental approach to the subject. That's over with. There's only one way to deal with their type of person."

I offered him a cigarette. "What are you going to do?"

"I'd like to borrow that invisibility suit you mentioned."

I brought the two suits out without a word, and offered him the larger: "We're much of a height," I said, "but you swell out more around the shoulders and chest. I've always used the big one when I'm carrying equipment."

I saw his gaze on me oddly, as I pulled the second suit over my clothes. "Where do you think you're going?" he said coolly.

"You're heading for Apartments 300–308, aren't you?"

"That's right but—"

"I feel sort of responsible for you," I said. "I'm not going to let that girl be stuck in her job, or be forced to marry some tenth-rater because you get killed at the last minute."

Rand grinned boyishly. "You sort of like her looks, eh? O.K., you can come along."

Just before he put on his headpiece, I brought out the glasses. I said: "We might as well be able to see each other."

For the first time, then, since we had met, I saw Jim Rand change color. He stood for a moment as if paralyzed; and then his hand reached gently forth and took the glasses. He stood there with them in his fingers, staring as at a priceless gem.

"Man!" he whispered finally, "man, where did you get these? I've been trying for fifteen years to get hold of a pair."

"There was a shipment," I said, "of five dozen to the patrol police on Chaikop. Four dozen and twelve thousand stellors arrived. I figured they were worth a thousand apiece."

"I'll give you," Rand said tensely, "ten million stellors for this pair."

I could not for the life of me suppress a burst of laughter. He scowled at me, snapped finally: "All right, all right, I can see you won't sell. And besides you're right. What the devil does a family man want with them on Earth anyway!" He broke off. "How well can you see with them?"

"Pretty good. Help me switch on the lights. That'll give you a better idea."

It's really startling how little is known about invisibility suits. They were invented around 2180, and were almost immediately put under government control.

Almost immediately. It was soon evident that someone else was manufacturing them secretly, and selling them at enormous prices. The traffic was eventually suppressed on all the major planets, but it followed the ever receding starry frontiers, its sale finally limited by a single fact:

Only one man in a hundred thousand was willing to pay the half million stellors asked for an illegal suit.

The cost of manufacture, I have been told, is three hundred stellors.

Try and suppress that kind of profit. Fifty years have shown that it can't be done.

The strangest thing about the suits is that they work best in bright sunlight. Come twilight, or even a dark cloud, and the wearer takes on a shadowy appearance. In half darkness, a suit is practically worthless.

When the power is switched off, an invisibility suit looks like a certain type of overalls extensively used for rough work. It takes a very keen eye to detect the countless little dark points of—not cloth—that make up the entire surface.

Each one of these points is a tiny cell which, when activated, begins to absorb light. The moment this occurs the cell goes wild. The more light turned on it, the wilder it becomes. The limiting factor is the amount of light that is available.

That was why I had the lights switched on in my apartment, so that Jim Rand could look at me under conditions where, without the glasses, I would have been completely invisible to him.

It was day-bright in the big hallway, too. These enormous ships always try to give the impression of sunniness even in deepest space. It's supposed to be good psychology. No one with an invisibility suit could ask for a better light.

As I closed the door of my suite, I could see Rand just ahead of me, a shimmering shape. His suit glittered as he walked, and took on strange, shining light-forms. It blazed with shifting points of color, like ten thousand diamonds coruscating under a brilliant sun.

It was the sleeping hour; and the long corridors were empty. Once, a ship-officer passed us, but both Rand and I were accustomed to the curious sensation of watching a man walk by with unseeing eyes.

We reached Apartment 300. I used my key of ten million locks—and we were in. All the lights were on inside, and a man lay on the living-room floor, very still. It was one of the men who had been watching Rand in the ship's lounge. Not the leader, Tansey.

Automatically, Rand floated off like a god of light into the bedroom. I headed for the bathroom, then the spaceroom. When I came back, Rand was kneeling beside the man.

"Been dead," he whispered to me, "about an hour."

He began to go through the fellow's pockets, pulling out papers. That was where I stepped forward, and put a restraining hand on his wrist.

"Rand," I whispered, "do you realize what you're doing?"

"Eh?" He looked up at me. His face showed as a blurred pool of light, but even in spite of that I could see the surprise in it. "What the devil do you mean?"

"Don't look any further," I said. "Don't try to find out any more."

His low laughter mocked me. "Man, are you harping on that again? For all I know, in a minute I'll find out from these papers what this is about."

"But don't you see," I said earnestly. "*Don't you* see—it doesn't matter what it is. It's simply another big Ridge deal; it can't be *more* than that. You know that. There have been thousands like it; there'll be millions more.

"It may be a new city; it may be mining, or any one of a dozen other things. *It doesn't matter.*

"Here's your test. You can't leave half your soul on the Ridge and take half with you. For you, it's all or nothing. I know your type. You'll always be coming back, ruining your life and hers.

"But if you can stop yourself now, this minute, this second, and go out of here, and dismiss the whole affair from your mind—"

He had been listening like a man spellbound. Now, he cut me off brutally: "Are you crazy? Why, I'll lie awake nights from sheer curiosity if I don't find out what this is, now that I've been dragged into it."

His voice took on an arrogant note: "And suppose I do get off at Zand tomorrow, and stay for a few weeks. Am I a slave to the idea of retirement? It was never my intention to be anything but free to act as I pleased. I—"

"*Ssshh!*" I said. "Here comes somebody."

Rand stood up in a leisurely fashion, the true sign of the experienced invisible man. No quick movements! Soundless action. We stepped back from the body as near the door as possible.

It was in such moments that the glasses were priceless. Ordinarily, in a crisis, two invisible men working together are a grave danger to each other's movements.

The door opened, and four men came in, the last of them being Tansey. He had a white bandage on his nose.

"Price was a damned fool," he said coldly. "He should have known better than to try to murder a fellow like that. Just because we received the eldogram from Grenville telling us that he'd never sent that other message, he—"

Another man cut him off: "The important thing is to slip him into this invisibility suit and dump him through the refuse lock."

They trooped out into the empty corridors, carrying their invisible burden.

When they had gone, Rand said slowly, grimly: "So Grenville's in on this—"

I stood at the great entrance lock, watching the ship cranes load Rand's baggage onto the surface craft that had soared up from Zand II.

The planet rolled below, a misty ball of vaguely seen continents and seas, a young, green, gorgeous world.

Rand came over and shook my hand, a big man with a strong, fine face. I couldn't help noticing the way his hair was graying at the temples.

"I've eldogrammed Gady," he said, "that I'll be there in two or three weeks."

He saw the look on my face, and laughed. "You must admit," he said, "that the opportunity is one that I can't afford to miss."

"Don't kid me," I said, "you don't even know what it's all about."

"I will," he said, smiling. "I will."

I knew that.

His last words to me were: "Thanks for the loan of the suit and glasses. That cuts you in for twenty-five percent of anything I make."

I said: "I'll see that my agents contact you."

I watched his big form move off through the lock. Steel doors clanged between us.

As soon as the ship started to move, I went to the purser's office. He looked surprised.

"Why, Mr. Delton," he said, "I thought you were leaving us at Zand."

"I changed my mind," I said. "Book me through to Earth, will you?"

That was three years ago.

My wife is looking over my shoulders as I write this. "You can at least," she says, "explain."

It's really very simple. When I saw Rand come aboard, I eldogrammed my agent on Zand II. He sent a message to Tansey, purporting to come from Grenville, describing Rand, and stating that the man of that description was Artur Blord, who, the eldogram said, must be prevented from landing.

Rand reacted the way I expected. The only thing was, when I saw the girl, I changed my mind. I had my agent wire Tansey that a mistake had been made and that Rand was—Rand.

Tansey grew suspicious, and wired Grenville, who disclaimed all knowledge of the previous eldograms. At this point Price came to my suite to kill me. I used the large invisibility suit to cart his body to Apartment 300; and it was still lying there when Rand and I entered.

The reason I interfered in the first place with Rand's purpose of retiring was because I wanted to use him to force my interest into the tremendous uranium find that had been made on Zand. I've found that I become bored with the actual details of organizing a great mining development, and I do it only when I can't find a man to whom such details are life's blood. A man who will moreover let me buy in in some fashion.

Naturally, I used my knowledge of the psychology of spacemen. It's clear to me now that, once those kind of forces are set in motion, they can't be stopped.

I looked up at my wife. "Well, Gady," I said, "will that do?"

"Except that like a good sport, Mr. Rand sold us the house."

Gady has insisted on calling our first-born by my full name: Artur Christopher Blord Delton.

You see, Rand convinced me. A man has to retire sometime.

ABOUT THE EDITOR

FREDERIK POHL has won three Hugos as best editor, one for best short story—the only person ever to have won this coveted award both as writer and editor. He was himself Guest of Honor at the World Science-Fiction Convention in Los Angeles in 1972. He has written about seventy-five books. In addition to science fiction, they include writing on number theory, astronomy, etc. He has contributed to some three hundred magazines all over the world and is the *Encyclopaedia Britannica*'s authority on the Roman Emperor Tiberius. He has lectured in some two hundred and fifty colleges and has appeared on about four hundred radio and television programs, including Johnny Carson's *Tonight Show*. He is currently the science-fiction editor for a large publishing firm.